# Energy
# and
# Environment

---

*The Unfinished Business*

# Energy
# and
# Environment

---

## *The Unfinished Business*

Congressional Quarterly Inc.
1414 22nd Street N.W.
Washington, D.C. 20037

# Congressional Quarterly Inc.

Congressional Quarterly Inc., an editorial research service and publishing company, serves clients in the fields of news, education, business and government. It combines specific coverage of Congress, government and politics by Congressional Quarterly with the more general subject range of an affiliated service, Editorial Research Reports.

Congressional Quarterly publishes the *Congressional Quarterly Weekly Report* and a variety of books, including college political science textbooks under the CQ Press imprint and public affairs paperbacks on developing issues and events. CQ also publishes information directories and reference books on the federal government, national elections and politics, including the *Guide to Congress,* the *Guide to the U.S. Supreme Court,* the *Guide to U.S. Elections* and *Politics in America.* The *CQ Almanac,* a compendium of legislation for one session of Congress, is published each year. *Congress and the Nation,* a record of government for a presidential term, is published every four years.

CQ publishes *The Congressional Monitor,* a daily report on current and future activities of congressional committees, and several newsletters including *Congressional Insight,* a weekly analysis of congressional action, and *Campaign Practices Reports,* a semimonthly update on campaign laws.

An electronic online information system, the Washington Alert Service, provides immediate access to CQ's databases of legislative action, votes, schedules, profiles and analyses.

---

Printed in the United States of America

**Library of Congress Cataloging-in-Publication Data**

Main entry under title:

Energy and environment

Includes index.
1. Energy policy — United States.    2. Environmental Policy — United States.
I. Congressional Quarterly, inc.
HD9502.U52E4524    1985                      333.79′0973                      85-25471
ISBN 0-87187-360-5

*Major Contributor:*  Thomas Arrandale
*Other Contributors:*  Robert Benenson, Joseph A. Davis, Stephen Gettinger, Roger Thompson
*Editors:*  Carolyn Goldinger, John L. Moore
*Cover:*  Robert Redding
*Photo Credits:*  p. 5, UPI; p. 11, Metropolitan Edison Co.; p. 15, Agriculture Department; p. 21, Steven Karafyllakis; p. 27, Energy Department; p. 45, Mike McClure; pp. 58, 135, 159, Wide World; p. 67, E. I. du Pont de Nemours Co.; pp. 109, 113, 143, 165, Environmental Protection Agency; pp. 124, 127, 131, 148, 170, 175, 178, Interior Department; p. 160, *Washington Post*; p. 179, Hank Lebo/Jeroboam Inc.
*Indexer:*  Toni Gillas

# Contents

# Editor's Note

Less than a month after taking office in 1981, President Ronald Reagan outlined his economic agenda before a joint session of Congress and a nationwide television audience. Among his tax and budget proposals was another idea — that of reversing what he described as a "virtual explosion of government regulation during the past decade."

In his presidential bid, Reagan had campaigned against regulation, saying that it hampered economic growth. He advocated letting the marketplace control supply and demand of energy. And, although the president was on record as favoring environmental protection, many of the regulations he wanted "reviewed" dealt with public health and safety.

This policy was a sharp change from the past several administrations, and it presented Congress with a dilemma — how to give the economy a much-needed boost and at the same time continue environmental policies that had tremendous grass-roots support. This book examines what Congress and the Reagan administration did concerning energy and the environment during the president's first term and, perhaps more important, what they left undone.

President Richard Nixon had ushered in the "environmental decade" in 1970 by signing the National Environmental Policy Act. The law stated that it was the goal of the federal government "to use all practicable means and measures, including financial and technical assistance ... to create and maintain conditions under which man and nature can exist in productive harmony, and fulfill the social, economic, and other requirements of present and future generations of Americans." This measure, however, was only the beginning of an outpouring of environmental legislation.

With passage of the Clean Air Act in 1970 and the Federal Water Pollution Control Act in 1972, Congress launched the nation on an all-out effort to improve the environment. Other new laws — to control the use of pesticides, to monitor the disposal of hazardous materials, to protect natural resources, for example — had the support of presidents and Congress alike. But with improvement to the environment these measures also brought mountains of regulations and increased costs to producers and consumers.

The 1970s were also the decade in which the United States learned some harsh truths about energy. Far too much of the oil used by Americans was imported from countries in the politically unstable Middle East. The lifestyle of much of the country — big cars, urban sprawl and homes that were not energy efficient — was based on a plentiful supply of cheap oil.

In 1973 several countries belonging to the Organization of Petroleum Exporting Countries (OPEC) showed their disapproval of U.S. policy toward Israel by imposing an embargo on oil shipments to the United States. OPEC already had nearly doubled the price of a barrel of crude oil, but the shortage created by the embargo caused prices to go even higher.

A revolution in Iran in 1979 brought about the cessation of oil shipments to the

United States and resulted in a second energy crisis. Even when oil once again flowed, the increased cost of fuel raised the price of just about everything Americans bought.

President Jimmy Carter, who came into office between these two "energy shocks," tried to convince the country to conserve and, through developing alternative energy sources, to become less dependent on foreign sources. President Reagan, also a strong advocate of energy independence, had vastly different ideas on how to go about it.

Carolyn Goldinger
John L. Moore
September 1985

# Part I

---

# Energy

# 1

# Energy: Unanswered Questions

In the mid-1980s the United States all but forgot the national energy problems it had struggled with throughout the previous decade. As Americans suffered through serious fuel shortages and rapidly escalating energy costs after the 1973 Arab oil embargo, the federal government fought to cope with an energy "crisis" that President Jimmy Carter in 1977 declared "the moral equivalent of war."

But in the early 1980s Congress and the federal government stepped aside while world market forces granted the nation a reprieve, at least temporarily, from its energy nightmares of 1974-80. As soon as he became president in 1981, Ronald Reagan abandoned Carter's call for energy-conserving sacrifices to curb U.S. dependence on foreign oil imports. Instead, he promised that the nation could produce its way out of energy problems by spurring development of its own domestic fuels, if only the U.S. government let market incentives operate.

In the following years energy demand fell off dramatically as the crude oil price increases during the late 1970s contributed to a worldwide economic recession and forced the United States and other nations to curtail their use of fuel. World crude prices, once expected to top $50 a barrel in 1982, instead dropped from $35 a barrel to $28 a barrel; economists talked of an international oil glut. U.S. oil imports fell significantly, and the Organization of Petroleum Exporting Countries (OPEC) lost its power to keep world crude prices rising.

By 1985 the stormy political debates over energy policy of the 1970s had lost their thunder. With gasoline plentiful — in some regions selling for less than $1 a gallon for the first time in five years — energy no longer ranked among the American public's central worries. With no crisis to raise an alarm, members of Congress who were still concerned about the adequacy of the nation's long-term fuel supplies could generate little political momentum for challenging Reagan's determination to scale back federal control over U.S. energy markets.

## 1970s Energy Strategy

Throughout the 1970s Congress and three presidents had searched, at times in near-desperation, for actions the federal government could take to control or at least soften the blow from the nation's severe energy problems.

The American way of life suffered major dislocations following the "oil shock" of 1973. The price of oil climbed from $3 to $11.65 per barrel in three months in 1973, and it zoomed to more than $30 per barrel following the cutoff of Iranian oil in 1979.

3

Natural gas shortages closed factories and schools during the winters of 1972-73 and 1976-77. Speed limits, thermostats and industrial output were lowered, while inflation and international debt soared.

Congress responded between 1974 and 1980 by trying to boost production, reduce demand, stockpile reserves and find new fuels. The government tried to soften the economic impact by price and allocation controls.

But with the United States depending on imported foreign crude for nearly half of its critical oil supplies in 1977, the government could do little to insulate the U.S. economy from the OPEC cartel's successful campaign for tenfold increases in crude oil prices. The nation's own oil production had peaked in 1970, and the U.S. energy industry could pump only part of the oil and natural gas the United States needed to fill an ever-growing appetite for liquid fuels for industry, residential use and transportation.

The government's efforts to regulate how those domestic supplies were used — while holding their prices below accelerating world market levels — seemed only to discourage new production and encourage fuel-wasting uses. So Congress in 1978 set in motion gradual deregulation of natural gas prices, and Carter the following year began phasing out federal price ceilings on domestic oil.

During Carter's four-year term, between 1977 and 1981, Congress also created a separate Cabinet-level Department of Energy (DOE), regulated industrial fuel consumption, provided federal tax and subsidy incentives for energy conservation investments, imposed a "windfall profits" tax on rising oil prices and launched what members expected to be a crash program to develop synthetic liquid fuels from coal, oil shale and other resources. Carter's successor, however, had vastly different ideas about energy.

# Reagan Energy Strategy

Just days after replacing Carter in the White House, Reagan in January 1981 lifted remaining federal oil price controls that President Richard Nixon had first imposed a decade earlier. Although Carter already had scheduled complete oil decontrol within another nine months, the new president's step signaled that Reagan meant what he had said during the 1980 presidential campaign about cutting back the government's efforts to manage U.S. energy markets.

During the campaign Reagan had contended that federal actions had caused, rather than helped, the nation's energy problems. Declaring that "America must get to work producing more energy," he pledged to keep the government from interfering with marketplace supply-and-demand incentives that would encourage domestic fuel development. Reagan vowed to abolish the Department of Energy, an agency that conservatives viewed as an unneeded instrument for federal meddling in energy matters.

With two notable exceptions Reagan's conservative-dominated administration followed a free market philosophy that assigned the federal government a minimal role in dealing with energy supplies and prices. Congress refused to dismantle DOE, but Reagan's first-term energy secretaries — former South Carolina Gov. James B. Edwards, an oral surgeon, and Donald P. Hodel, former deputy secretary of the interior — de-emphasized the department's programs to promote conservation, encourage solar and other alternative technologies, and develop new ways to burn fossil fuels. While Edwards and Hodel gave DOE a low profile, Secretary of the Interior James G. Watt took the lead as chairman of Reagan's Cabinet Council on Natural Resources and the Environment in shaping the administra-

The first day of odd/even gas rationing in Los Angeles May 9, 1979. Long lines of cars waiting for scarce gasoline were tangible evidence of an "energy crisis" to most Americans.

tion's agenda for easing federal regulatory restraints on the U.S. energy industry.

In two policy areas the administration stepped up federal action to promote nuclear power and to open the government's own federally owned lands and waters for fossil fuel development. Warning that the nation in the 1990s faced a "capacity crunch" in electrical power generation, DOE officials tried to bolster the nation's faltering nuclear power industry by seeking solutions to safety concerns, construction delays and financial troubles that were forcing utilities to mothball ambitious plans to build new reactors. Before resigning under congressional fire in 1983, Watt moved aggressively with controversial plans to accelerate federal coal and oil and gas leasing

on public lands, while opening pristine wilderness areas and vast Outer Continental Shelf tracts for exploratory drilling. *(Mineral leasing, p. 39)*

Through those DOE and Interior programs — and through Environmental Protection Agency stands on federal clean air regulations — the administration pursued a policy of spurring domestic energy production by easing environmental restraints on the nation's petroleum, coal and electric power industries.

Congress resisted Watt's leasing program, and members remained skeptical about the safety of nuclear power. But in addition to political opposition, the administration's pro-growth strategy ran into trouble from market conditions created by am-

# Reagan's Energy Secretaries: . . .

Three men have served as secretary of the Department of Energy (DOE) under President Reagan. With the administration favoring de-regulation of energy markets, none took a prominent role in dealing with U.S. energy concerns.

Reagan's first energy secretary, former South Carolina Gov. James B. Edwards, frequently spoke about abolishing the department he headed in 1981-82. His successor, former Under Secretary of the Interior Donald P. Hodel, proved an effective manager for the department but followed the administration's policy of de-emphasizing most DOE functions except for those promoting nuclear power. Hodel's successor, John S. Herrington, acknowledged during his confirmation hearings that his energy background was strictly personal: he had waited in lines during gas shortages and had insulated his home to conserve energy.

Before replacing Edwards Nov. 5, 1982, Hodel served as chief deputy to Interior Secretary James G. Watt, who dominated the administration's natural resource policies as chairman of the Cabinet Council on Natural Resources and Environment.

Reagan in January 1985 nominated Hodel to replace William P. Clark, Watt's successor, as interior secretary. Reagan asked John S. Herrington, his White House assistant for personnel, to replace Hodel as energy secretary.

Congress had created the Department of Energy in 1977 at President Carter's request. Carter's energy secretaries, James R. Schlesinger and Charles W. Duncan Jr., had played leading roles in government attempts to counter rising energy prices and develop long-term supplies of fuel.

## James B. Edwards

Reagan defeated Carter in the 1980 presidential election after campaigning on a pledge to reduce government interference in energy markets and abolish the Energy Department. In selecting Edwards, an oral surgeon, as his first energy secretary, Reagan found someone who shared his basic philosophy: get government out of the way so private industry could produce more energy.

Shortly before Reagan appointed him to the DOE post, Edwards had stated. "I'd like to go to Washington and close the Energy Department and work myself out of a job." The Senate confirmed his appointment by a 93-3 vote on Jan. 22, 1981.

Edwards had little experience in dealing with energy issues. But as South Carolina governor, he had been an unabashed advocate of developing nuclear power. Environmental groups were dismayed by Edwards' strong backing for commercial reprocessing of spent nuclear fuel into fresh fuel, plutonium and liquid wastes.

As energy secretary, Edwards continued to back nuclear research and development as offering the best long-term solution to U.S. energy needs. On most energy matters, however, Edwards kept a low profile as Watt took the lead in pushing more rapid development of domestic fuels, especially coal, oil and natural gas from federally owned lands and Outer Continental Shelf waters that were leased by the Interior Department.

During Edwards' tenure the administration drew up plans to dismantle DOE and transfer most government energy programs to the Commerce Department. But Congress

# ... Edwards, Hodel, Herrington

took no action on the reorganization plan. Edwards, who had made it clear he would leave the government before the expiration of Reagan's first term, resigned Nov. 5, 1982, to become president of the Medical University of South Carolina.

## Donald P. Hodel

In selecting Hodel to replace Edwards, the administration ignored environmental group critics of his close ties to Watt and his record of supporting nuclear power.

Before being named interior under secretary, Hodel was administrator from 1972 to 1977 of the Bonneville Power Administration (BPA), a federally owned agency that marketed hydroelectric power from 30 federal dams to states in the Pacific Northwest. During Hodel's tenure, BPA joined many U.S. utility companies in predicting that demand for power would far outstrip supply by the early 1980s. The agency stopped selling cheap federal power to investor-owned utilities in 1973, putting public utilities on notice in 1976 that it would not be able to meet their additional power demands after July 1983.

That warning, according to critics, led to an explosion of high-cost power plant construction. The Washington Public Power Supply System (WPPSS) — nicknamed "Whoops" by critics — embarked on an ambitious program to build five new plants. Two nuclear plants were later canceled, leading to the default of $2.25 billion in WPPSS bonds in July 1983.

The Senate confirmed Hodel as energy secretary by an 86-8 vote on Dec. 8, 1982. Hodel improved DOE employee morale by playing down talk of abolishing the department. He also won praise from some members of Congress, even Democrats who opposed his policies.

After Hodel was nominated to be interior secretary in 1985, House Energy Committee Chairman John D. Dingell, D-Mich., said that he and Hodel "enjoyed a pretty good relationship." House Interior Committee Chairman Morris K. Udall, D-Ariz., criticized the Hodel and Herrington appointments in 1985 but said that he had worked effectively with Hodel on 1982 nuclear waste legislation.

## John S. Herrington

The president named Herrington to succeed Hodel on Jan. 10, 1985. Herrington was a California lawyer and a veteran of past Reagan campaigns. He served as assistant secretary of the Navy from 1981 to 1983 before taking the White House position.

Reagan's deputy press secretary, Larry Speakes, said of Herrington: "He knows the president's policies and desires ... and he brings to the Energy Department a combination of the knowledge of civilian management and organization."

When questioned by the Senate Energy Committee, Herrington admitted ignorance of particular laws, policy and problems. Committee members appeared satisfied with his declaration that he had an open mind regarding matters he did not know about. Sen. John Warner, R-Va., described Herrington as "a quick study." The Senate confirmed the nomination Feb. 6, 1985, by a 93-1 vote.

ple supplies and falling energy consumption. With electric power demand lagging far below previous projections, electric utilities mothballed partly built nuclear plants and canceled expensive capacity expansion plans. And with coal markets depressed, Congress halted Watt's expansive coal leasing plans after critics charged that the Interior Department was selling federally owned reserves at prices below fair market value.

In most energy and environmental policy areas administration officials pursued their agenda through budget decisions and administrative changes. The White House sent Congress only limited legislative proposals, backing efforts to speed nuclear plant licensing, provide for nuclear waste disposal and tighten accounting procedures for oil and gas production from federal lands. But with deep divisions in Congress dimming prospects for tackling controversial matters, the administration backed away from expected efforts to speed up natural gas deregulation and overhaul federal clean air standards.

## Congressional Reconsideration

Given administration hostility to active federal intervention, Congress spent most of 1981-84 reconsidering old energy policy decisions instead of launching new programs.

Not sharing the administration's enthusiasm for free market policies, members of Congress by and large still were oriented toward federal efforts to conserve energy and prepare for future emergencies. Many members, especially Democrats who held key energy policy-making posts in the House leadership and committees, doubted that U.S. oil and gas reserves could be expanded significantly by drilling previously unexplored federal lands and coastal waters. Concerned by safety and environmental problems, members no longer looked

to nuclear power to meet the nation's long-term electrical energy needs. In alliance with politically influential environmental groups, House Democrats stood guard against what they considered administration plans to sacrifice the environmental safeguards enacted during the 1970s to promote domestic fuel supplies.

Yet in balancing energy concerns with environmental and economic goals, Congress concluded that some decisions the government made during the 1970s had been mistaken. After several years of debate, for instance, lawmakers in 1983 halted federal financial support for building the Clinch River breeder reactor at Oak Ridge, Tenn. In approving the Clinch River project, intended to demonstrate "fast breeder" technology for generating electricity while producing more fuel than was consumed, Congress had hailed it as the solution to U.S. energy problems. But sharply rising costs, flattening electric power demand and nuclear safety concerns gradually eroded congressional support for finishing the project. Finally, fiscal conservatives and environmentalists teamed up in 1983 to cancel further funding for Clinch River.

Bowing to similar second thoughts, Congress in 1984 cut in half federal funding for promoting a synthetic fuels industry. In the wake of 1979 Iranian oil cutbacks Congress in 1980 set up a federally funded U.S. Synthetic Fuels Corporation (SFC) to stimulate development of fuels from coal, oil shale, tar sands and other sources.

The SFC had been plagued by management troubles almost since its inception, and these reached crisis proportions by early 1984 as resignations left the SFC board without the quorum it needed to conduct business. With a worldwide oil glut making energy cheap and plentiful, few companies had any interest in pursuing costly synfuels development. Congress lost patience with the fumbling SFC, and began eyeing its rich cache of funds for possible savings in an era of high deficits. By late 1985 Congress was close to putting the synfuels corporation out of business. *(Synfuels, p. 35)*

## World Oil Market Turnaround

In putting the various programs in place, federal energy planners during the 1970s expected world oil prices to keep escalating. But nobody, either in the White House or Congress, could have predicted the dramatic turnaround in world oil markets during the early 1980s.

From 1973 on it appeared that the OPEC cartel of oil-producing nations held power to keep world crude prices rising indefinitely. But during the late 1970s a worldwide recession cut energy demand; industrial nations meanwhile found new sources of fuel to replace imports from the politically unstable Persian Gulf region. Throughout the industrial world, consumers adopted fuel-saving practices as higher energy costs increased incentives for conservation.

The resulting slump in world oil demand left a large glut of oil and international markets that put downward pressure on prices. A week before Christmas in 1982, oil ministers from the 13 OPEC nations met in Vienna, Austria, but adjourned in disarray, unable to reach agreement on production quotas for OPEC member countries. Two years later, with member nations unilaterally discounting their oil, OPEC cut its official price below $30 a barrel. Unable to agree on production cutbacks to defend its official price, the organization, for the time being at least, had lost its ability to control world energy markets.

While European nations and Japan still relied heavily on Middle East oil, the United States began buying most of its imported oil from Mexico and Venezuela. As total oil demand fell, the nation depended less on foreign crude suppliers. U.S. oil imports, which peaked at 47 percent of national consumption in 1977, fell to 28 percent by 1983.

Declining world energy demand badly hurt Third World nations, notably Mexico, that had counted on rising oil revenues to pay off heavy debts to international banks. In the United States petroleum industry profits plunged, and exploratory drilling for new reserves fell off with the drop in oil prices. Carter's 1979 decontrol decision helped spark a drilling boom in 1980-81 as major oil companies and independent "wildcat" drillers stepped up their search for domestic oil and natural gas that could be sold at world price levels. But many independent oil companies, drilling rig suppliers and other oilfield businesses went bankrupt in the following years after borrowing heavily in anticipation of rising prices.

Even major international oil companies went through a period of consolidation. In a series of mergers, giant energy companies eager to expand their dwindling oil reserves acquired other major oil companies. Members of Congress expressed alarm that the mergers increased industry concentration and consumed financial resources that otherwise could be spent to discover new petroleum resources. But the administration refused to intervene, and Congress sidetracked proposals for a temporary moratorium on major oil company mergers.

## Natural Gas Prices

Reagan's decision to lift all oil price controls encouraged natural gas producers to expect that the administration would follow up by asking Congress to speed deregulation of natural gas as well. But although Reagan's Cabinet in 1981 recommended prompt deregulation, congressional protests over rising prices allowed by the Natural Gas Policy Act of 1978 foreclosed chances for ending federal ceilings on natural gas prices ahead of schedule.

Like oil, gas was in surplus. But while oil prices fell, natural gas prices rose as the 1978 law gradually raised federal price ceilings. Natural gas warmed about 55 million households and supplied 25 percent of U.S. energy needs, including those of important industries. Business and consumer groups howled as higher cost gas flowed through interstate pipelines, sending gas bills soaring through most of the nation.

Members of Congress, responding to those complaints, introduced dozens of bills for dealing with the problem. Some members suggested the solution to rising prices was the reimposition of price controls, which were being removed gradually according to the schedule established by the Natural Gas Policy Act of 1978.

The Reagan administration, on the other hand, attributed the problems to the controls themselves. Oil prices, administration officials noted, had been decontrolled and were behaving admirably in the face of a glut. Immediate, full decontrol of natural gas producer prices would enable that market to operate properly too, and cause prices to fall, these officials predicted. *(Natural gas deregulation, p. 28)*

Both arguments were somewhat simplistic. Strict controls on the wellhead price of gas probably would have resulted in supply shortages at some point in the future, just as they had in 1976 and 1977. But immediate and full decontrol of wellhead prices could have led to even faster price hikes, since many gas pipelines were tied to long-term contracts that forced them to buy more expensive gas even when cheaper gas was available. Futhermore, federal regulation of the pipelines — which Reagan did not propose to eliminate — enabled them to pass on the cost of gas to the consumers,

thus reducing incentives to bring prices down.

Neither the 97th nor the 98th Congress could resolve the difficult technical and economic questions posed by natural gas deregulation. A natural gas bill did reach the Senate floor late in the 1983 session, but members soundly rejected competing proposals to phase out all remaining federal price controls on natural gas or, alternatively, to retain existing controls and roll back prices to August 1982 levels. The House in 1984 scrapped Energy and Commerce Committee legislation that attempted to iron out problems in natural gas markets but threatened a bitter regional fight on the floor that would divide both Democrats and Republicans.

Congressional inaction allowed price controls to expire on roughly half of all U.S. gas supplies on Jan. 1, 1985, as Congress had scheduled in the 1978 law. Despite warnings that continued deregulation would produce a sudden price "fly-up," gas prices leveled off during the first months of 1985.

# Nuclear Industry Troubles

Reagan gave the nuclear industry a boost in 1981 with a policy statement that overturned his predecessor's ban on the reprocessing of burned nuclear fuel into more fuel, waste and plutonium. He also promised to cut government red tape and increased the nuclear energy budget while cutting all other energy programs.

But Reagan's support was insufficient to rescue the industry from its troubles. Still on the defensive after the 1979 Three Mile Island nuclear reactor accident in Pennsylvania, nuclear power companies lost public confidence in the ability of nuclear reactors to generate electric power without risking public health and safety.

The congressional decision to cancel the Clinch River breeder project symbol-

Cooling towers and reactor while under construction at the Three Mile Island nuclear station, located on the Susquehanna River near Harrisburg, Pa. The towers have come to symbolize the dangers, not the benefits, of nuclear energy.

ized the nation's growing disillusionment with nuclear technologies that once had promised nearly limitless supplies of electric power. Environmental group challenges, financial woes and growing antinuclear political sentiment combined to make the industry's prospects for future expansion doubtful.

With electricity demand lagging below projections made a decade earlier, U.S. electric utilities had placed no new reactor orders for several years. While some new plants were brought on line, utilities canceled or delayed construction of other planned units that had been plagued by faulty designs, construction problems, legal challenges, labor disputes or rising interest rates that made them too costly to finish.

In the Pacific Northwest souring prospects for nuclear power were magnified by the largest municipal bond default in U.S. history. The Washington Public Power Supply System (WPPSS), nicknamed "Whoops" by its critics, during the 1970s drew up plans to build five huge nuclear plants to meet the region's projected electric power demand. But the demand never materialized, and cost overruns were enormous. Project sponsors canceled two partly built plants, but the project remained saddled with huge long-term debts. In 1983 WPPSS defaulted on $2.25 billion in bonds it had issued to build the two canceled plants.

Congress took some steps to deal with the industry's problems. In 1982 it authorized the Nuclear Regulatory Commission (NRC) to issue temporary licenses to permit utilities to start operating newly built reactors before full-scale NRC hearings had

# The Nation's Electricity Supply...

The specter of regional electric power shortages by the early 1990s loomed large at Senate hearings in late July 1985. At the hearings, entitled "When Will the Lights Go Out?" representatives of private, investor-owned electric companies, economic analysts and government officials warned that the current surpluses of electric generating capacity could be used up within the next decade. "Without new generating capacity, the lights ... *will* start to go out some time in the 1990s and will do so increasingly as the decade progresses," Deputy Secretary of Energy Danny Boggs said.

A Department of Energy (DOE) report released in June 1983 sparked the current debate about a potential electricity shortage in the 1990s. The report said that the nation would require 438 gigawatts (438,000 megawatts) in additional generating capacity by the year 2000. The DOE prediction was based on several assumptions. First, a 3 percent annual growth in electricity demand was expected to require 329 gigawatts (GW) of new generating capacity — nearly 50 percent more than was currently available. Another 71 GW would be needed to replace aging or retired plants, while 38 GW would be needed to replace power plants that used high-cost fuels, including oil, which the report predicted would cost $42 per barrel.

Many of the witnesses at the Senate Energy and Natural Resources Committee hearings also predicted the need to build new generating capacity. However, they differed on the size of electrical demand growth and the amount of new capacity needed. Updating DOE estimates, Boggs reported that growth in electricity demand was expected to parallel growth in the gross national product (GNP), the total value of all goods and services produced. With GNP growth expected to be between 2.5 and 4 percent through 2000, electricity growth would be 1.7 to 4.4 percent, he said, requiring a generating capacity increase of 100-475 gigawatts. With retirements (70 GW) and uneconomical generation (40 GW) near levels predicted in 1983, Boggs estimated the actual generating capacity need at 210-585 GW.

Using somewhat different assumptions about growth, Helmut A. Merklein, head of DOE's Energy Information Administration, said new generating capacity would keep up with new demand but would not replace old and expensive power plants. Projecting a shortfall in 1995 of 3 to 24 gigawatts, Merklein said the West was likely to need capacity additions that were not being planned, and that New England, the Mid-Atlantic and Central regions and the Southwest could experience difficulties.

Given the national surplus that existed in the mid-1980s, the idea of widespread electricity shortages seemed far-fetched. "Reserve" margins in every region of the country topped the 20 percent figure traditionally thought necessary to ensure reliable electric service; in most regions the margin was well above 20 percent. Blackouts and brownouts were rare, localized and usually resulted from mechanical failures rather than lack of generating capacity.

# ...Surplus or Shortage in the 1990s?

Electric utility leaders claimed the surplus would not last. Demand for electricity was expected to increase, although predictions of the rate of growth varied widely. At the same time, aging power plants were scheduled for retirement, and oil- and gas-fired plants could become too costly to operate if fuel prices increased.

Most of all, utility executives said, the nation would suffer from a lack of new power plant construction. Failing to anticipate a slowing growth rate in electricity demand in the 1970s, utilities plunged into a huge construction program just as inflation, high interest rates, construction delays and intensified environmental regulation sent the cost of building power plants, especially nuclear facilities, soaring. Numerous projects were abandoned, some after the expenditure of billions of dollars. State regulatory bodies were reluctant to allow utilities to pass on to consumers the full costs of completed plants, let alone abandoned ones. Several electric companies were pushed to the brink of bankruptcy, and even financially solvent companies were reluctant to expand current construction plans. Private utility executives said the current plans were not enough to overcome anticipated shortages.

However, there was no consensus on the certainty of an electricity shortage or the need for new construction. Skeptics who questioned the claims of near-term electricity shortages included traditional utility critics, such as residential ratepayer and environmental groups. They were joined by steel, automobile and aluminum manufacturers who feared higher electricity prices would make their products even less competitive with foreign manufacturers. John A. Anderson, executive director of the Electricity Consumers Resource Council (ELCON), testified that his group found "no [supply] problems on either a national or regional basis." Representatives of public power systems — those owned by state and local governments — also rejected the crisis predictions of their private-sector counterparts.

Industry critics said the utility executives had not proved their case for a massive program of new construction. Roger F. Naill, vice president of Applied Energy Services of Arlington, Va., a private, for-profit energy consulting firm, said that while high annual demand growth of 3.1 percent might require new capacity as soon as 1992, a low growth rate of 1.8 percent would enable utilities to put off new construction until after 2000. Ralph Cavanagh of the Natural Resources Defense Council observed that even DOE estimates had a 300-gigawatt margin of error, which he equated to 600 coal-fired plants.

Various alternatives to large plant construction had been proposed to cover any electricity shortages. Refitting old plants and building smaller units could enable utilities to match generating capacity to demand. Cogeneration, the use of waste heat from industrial processes to create electricity, may have growth potential. Conservation, load management and more efficient energy use could slow the growth of demand. Improved transmission networks between regions could ease whatever localized shortages developed. But electric industry spokesmen insisted these were stopgap measures that would merely delay the day of reckoning.

been completed. NRC never used that authority, however, and Congress refused to renew it.

Also in 1982, after four years of bickering, Congress completed work on a plan to provide both temporary and permanent repositories, operated by the federal government, to dispose of spent nuclear fuel that had been piling up at civilian power plants throughout the country. But the disposal of highly radioactive nuclear waste remained an inflammatory political issue, and congressional delegations and local residents quickly protested at the end of 1984 when Energy Department officials identified three regions they were considering for a permanent disposal facility. *(Nuclear power, p. 65)*

## Conservation Cutbacks

Following up on his campaign pledge, Reagan asked Congress to abolish the Energy Department and turn most of its programs over to the Department of Commerce. But influential Republican senators resisted the plan, and Congress took no action.

Through budget reductions, however, the administration significantly shifted DOE's focus. During Carter's term Congress substantially bolstered federal funding for DOE conservation programs and for research on solar energy and other renewable energy technologies that promised to curb the nation's appetite for fossil fuels. *(Renewable energy, p. 34)*

But the Reagan administration contended that rising energy prices should offer sufficient incentives for business and individuals to invest in conservation and renewable energy technologies. The administration curtailed funding for conservation efforts, trying to eliminate some federal assistance programs that were popular in Congress. The administration drastically

cut funds for solar research, arguing that it was time to turn the task of demonstrating commercial solar equipment to private industry. It also curtailed DOE research on fossil fuel technologies to develop cleaner, more efficient ways to burn coal and petroleum.

Congress restored some of Reagan's cuts, but funding fell well below the levels during Carter's administration. Congressional critics complained that by shifting limited funds toward nuclear programs, the administration was cutting short conservation and alternative energy programs that could yield long-term benefits by reducing demand for imported oil.

Before Reagan took office, "we had a very balanced energy budget — spending was spread reasonably among all energy technologies," Rep. Richard L. Ottinger, D-N.Y., chairman of the House Subcommittee on Energy Conservation and Power, argued during 1984 debate on DOE's conservation budget. But during Reagan's first term "this balance was destroyed," Ottinger claimed. "Since 1981 solar energy programs have been cut by 70 percent. Conservation programs have been cut by 50 percent. Fossil energy was cut by over 80 percent. Meanwhile, nuclear fission (including waste) and nuclear fusion have remained about the same.

"The net result," he said, was a "shift toward an all-nuclear budget."

## Preparing for Future Shortages

Congress offered only token protests when Reagan in 1981 ended federal oil price controls, along with the mechanism for allocating petroleum products that the government used during shortages. But the administration and Congress differed over whether the government should keep presidential authority to control oil markets in place, ready for use in future emergencies.

At the Agriculture Department's Animal Genetics and Management Laboratories in Beltsville, Md., scientists heat water and the milking parlor with energy from the sun. Four different types of solar collectors are being compared for efficiency and durability.

Administration officials and many congressional Republicans maintained that oil price and allocation programs during the 1970s had exacerbated, if not actually created, the shortages the nation endured. While defending the price and allocation controls as a necessary if unsatisfactory response to critical problems, congressional Democrats acknowledged that the previous decade's battles over routine federal regulation of the day-to-day marketplace in petroleum and natural gas had been settled in favor of deregulation. But many members, including conservative Republican senators, contended that public clamor in the event of another oil shortage would force Congress and the government again to step in to regulate petroleum markets.

Senate Energy and Natural Resources Committee Chairman James A. McClure, R-Idaho, for one, tried unsuccessfully to persuade the White House to accept some standby emergency planning that would head off more intrusive congressional action after a shortage had developed. But the Senate in 1982 unexpectedly upheld the president's veto of legislation granting him standby authority to control oil markets. Congress thereafter gave up efforts to force the administration to draft plans for dealing with energy emergencies. But it continued to prod the administration to fill the Strategic Petroleum Reserve, created in 1976 as a backup national oil supply during market shortages, more rapidly than White House budget makers wanted. *(Allocation authority, p. 23; SPR, p. 25)*

## Long-Term Energy Worries

Although the U.S. energy situation undeniably brightened in 1983-84, skeptics still warned that the nation remained vulnerable to future oil supply disruptions.

Critics of Reagan administration policies maintained that most cutbacks in national energy consumption were produced by declining industrial activity, not by true conservation. That conclusion suggested that the U.S. economy would have a hard time recovering from the oil shocks of the 1970s, since industries that had depended on cheap oil probably would never revive. Even if the economy rebounded, growing energy demand would quickly make the nation dependent on foreign oil, restoring OPEC's stranglehold on the U.S. economic future.

Although the United States had curtailed its reliance on imports in the early 1980s, experts warned that several factors kept the nation's energy security in doubt:

—Oil prices were set in the international marketplace, over which the United States had little direct control. Excess capacity in the Western world helped keep OPEC from raising prices, but there was not a lot of breathing space. Some major reserves, such as Great Britain's North Sea and Alaska's Prudhoe Bay fields, would soon begin to decline. World demand was growing, particularly in communist and developing countries. If things reached the point where the rest of the world was producing petroleum at capacity without meeting demand, the Middle East again would control the price of oil.

—The long-term outlook was not good. The Middle East had 55 percent of the world's proven oil reserves, the United States only 4 percent.

—The federal Strategic Petroleum Reserve held 484 million barrels of oil in mid-1985, enough to make up for the loss of all imports for nearly 100 days at existing rates of consumption. But the practical value of the SPR was unknown. Its existence may have helped forestall panic buying in 1984, during the Iran-Iraq war, but the United States had no concrete plan for how or when to use it. Debates continued over whether to tap the reserves in the event of a shortage to keep prices from rising, or to save them for a major catastrophe.

—While the United States had shifted its import patterns, its allies remained heavily dependent on Persian Gulf oil. Japan imported 60 percent of its supplies from the gulf, Western Europe 20 to 40 percent. In the event of a shortage, would the United States use its reserves to bail out these countries, possibly subjecting U.S. consumers to gas lines and price rises, or would it stand by while other nations bid up the price?

—U.S. consumption of petroleum had begun to rise again, and production, which had remained essentially flat in recent years, had not met that new demand. Production was still 8 percent below the peak year 1970.

A 1984 report by the congressional Office of Technology Assessment concluded that the nation was in far better shape than in 1973, but "a large and enduring shortfall and oil price increase would have severe economic consequences on the United States, even with full drawdown of the Strategic Petroleum Reserve and available private stocks."

## Environmental Outlook

For almost every type of energy production in the United States there is a direct environmental consequence. One major cause of air pollution is the nation's heavy dependence on non-renewable fossil fuels — petroleum, natural gas and coal. If these fuels are replaced with nuclear power in the future, however, the dangers to the environment could be even more serious. In other parts of the world the use of wood for fuel leads to the loss of arable land.

The burning of fossil fuels in the United States has had the following results:

—Each year transportation and fossil-fuel fired electric generating plants produce 36 percent of the particulates, 37 percent of the hydrocarbons, 83 percent of the carbon monoxide, 84 percent of the sulfur oxides and 95 percent of the nitrogen oxides emitted into the atmosphere as pollutants.

—In 1982 the National Academy of Sciences warned that the "continued rise in atmospheric $CO_2$ (carbon dioxide) concentrations poses potentially severe long-term risks to the global climate and to the biological systems that depend upon it." The academy was describing the so-called "greenhouse effect," or the unnatural warming of Earth's atmosphere.

—About 30 million tons of sulfur dioxide and 20 million tons of nitrogen oxide yearly rise into the atmosphere from the nation's industries, public utilities and motor vehicles. High-level winds can carry these gases hundreds of miles from their origin. Forming sulfate and nitrate aerosols, they combine with water vapor and return to Earth as acid rain or snow. Acid precipitaiton, now found throughout the United States, has become common in the Northeast and in eastern Canada. A federal interagency task force reported in 1981 that the average northeastern rainfall had increased 10 times above normal acidity — in some areas, a thousandfold. Acid rain is suspected of rendering hundreds of mountain lakes in the United States and Canada ecologically sterile and disrupting the related forest ecosystems. The Reagan administration has responded to this international problem by calling for further studies.

The 1978 nuclear reactor accident at Three Mile Island near Harrisburg, Pa., alerted the nation to the potential dangers of nuclear power generating plants. Since then the Nuclear Regulatory Commission has reported that other plants suffer from design, construction and operating errors. Even when nuclear plants are operated with perfect safety, however, the problem of how to dispose of the waste they generate continues to concern environmentalists.

## Looking Forward

Although the U.S. energy picture undeniably brightened during Reagan's first term, administration critics contended that the nation remained vulnerable to foreign oil disruptions as energy demand picked up. Even with no crisis, Congress still could be forced to deal with prickly energy issues during Reagan's second term.

The 99th Congress, which convened in 1985, was expected to debate nuclear licensing, which the administration would like to streamline, and federal support for conservation efforts, which the administration would like to cut.

Other battlegrounds of the past, such as natural gas regulation and emergency planning, will probably not be revisited. Even members who would most like to take the initiative on energy matters agree that without strong public interest, in Ottinger's words, "you just can't do it with a hostile administration."

In the mid-1980s there no longer was in Congress an issue known as "Energy," with a capital E. But subsidiary issues still aroused the lobbying pressures and regional battles that Congress experienced in past battles. It was seen as an environmental safety issue, but DOE's deliberations on selecting a site for disposing of high-level nuclear wastes promised to develop into an intense fight that could determine whether the nation in the future could rely on nuclear power for generating electricity.

"It's returned to specialized interests," said Sen. Bill Bradley, D-N.J. "I don't see energy politics. I see coal politics. Or natural gas politics. The nuclear boys don't scratch the backs of the oil boys. I don't see any coalition."

Another change for the 99th Congress

was that the "institutional memory" of the past energy crisis was weakening as veteran legislators were replaced. In both chambers of Congress, only a quarter of the members were in office in 1973, and almost half were not there to vote on the 1978 Natural Gas Policy Act. This could mean that Congress would have to re-invent the wheel in the event of a future crisis.

But McClure sees a brighter side as well. Perhaps, he said, energy veterans like himself were like old generals preparing to fight the last war. "Maybe we need some new perspectives," he said. But, he added, the rallying cry will be an echo of the past: " 'Congressman, *do* something!' "

# 2

# Energy Regulation

Scarcely more than a decade after it burst into public consciousness, the "energy crisis" seemed to evaporate as a political force in Congress. Energy policy was *the* issue of the 1970s — a national concern that President Jimmy Carter called "the moral equivalent of war." In 1985 falling oil prices washed away public concern, and the Reagan administration's reluctance to intervene in the energy marketplace sapped congressional initiative. Although the crisis atmosphere had gone, for key members of Congress the concern — and the rhetoric — remained.

"We're all so fat, dumb and happy again," said Sen. James A. McClure, R-Idaho, chairman of the Senate Energy and Natural Resources Committee. In June 1984, as oil tankers were being sunk in the Persian Gulf during the Iran-Iraq war, McClure could not muster a quorum of his committee to consider a bill requiring preparations for an oil shortage.

"I feel frustrated that nobody is aware of the fact that the problem is still there, like a sleeping vampire that waits to rise," said Rep. John D. Dingell, D-Mich., chairman of the Energy and Commerce Committee and the most influential remaining member of the group that steered energy legislation through Congress in the 1970s. Energy "has ceased to be a political ques-

tion," Dingell added.

The American way of life had suffered major dislocations following the "oil shock" of 1973. The price of oil climbed from $3 to $11.65 per barrel in three months in 1973, and it zoomed to more than $30 per barrel following the cutoff of Iranian oil in 1979. Natural gas shortages closed factories and schools during the winters of 1972-73 and 1976-77. Speed limits, thermostats and industrial output were lowered, while inflation and international debt soared.

Congress responded between 1974 and 1980 by trying to boost production, to reduce demand, to stockpile reserves and to find new fuels. The government tried to soften the economic impact by price and allocation controls. But that strategy seemed only to make things worse, so Congress allowed gradual decontrol of oil and natural gas prices. As prices rose, Congress enacted the largest single tax ever imposed on an industry, the windfall profits tax on oil.

The Reagan administration approach to energy was quite different from Carter's. Regulation of the marketplace was a bête noire of conservatives. Their view was that the price controls on petroleum products imposed by President Richard Nixon in 1971 and the allocation mechanisms set up to support had created the energy crisis.

Rep. James T. Broyhill, R-N.C., ranking Republican on the House Energy and Commerce Committee, said, "I voted for the first bill [imposing allocation controls in 1973] and it was a mistake."

Democrats continued to defend the price and allocation controls as an unsatisfactory but necessary response to a real crisis. Most members agreed, however, that the battle over regulation of the day-to-day marketplace in petroleum and natural gas was over. The most stirring battles of the period were fought over this question, and they were decided in favor of deregulation.

Bowing to President Ronald Reagan's free-market philosophy, the 97th Congress accepted the president's determination to end the government's efforts to regulate oil prices and allocate petroleum supplies during shortages. In the process, Congress repealed or allowed to expire several laws enacted during the 1970s to give the government power to manage energy problems.

Those decisions continued the process, launched by President Carter, of freeing U.S. oil production from federal regulations. The House and Senate offered few objections when Reagan lifted all remaining oil price controls eight months ahead of schedule. After months of maneuvering, Congress gave up attempts to extend standby presidential authority to control oil prices and supplies that Reagan vowed never to use.

To augment U.S. petroleum supplies, Congress pushed to fill the U.S. Strategic Petroleum Reserve (SPR) and encourage construction of a natural gas pipeline from Alaska.

With natural gas prices escalating through 1981-82, congressional concern forced Reagan to put off his Cabinet's proposal to speed the previously scheduled deregulation of natural gas prices. But members also were unable to forge agreement on counterproposals to reimpose federal gas price controls that were being phased out by 1985 under the Natural Gas Policy Act of 1978.

# Oil Price Decontrol

President Reagan, in one of his first acts in office, Jan. 28, 1981, terminated remaining federal regulations on domestic oil prices and supplies. That action freed U.S. oil prices for the first time since 1971 to rise and fall with world petroleum market levels.

Reagan's decision completed, eight months ahead of schedule, a gradual decontrol process that his Democratic predecessor, Jimmy Carter, had started in 1979. While final decontrol had little economic impact, Reagan's action demonstrated a conservative administration's determination to rely on free market forces to regulate the nation's energy supply and demand.

Through most of the 1970s a Democratic-controlled Congress had insisted that the federal government maintain controls over the price of oil produced in the United States while foreign oil prices climbed dramatically. But by 1981 most members of Congress evidently agreed that holding domestic oil prices below foreign levels discouraged exploration for new U.S. reserves and reduced incentives for Americans to cut oil consumption.

## A Decade of Controls

President Nixon first imposed oil price controls on Aug. 16, 1971, as part of a general freeze on wages and prices throughout the U.S. economy. As federal energy policy debates dragged on over the following years, Congress refused to allow Nixon and President Gerald R. Ford to lift federal controls. Democratic members contended the controls were protecting American consumers against the full brunt of rapid oil price increases determined by the Organiza-

At the height of the energy crisis in 1979, motorists often encountered closed pumps or limits on what gas they could buy.

tion of Petroleum Exporting Countries (OPEC) cartel.

The Nixon administration's Cost of Living Council in 1973 devised a two-tier oil pricing system that removed controls from oil produced from newly drilled wells but limited prices for "old" oil from wells drilled before that year. Less than a month after Arab oil-producing nations imposed an embargo on shipments to the United States, Congress wrote similar controls into law as part of the Emergency Petroleum Allocation Act of 1973. That measure was temporary, scheduled to expire in 1975. But Congress kept oil price controls in effect for another six years through subsequent laws.

Contending that higher oil prices would encourage energy conservation, Ford in 1975 proposed lifting price controls while imposing a "windfall profits" tax on the resulting revenues unless oil companies reinvested them in exploring for new reserves. But the Democratic-dominated Congress protested, arguing that decontrol would benefit the oil companies at the expense of the already hard-pressed consumer. The result was the extension, in the 1975 Energy Policy and Conservation Act, of mandatory price controls on oil until June 1, 1979. After that date, the act gave the president power to continue, modify or remove the controls.

## Movement for Decontrol

But energy prices rose despite controls, and supplies diminished in the four years between 1975 and 1979. Support for continued controls ebbed during Carter's term, as a Democratic White House and Congress struggled to fashion an energy conservation strategy. Congress in 1977 turned down Carter's plan to impose new taxes on U.S. oil production to bring its cost up to world levels. And Congress continued to find politically unacceptable strict government regulations to force Americans to curb energy consumption.

At the same time taxes and rules were going down in defeat, there was a growing acceptance of the idea that higher prices could spur conservation. By the late 1970s articulate defenses of that position were coming from academicians with liberal credentials and from some interest groups, such as environmentalists. They contended that conservation and alternative energy sources, such as solar power, would be more competitive economically if oil and gas prices were decontrolled. So long as oil and gas remained relatively inexpensive, they argued, people had no reason to adapt to the new energy era. The oil companies and Republicans who had fought for years against controls suddenly had company.

In 1979 revolution in Iran slowed that country's oil production and set off another round of price increases that broadened the gap between world market levels and prices that federal controls set on a portion of U.S. oil production. Carter went on television April 5, 1979, to announce he would use presidential authority that Congress had granted in the 1975 Energy Policy and Conservation Act to wind down domestic oil price controls. The Carter administration began the decontrol process on June 1, 1979, and scheduled the lifting of all controls by Oct. 1, 1981, when the 1975 law's price control provisions were due to expire. Carter's decontrol program meant that domestically produced oil then selling for $6 to $13 a barrel would be freed to climb to world market levels. That price was in the process of doubling, to more than $30 a barrel, as the Iranian crisis squeezed supplies from Middle East nations.

Carter proposed a "windfall" profits tax to accompany decontrol. The tax, approved by Congress in 1980, satisfied most remaining concerns for a majority of members by preventing the oil industry from getting an undeserved windfall from sharply rising prices. It also provided revenues to finance federal assistance to help low-income families cope with energy costs and to subsidize development of synthetic fuels and other alternative energy sources.

## Reaction to Reagan Decontrol

Reagan had defeated Carter in the 1980 presidential election after pledging to promote production of additional domestic energy. The new president's decision to move up complete decontrol confirmed the oil industry's hopes that the conservative administration would back all-out exploration while scaling back federal energy regulation. Consumer groups opposed immediate decontrol, predicting that Reagan's action would prompt large price increases for gasoline and fuel oil.

Senate liberals mounted one unsuccessful legislative challenge. In March Sen. Howard M. Metzenbaum, D-Ohio, offered provisions reimposing price controls on oil and gasoline as an amendment to related legislation. Metzenbaum called the decontrol action "hasty and ill-advised," and he contended it would cost U.S. consumers $10 billion while adding an extra 1.1 percent to 1.4 percent to the U.S. inflation rate. Senate Energy Chairman McClure retorted that recontrolling oil would be a "monumental mistake." McClure maintained that decontrol would ease U.S. dependence on foreign oil imports and increase domestic production.

The Senate defeated the Metzenbaum amendment, 24-68. Most of the 24 senators who voted for the amendment were from the Midwest and Northeast, regions that had been hit hard by rising fuel prices. The

House never considered legislation to extend oil price controls.

Metzenbaum, along with several other members of Congress, labor unions and consumer groups, filed a lawsuit to block Reagan's decontrol order. But a federal court in Washington, D.C., rejected their challenge.

## Oil Allocation Authority

Congress in 1982 gave up a two-year effort to force President Reagan to accept standby power to control oil prices and supplies in the event of an energy emergency. The president had sparred with Congress throughout 1981 over whether the federal government or private energy markets should allocate oil and set its price during future petroleum shortages. Both the House and Senate passed legislation directing the president to draw up contingency government plans for managing petroleum supplies despite Reagan's insistence that he did not want that authority.

The Republican-led Senate in March upheld Reagan's veto of standby allocation authority. The 97th Congress later settled for compromise legislation that instead ordered the president to buy oil more rapidly than the administration had planned to fill the U.S. government's Strategic Petroleum Reserve in the Gulf Coast salt caverns of Texas and Louisiana. *(SPR, p. 25)*

In signing that measure, Reagan agreed to some House-drafted provisions that ordered the president to send Congress a plan for drawing oil from the strategic reserve to tide the nation through shortages. The bill also required the administration to keep collecting data on petroleum supplies and to submit various plans and reports on how it would respond to future supply curtailments. But the law essentially left Reagan free to let marketplace forces determine how oil would be shared if future

production cutbacks confronted the nation with severe energy shortages.

Through the veto Reagan successfully resisted bipartisan congressional proposals to extend presidential authority, first provided during the 1973 Arab oil embargo, to set oil prices and ration supplies among competing regions and industries. Administration officials maintained that the federal government's efforts to manage petroleum shortages in 1973 and again in 1979 actually had made them worse. In any future shortage, they contended, the government should let market adjustments run their course as prices rose to levels that would shrink energy demand to match reduced oil supplies.

### Background

President Reagan came into office with a conservative's trust in private market incentives, along with a distrust of the government's ability to manage energy supplies fairly and efficiently. In winning the presidency, he had pledged to dismantle most of the federal bureaucracy and regulations that Congress and previous presidents had put in place to handle the nation's energy policy during the shortage-plagued 1970s.

Reagan backed away from his campaign pledge to dismantle a separate Department of Energy (DOE) that Congress created in 1977. But the new administration, insisting that the market could do a better job of allocating oil during shortages than the government could, in 1981 opposed extension or replacement of the mandatory price and allocation regulations that Congress had required since the 1973 oil embargo.

**1973 Act.** In the midst of that embargo, Congress passed the Emergency Petroleum Allocation Act of 1973 (EPAA). That law directed the president to issue mandatory regulations for allocating and pricing crude oil and oil products. An earlier voluntary distribution program had proved ineffective in allocating supplies evenly. By the time Congress cleared EPAA in mid-November, long lines of cars at gasoline stations were making the nation's energy problems plain to the American people.

The legislation required the president to set up a comprehensive program to allocate oil and oil products among different regions and sectors of the petroleum industry. (It also directed the president to set prices — or set out a formula for determining them — for crude oil, residual fuel oil and refined petroleum products.) The law protected some oil users by requiring that independent refiners and retailers receive the same proportion of total crude or petroleum product supplies as they had in 1972. Major oil companies opposed mandatory allocations, but independent oil marketers favored a mandatory system that they contended would keep suppliers from driving them out of business by cutting off all their oil deliveries.

Congress extended the law in 1975 but modified the mandatory control provisions to make them discretionary starting in 1979. At the same time Congress provided for those standby authorities to expire altogether on Sept. 30, 1981. President Carter in 1979 used that discretionary power to begin gradually phasing out remaining oil price controls. Reagan lifted the controls completely on Jan. 28, 1981, eight months before allocation authority expired.

**Administration Position.** The administration took several months, however, to develop a position on extending the president's allocation authority beyond Sept. 30. Congressional committees held hearings in May and June, and witnesses generally agreed that the president should have the power to intervene in the market during severe petroleum shortages. But there was no agreement on how scarce oil would have to be before the president stepped in.

Tired of waiting for the administration to take a stand, McClure and Rep. Philip R. Sharp, D-Ind., chairman of the House Energy and Commerce Subcommittee on Fossil and Synthetic Fuels, introduced their own legislation to extend the 1973 law.

But at hearings Deputy Energy Secretary W. Kenneth Davis expressed opposition to any extension. Davis contended that government management of past petroleum shortages had "seriously hampered the ability of the marketplace to respond to short-term problems and actually contributed to the supply shortage. He said the nation was in a better position to weather future oil import curtailments because the SPR was being filled and privately held stocks were high.

But the congressional General Accounting Office (GAO), in a report released the day before the 1973 law expired, found that the country remained "grossly unprepared" to cope with a major shortage. The report criticized the administration's plan to let market adjustments manage shortages as "inappropriate."

## Vetoed 1981 Legislation

The president's authority to allocate oil expired on schedule on Sept. 30, 1981. In the months that followed, both the House and Senate ignored Reagan's objections by overwhelmingly approving bills to renew his standby allocation powers. The legislation, as cleared by Congress March 3, 1982, required the president to send to Congress within 180 days a standby petroleum allocation regulation, which would include a program for allocating crude oil among refiners. It also required the president to declare that there was a "severe shortage" (undefined) before putting the regulation into effect and placed a 90-day limit, which could be extended for 60 days, on any regulation. The law exempted certain "old" oil from the allocation plan.

The president vetoed the legislation March 20. In his message, Reagan contended that the bill could be counterproductive to preparedness if businesses and individuals believed that the government would come to their rescue during shortages.

The Senate attempted to overturn the veto on March 24, but failed. The vote, 58-36, fell five shy of the two-thirds majority required. Metzenbaum said the veto meant that "if there is another supply cutoff from the Middle East, the oil companies will decide who will get the scarce supplies of crude oil, gasoline and heating oil. And the oil companies, not the federal government, will decide what the price will be for the fuels that make this country run."

# Strategic Petroleum Reserve

Congress pressed the Reagan administration in 1981-82 to fill the federal government's Strategic Petroleum Reserve (SPR) more rapidly. In both years Congress approved legislation that urged the president to add at least 300,000 barrels of oil a day to the reserve as insurance against future energy shortages. But Congress in 1982 settled for a less costly compromise to fill the reserve at a rate of 220,000 barrels a day until it held 500 million barrels, two-thirds of its authorized capacity.

Congress established the strategic reserve in 1975 to give the nation a backup supply if it lost access to foreign oil markets. Since 1977 the government had been stockpiling oil in salt caverns along the Gulf of Mexico coastline in Texas and Louisiana.

After taking office in 1981, the Reagan administration stepped up oil purchases for the reserve to take advantage of falling prices and ample supplies on international markets. But Congress wanted DOE to buy oil even faster to build up a larger stockpile.

Through its massive budget reconcilia-tion measure enacted in Reagan's first year in office, Congress also tried to disguise the SPR's cost by establishing a special off-budget account so its funding would not count against the federal deficit.

The strategic reserve enjoyed as much bipartisan support in Congress as any government energy program. Members pushed hard to accelerate filling the reserve in the early 1980s, especially after Reagan vetoed the bill that would given him renewed authority to allocate oil during an energy shortage. But concerned about soaring budget deficits, Congress ultimately accepted a compromise that allowed Reagan to buy oil at a slower rate.

Congress had authorized storage of 750 million barrels of oil in the reserve. In mid-1985 the reserve held 484 million barrels. A barrel equals 42 gallons of liquid petroleum.

## Background

At President Ford's request, Congress created the strategic reserve as part of the Energy Policy and Conservation Act of 1975, a law that extended presidential powers to control oil prices and allocation. Congress approved government proposals to stockpile as much as one billion barrels within seven years as a hedge against import disruptions.

Federal energy officials selected underground storage sites in Texas and Louisiana near existing Gulf Coast oil fields and distribution pipelines. The oil was stored in evacuated salt domes, geologic formations where massive salt deposits were surrounded by rock. To create space for the reserve, the salt was flushed out with water, leaving a huge cavity. Energy officials also planned additional storage sites in other regions closer to where oil would be needed in emergencies. But in the late 1970s sharp world oil price increases, Middle East politics and technical problems in preparing the salt caverns as storage tanks combined to slow the filling of the reserve and to boost its expected cost.

President Carter took office in 1977 and moved to buy 500 million barrels of oil for the reserve by the end of 1980, two years ahead of the Ford administration's schedule. Although the first oil was placed in reserve in July 1977, DOE officials admitted that the program was initially plagued by overambitious goals. By early 1979 the government had stored 91 million barrels in the SPR, but pumps had yet to be installed to withdraw the oil for use.

In that year revolution in Iran curtailed that country's oil production and disrupted world petroleum markets. The price of oil escalated from $13 a barrel in late 1978 to $30 or more a barrel in early 1980, sharply increasing the cost of purchasing oil for storage. The Carter administration stopped buying oil for the reserve altogether between March 1979 and September 1980.

Yielding to pressure from Saudi Arabia, the administration held off on filling the reserve even after world supply restrictions eased later in 1979. Saudi Arabia, the largest oil producer belonging to OPEC, stepped up its production to stabilize the international market after the Iranian revolution and resisted higher prices sought by other OPEC nations. Saudi officials had long been opposed to the U.S. stockpile, and they worried that new SPR purchases would tighten world supplies and heighten pressure from some Saudi political groups that wanted to cut back the nation's production. So the Saudi government quietly threatened to cut back its output if the United States resumed filling its reserve.

But Congress ordered stockpiling to resume in 1980. Sen. Bill Bradley, D-N.J., a Senate Energy Committee member, in 1979 traveled to Saudi Arabia to confer with officials; he came back convinced that benefits from filling the reserve far outweighed the risk of Saudi cutbacks. Included in legislation setting up the Synthetic Fuels Corporation was a provision ordering the president to start putting 100,000 barrels a day into storage on Oct. 1, 1980.

## 1981 Energy Reconciliation

Following congressional orders, the Carter administration again started filling the reserve on Sept. 23, 1980. The Reagan administration, in 1981 revisions to the fiscal 1982 budget, planned to pump 230,000 barrels a day into the SPR. But Congress, through the 1981 budget reconciliation package, raised the rate to 300,000 barrels a day.

Even as Congress pushed to stockpile more oil, however, members were looking for alternative ways for the government to finance the growing cost of the reserve. The government had spent nearly $7 billion on the SPR since the mid-1970s, and it was estimated that another $40 billion would be required during the 1980s. Concerned by the potential impact on its budget-balancing efforts, Congress voted not to count SPR spending in the government's annual budget. In what members freely admitted was "creative accounting," the reconciliation bill authorized $3.9 billion to buy and store crude oil but established a special off-budget account for it.

Another $260 million was included on-budget to administer the program and to expand the storage facilities. The administration had requested all on-budget funding for the reserve.

Some members, principally on the Budget committees, believed that private funding, such as oil bonds, could be found to pay for the oil, so the funds were knocked out of the budget. But the financial community and the administration opposed private financing, and with no alternative in sight, Congress was faced with either increasing the budget by $3.9 billion or leaving fund-

**Workers preparing strategic petroleum reserve site in abandoned salt mine at Weeks Island, La.**

ing for the SPR off-budget. It decided to authorize the spending but simply not count it.

### 1982 Preparedness Bill

Congress repeated its instructions for filling the strategic reserve in a 1982 compromise on energy preparedness policy. The Senate, unable to override Reagan's veto of an earlier measure granting the president standby oil allocation powers, joined the House to prod the president again to build up oil stockpiles more rapidly than the administration had planned.

The compromise measure directed the president to fill the SPR at a rate of at least 220,000 barrels a day. It also ordered the administration to submit plans for distribut-

ing oil from the reserve in times of shortage. The measure repeated the previous goal of adding 300,000 barrels a day to SPR storage. Congress empowered the president to waive that target, however, and instead set a minimum fill rate of 220,000 barrels a day until the stockpile reached 500 million barrels. The measure also carried several provisions ordering the administration to submit various reports on its plans for coping with emergency energy shortages.

### 1983-84 Action

Congress and the White House compromised in 1983 on the rate at which the nation should fill the reserve. Congress approved a reduction from 220,000 barrels per day to 186,000 barrels per day as the minimum rate at which the reserve was to be filled. The administration had wanted to slow the rate to 145,000 barrels a day.

In proposing the slowdown, primarily as a money-saving measure, administration officials maintained that because oil imports had decreased and the possibility of an oil embargo was less likely, it was no longer imperative that the nation move quickly to build its reserve.

Acting on the only energy preparedness measure that received much congressional attention, the House Sept. 18, 1984, approved a bill that directed the government to conduct a test sale of 1.1 million barrels of oil from the SPR. But the Senate did not consider the proposal.

Supporters of the bill argued that a test sale was needed to boost public confidence in the reserve and to work out technical problems in the paperwork and actual transfer of the oil from underground storage to refineries. The administration did not oppose the bill but said a test sale in times of an oil surplus would be of little help in indicating problems that could arise in using SPR oil in times of an energy crisis.

# Natural Gas Deregulation

Despite the protests concerning rising natural gas costs, Congress during President Reagan's first term was unable to deal with the problem. Members remained badly divided over whether the federal government should roll back gas prices or lift its remaining controls on the prices that producers charged at the wellhead. The president, as a result, backed away from a 1980 campaign pledge to deregulate natural gas prices completely. And congressional leaders sidetracked consumer groups' demands that Congress legislate stricter controls that would reduce prices.

Although natural gas was in plentiful supply, prices continued to climb. The price

of gas for heating homes in 1982 rose nearly 18 percent above year-earlier levels, according to Department of Energy estimates.

Most experts blamed the workings of the Natural Gas Policy Act of 1978, passed by Congress as part of the Carter administration's responses to gas shortages in the mid-1970s. To encourage gas producers to find and develop new supplies, the law scheduled periodic large increases in the wellhead prices that federal regulations set for various categories of gas production. It allowed prices to rise until 1985, then freed roughly half of all gas supplies from all federal price limits.

## Background

The 1978 law had ended four decades of comprehensive federal regulation of natural gas prices. Federal controls, in combination with local utility commission authority over retail gas rates, imposed "wellhead to burner-tip" regulation that created a tremendously complex industry, fraught with problems.

The natural gas industries operated in three segments: major oil companies and independent producers who drilled wells and sold gas to pipelines; pipeline companies who transported the gas from oil fields to distant markets; and local gas utilities who bought gas from the pipelines and resold it to industrial and residential users.

**FPC Regulation.** In the Natural Gas Act of 1938, Congress gave the Federal Power Commission (FPC) the power to regulate wholesale gas rates that pipelines charged for gas shipped in interstate commerce. The Supreme Court, ruling on the *Phillips Petroleum* case, extended FPC regulation to the wellhead prices that producers charged for gas they sold to those pipelines. Until 1978 the federal government imposed no controls on gas that was sold in intrastate markets without crossing state lines.

Congress in 1956 passed legislation to exempt gas producers again from federal regulation, but President Dwight Eisenhower vetoed the bill because an oil company lawyer lobbying on its behalf had offered Sen. Francis Case, R-S.D. (Senate, 1951-1962), a $2,500 campaign contribution. The scandal caused Congress to shy away from deregulation proposals over the following decades, but the U.S. petroleum industry continued to protest what it regarded as troublesome federal interference in natural gas markets.

In 1975 natural gas sold within the state where it was produced for prices three or four times the top regulated interstate price of 52 cents per thousand cubic feet. With the nation facing difficult energy shortages, Presidents Nixon and Ford asked Congress to end federal price controls to let interstate prices rise to the level of intrastate markets. Deregulation proponents argued that higher interstate prices would encourage producers to channel more gas into interstate markets and step up exploration for new gas reserves.

The Senate in 1975 approved legislation to gradually remove federal price ceilings from natural gas. But the House in 1976 approved much different legislation to lift controls over small gas producers but extend federal regulation to the gas that major companies sold on intrastate markets. Senate deregulation supporters chose not to go to conference, and the FPC reduced the pressure for legislative action with a 1976 administrative decision that raised the top nationwide price ceiling from 52 cents per thousand cubic feet (mcf) to $1.42.

**1978 Deregulation Law.** Alarmed by severe natural gas shortages in the Northeast and Midwest during the winter of 1976-77, President Carter in his 1977 energy program proposed extending federal price ceilings to intrastate markets in gas-producing states. The House accepted Carter's plan, which allowed gas prices to rise to slightly higher levels. But the Senate, after overcoming a lengthy filibuster by deregulation foes, again approved a gradual deregulation measure. After long negotiations that carried nine months into 1978, House-Senate conferees fashioned a compromise bill that Congress cleared as the 1978 Natural Gas Policy Act.

In the 1978 law Congress tried to combat natural gas shortages by increasing incentives to search for new gas supplies. Extending federal controls to intrastate gas markets, the law divided gas production into various categories, subject to price ceilings set by the Federal Energy Regulatory Commission (FERC), the agency that Congress had set up to replace the FPC in 1977. While holding "old" gas prices at lower levels, the law allowed large periodic increases in the producer price of newly discovered gas, defined as production from wells drilled after April 20, 1977, the date of Carter's energy message to Congress. It allowed regulated gas prices to rise steadily through 1984, then freed all "new" gas from federal price ceilings on Jan. 1, 1985.

The 1978 law also ended controls altogether on high-cost gas that was difficult to find and produce. Eager to assure themselves adequate supplies, pipeline companies that bought and transported gas for resale signed long-term contracts in the following years that committed them to purchasing large amounts of higher priced gas. As a result of those contracts, pipeline companies were forced to buy more expensive gas even when cheaper supplies were available. Passed through to consumers at the end of the pipelines, those costs produced rapid increases in natural gas bills for heating homes and firing industrial furnaces. The resulting outcry sparked new debate in Washington over federal natural gas policy.

### New Problems

The 1978 legislation had solved the supply problem. With the higher prices, gas shortages ended immediately, as gas companies rerouted high-cost gas from the intrastate markets in Texas and Louisiana, where prices had always been free from federal regulation, to the interstate market. Exploration for new supplies increased and in 1981, according to some producers, newly discovered supplies equaled depleted reserves for the first time since 1967.

But the 1978 law also heralded a new set of problems, nearly as vexing as those it solved. The legislation established a complex scheme for pricing gas reserves, based on their age and the difficulty of tapping them. Old gas — gas reserves discovered before 1977 — was priced the lowest; new gas was priced at a higher level; and certain kinds of high-cost gas, such as gas from wells deeper than 15,000 feet, were freed from price regulation altogether.

**Price Distortions.** In the years following passage of the measure, pipeline companies, which act as wholesalers for the gas industry, bid eagerly to contract for new supplies of gas. They were anxious to prevent shortages from recurring. And because FERC, which regulated pipeline prices, guaranteed pipeline companies a certain rate of return on their fixed assets, those companies had little incentive to keep gas costs down.

As a result pipeline companies agreed to long-term contracts requiring them to purchase large amounts of gas at the highest legal price. In some cases they agreed to buy deregulated gas at rates that far exceeded the price the market was willing to pay. But FERC allowed them to "roll in" this expensive gas with cheap, regulated gas and charge an average price. That average price climbed rapidly and steadily.

The upward pressure on gas prices was compounded by "take or pay" contracts that some pipelines signed. Those contract provisions obligated pipelines to pay for as much as 90 or 95 percent of the volume of gas they had agreed to purchase, whether or not there was demand for it when the time came for delivery.

**Natural Gas Glut.** As producers delivered more expensive gas, average prices throughout the nation rose rapidly. The average residential price per thousand cubic feet of gas jumped from $2.63 in 1978 to $4.90 in September 1981, then to $5.82 a year later. For consumers the price surge was all the more galling because it occurred at a time when gas was in ample supply.

Even as gradual deregulation expanded gas supplies on interstate markets, demand for gas fell off in the early 1980s as an economic recession cut industrial use, homeowners conserved more expensive energy, and businesses switched to alternative fuels. By 1982 gas prices in most parts of the country had caught up with the price of No. 6 residual fuel oil, a competing fuel that could be burned by factories and electricity-generating plants. In perfectly functioning markets, declining demand would have forced gas producers to cut the prices they charged pipeline operators. But with the deregulation format and contract provisions insulating producers from market forces, prices kept rising beyond the theoretical "market clearing price" that would balance supply with demand.

### Reagan Proposal Abandoned

Reagan's Cabinet in 1981 had recommended that the administration push for full natural gas deregulation. Arguing that price controls distorted market operations, officials suggested that removing controls could actually bring about a fall in prices. By 1982, however, congressional opposition and industry divisions forced Reagan to abandon the proposal.

Some gas-producing company officials lobbied hard for quick action on deregulation. But producers who sold high-priced gas from deep wells feared that lifting controls on lower-cost gas would drive their own earnings down. And gas pipeline companies and distributors shied away from deregulation proposals that might allow gas prices to rise so high that their customers would switch to other fuels.

With consumer groups calling for even tougher controls, senior congressional Republicans warned Reagan against pushing for 1982 legislation. On March 1 the president announced that he no longer intended to submit the issue to Congress. In April FERC issued a "notice of inquiry" indicating that it was studying administrative action to partially deregulate old gas prices. But congressional critics challenged the commission's authority to make major changes in pricing regulations.

### Congressional Response

As consumers' protests against gas prices rolled in, members of Congress introduced more than 100 bills dealing with natural gas. Through the summer months of 1982, the House Energy and Commerce Subcommittee on Fossil and Synthetic Fuels held extensive hearings on natural gas issues. But the 97th Congress never attempted to thrash out gas pricing problems fully through debate on legislation.

When Congress returned after the 1982 elections for a lame-duck session, several members offered gas-pricing amendments during debate on legislation raising gasoline taxes to pay for highway and other infrastructure repairs. With time too short for major action, however, the Senate adopted a resolution directing FERC to consider ways to correct the contract problems. The resolution, proposed by Energy Committee Chairman McClure, was adopted 90-3. The measure also said that

pipeline companies and producers should enter into negotiations to eliminate the problems, and that available federal aid should be provided to low-income natural gas consumers.

Congress in 1984 gave up attempts to revise federal controls on rapidly escalating natural gas prices. As natural gas rates continued to rise in 1982 and 1983, industrial and residential consumers put Congress under intense pressure to tighten the 1978 law. Energy experts on both sides of Capitol Hill worked on the controversial issue for months, but neither the House nor the Senate could develop a consensus approach for ironing out troubles in the nation's natural gas markets.

Members remained bitterly split over whether Congress should roll back natural gas prices or lift federal controls completely. And congressional leaders called off floor debate on compromise gas pricing bills that threatened to divide both Republicans and Democrats in bitter regional fights between delegations from gas-producing states in the Southwest and gas-consuming states in the Midwest and Northeast.

"It's just too controversial," House Speaker Thomas P. O'Neill Jr., D-Mass., told a Sept. 26, 1984, press conference in declaring natural gas pricing legislation dead for the 98th Congress.

## Alaska Gas Pipeline

In 1968 oil companies exploring Prudhoe Bay on Alaska's northern Arctic Coast discovered huge oil and natural gas deposits. The companies in 1977 finished building a $9 billion pipeline that shipped 1.7 million barrels of oil a day across the state to be loaded on tankers at Valdez. For years industry and government planners had studied proposals for piping Prudhoe Bay's extensive gas reserves across Alaska and Canada to reach markets in the lower 48 states.

Prudhoe Bay discoveries held 9 billion barrels of recoverable oil and roughly 26 trillion cubic feet of natural gas, an estimated 13 percent of known U.S. gas reserves. In the mid-1970s, when most U.S. energy experts concluded that the nation was starting to exhaust its natural gas supplies, Congress and President Carter moved to expedite a decision on several competing proposals for transporting Alaskan gas to the continental United States.

In 1976 Congress passed the Alaska Natural Gas Transportation Act, which directed the president to decide whether such an Alaskan gas transportation system should be built and to pick one of the competing proposals. The following year Carter decided the Alaska project should go forward.

He selected a proposal to build a pipeline that followed the route of the oil pipeline south from Prudhoe Bay past Fairbanks, and then followed the Alaska Highway through Canada to Calgary, Alberta. From there, the line would split, with one section going to the West Coast of the United States, the other to the Midwest. The pipeline would deliver about 2.5 billion cubic feet of Alaskan natural gas a day to the United States.

Carter's decision stipulated that the pipeline was to be financed by the private sector, not the government. It also specified that gas consumers could not be charged for construction costs until the entire system was finished. And to satisfy Justice Department antitrust concerns, the oil companies that owned the Prudhoe Bay gas were prohibited from owning any part of the pipeline.

But by 1981 the estimated costs of building the entire pipeline system had soared to $40 billion from the $10 billion projection in 1977. Technical problems involved in installing a 48-inch pipe in frozen tundra and cooling the gas to keep it from thawing the ground helped push the projected cost of the 745-mile Alaska portion from $3.3 billion to $27 billion. The lower legs from Canada to the Pacific Coast and Midwest were nearing completion. Northwest Energy Co. of Salt Lake City, Utah, the firm heading the consortium of gas companies planning the Alaska segment, had obtained most needed construction permits. But the banks that were considering financing the pipeline balked at lending the consortium $22.5 billion for construction unless the terms that Carter had set were altered.

Northwest responded by negotiating an agreement with Exxon, Standard Oil of Ohio (Sohio) and Atlantic Richfield (ARCO) — the oil companies that owned Prudhoe Bay gas reserves — under which those corporations would put up 30 percent of the financing in return for a 30 percent share of pipeline ownership. The banks also insisted that natural gas suppliers be allowed to "pre-bill" current consumers for pipeline costs as construction proceeded, not just after Alaskan gas began to flow.

Congressional debate over changes in financing the gas pipeline demonstrated continued divisions over how the government, consumers and industry should share the soaring costs of energy development efforts. Proponents contended that allowing oil company ownership and pre-billing of consumers would spread the financial risks of opening Alaska's natural gas reserves to help meet the country's energy needs. Opponents called the proposal "the greatest consumer rip-off in U.S. history" and warned that it might ultimately lead to the federal government's assuming the cost of building the pipeline.

Even after Congress agreed to the changes in 1981, high interest rates and technical problems combined with lagging energy demand to stall Alaskan pipeline construction. The project's uncertain prospects left in doubt how soon the nation could tap Alaska's huge natural gas reserves.

# Power Plant Conversion

Congress in 1981 scrapped a three-year-old law that ordered U.S. electric utilities to convert natural gas-burning power plants to coal or other fuels by 1990. That action responded to utilities' complaints that the 1978 law would force them to scrap perfectly good gas-fired generating stations after 1989 even though natural gas supplies probably would be plentiful.

The reversal illustrated the difficulties that Congress and federal energy agencies faced in trying to develop national plans for managing U.S. fuel supplies for the future. When Congress approved the 1978 Fuel Use Act, the Carter administration was predicting that the nation would start to exhaust its natural gas reserves in the 1990s. But in the following three years most energy experts concluded that newly discovered gas deposits and lagging energy demand would give the country ample natural gas supplies well into the 21st century.

Congress had enacted the 1978 coal conversion law as part of President Carter's plan to cut U.S. consumption of imported oil and then-scarce natural gas supplies. Its provisions barred industry from building new factories or power plants burning oil or gas and required that existing gas-fired power plants be closed or converted to other fuels by Jan. 1, 1990. Congress passed the Fuel Use Act as part of a five-measure legislative package that also granted tax incentives for conservation; promoted energy saving in homes, schools and hospitals; encouraged utility rate reform; and began gradually deregulating natural gas prices.

When Carter became president in January 1977, the country was suffering severe natural gas shortages in the Northeast and Midwest. Because of the federal price controls on interstate gas, producers in Texas, Louisiana and other producing states had been withholding supplies, preferring to sell gas at higher prices to users within their states. During the winter of 1976-77, unusually cold weather throughout the East inflated gas demand for heating and rapidly depleted interstate supplies. By the beginning of February, 11 states had declared emergencies and closed schools and factories, putting millions out of work.

Three months after taking office, Carter sent Congress a national energy plan built around the assumption that U.S. natural gas reserves were starting to run out. Part of his program was to discourage industrial use of natural gas, reserving most supplies for residential use. Congress, through an energy legislation package cleared on Oct. 15, 1978, approved those parts of Carter's plan.

Through the Fuel Use Act, Congress directed industry to switch from gas to oil or coal. At the same time, it regulated intrastate gas and set up a complicated system for phasing out federal price controls on most gas by 1985. It freed from price controls gas produced from deep wells drilled 15,000 feet into the earth.

But by the time Congress acted, Carter administration officials later acknowledged, new evidence indicated that the United States actually possessed plenty of natural gas. In the following years, deregulation brought additional gas onto interstate markets and encouraged a drilling boom that discovered large gas reserves in deep formations in Oklahoma's Anadarko Basin and the Rocky Mountain Overthrust Belt formation in southwestern Wyoming and northeastern Utah. When the Iranian revolution curtailed foreign oil supplies in 1979, the Department of Energy began granting exemptions from the 1978 fuel use law to allow industries that had shifted to oil to

# Renewable Energy Sources

The sun is this planet's most abundant source of energy. Only an infinitesimal fraction of the sun's energy strikes the Earth, but our share still equals about 180 trillion kilowatts of electricity, more than 25,000 times the world's present industrial capacity. According to scientists, the solar energy reaching the surface of the United States annually is greater than the total amount of fossil-fuel energy that will ever be extracted in this country.

This energy can be captured either directly through devices such as rooftop collectors, photovoltaic cells and building design features, or indirectly through the storage of solar energy in nature. The solar energy in organic materials such as trees, grasses, agricultural wastes and garbage can be burned to produce electricity or synthetic fuels. Even wind, which turns windmills to supply power, is an indirect form of solar energy. And so is water that has been heated by the sun to produce power.

Shocked by the energy crisis and awakened to environmental concerns, the United States began in the early 1970s to rediscover these ancient sources of energy. Congress for the first time in 1973 made money available for the development of solar energy. These funds grew steadily, peaking at $500 million in President Carter's fiscal 1981 budget.

Carter considered solar research and development an important part of his energy program, making it part of the new Department of Energy. He participated in Sun Day, May 3, 1978, to heighten public awareness of solar energy's potential as a national resource.

The same year Congress enacted energy tax credits for homeowners and businesses that installed solar equipment. A homeowner could claim a credit of 40 percent of the first $10,000 spent; a business could qualify for a 15 percent credit, in addition to the regular 10 percent business investment credit.

Then in 1979 Carter committed the United States to a goal of meeting 20 percent of its energy needs with solar and other renewable resources by the year 2000. In 1985 the country was half way to reaching that goal: renewable sources of energy were supplying 9.6 percent of all energy used — more than twice the amount supplied by nuclear power.

Carter's successor, Ronald Reagan, wasted no time in reversing those priorities. His administration instead emphasized petroleum and nuclear power. More important, according to Bill Holmberg, legislative director of the Solar Lobby, Reagan's tax reform proposals would not renew the investment tax credit, which was due to expire Dec. 31, 1985.

Holmberg claimed the tax credits permitted the still youthful solar energy industry to grow. While the industry had experienced increased investment and customer acceptance, it was not ready to stand alone. The tax credits had been passed as an "insurance policy" against the next energy crisis, which many observers felt could occur in the mid-1990s.

switch back to burning gas. By 1982, when the U.S. economic recession cut energy demand, the nation actually had a natural gas glut on its hands.

# Synthetic Fuels

Just four years after it launched the program, Congress in 1984 cut federal synthetic fuels development funding in half. In two deficit-cutting steps, Congress rescinded $7.375 billion in funds previously appropriated. President Reagan in May had asked Congress for a $9 billion rescission for the troubled synfuels corporation. With falling world oil prices undercutting synthetic fuel prospects, some members of Congress had demanded that the government scale back funding or scrap the program altogether.

Congress created the U.S. Synthetic Fuels Corporation (SFC) at President Carter's request in 1980, after a decade of energy disruptions. The corporation's mission was to funnel subsidies to help private business develop a commercial industry to convert coal, oil shale, tar sands and other raw materials into synthetic fuels.

At the time experts were predicting that world oil prices would keep soaring to $42.50 a barrel and beyond. Instead oil prices fell below $30 a barrel, far less than the level at which proposed synfuel processes could compete. The Reagan administration, which preferred to let energy markets provide the incentives for new forms of fuel, meanwhile gave the SFC program little priority in its energy strategy.

## Background

For at least half a century synthetic fuels had held out the promise of expanding U.S. supplies of critical liquid forms of energy that could be easily transported or burned in internal combustion engines. Despite decades of research, however, industry had yet to demonstrate technologies for making synthetic liquid fuels at a cost that could compete with petroleum or natural gas. As a result synthetic fuel conversion projects remained at the experimental stage.

The nation possessed ample coal reserves, including huge low-sulfur deposits beneath federal lands in the West. Colorado, Utah and Wyoming also held vast oil shale deposits, mostly federally owned, containing an estimated 400 billion to 700 billion barrels of oil that could be recovered by heating the rock to high temperatures. The nation also had available about 600 million tons of biomass — including farm and forest products and residues as well as municipal solid wastes — that could be converted to fuel oil and alcohol for blending with gasoline to make gasohol fuels.

**Sporadic Congressional Interest.** Congress began subsidizing synthetic fuels development in World War II, when experts were saying that domestic oil reserves would last only another dozen years. The Synthetic Liquids Fuel Act, passed in 1944, provided $30 million over the next five years for research and demonstration plants that converted coal, oil shale, trees and vegetative matter into liquid fuels. A three-year, $30 million extension was approved in 1948, with another $27.6 million voted in 1950, when the authorization was extended through 1955.

In the years following expiration of the act, the Bureau of Mines, under its basic research authorization, continued its experiments with oil shale and liquefaction and gasification of coal. A special coal research bill was approved in 1960, setting up a new office of Coal Research in the Interior Department.

The oil embargo and price increases by the Organization of Petroleum Exporting

Countries (OPEC) in 1973-74 renewed interest in synthetic fuels. President Ford called on Congress to provide new incentives to spur production by 1985 of the equivalent of one million barrels a day of synthetic fuels. Although the market was not ready for synfuels, Ford thought the government should help along a new industry that might be crucial during future embargoes.

The AFL-CIO and industry groups backed federal synfuels loan guarantees. But environmental groups, concerned about potential air and groundwater pollution from coal and oil shale conversion, lobbied against federal financial support for the industry. Western state governments also were alarmed by potential pollution, boomtown growth and demand for scarce water if a synthetic fuels industry suddenly took hold in their region.

President Carter in April 1979 called for massive federal financial support to spur synthetic fuels development as Iranian oil production cutbacks sent world oil prices soaring beyond $30 a barrel and created gasoline shortages in the United States. Carter asked Congress to create a synfuels corporation to manage $88 billion in federal financial incentives to spur synthetic fuels production reaching 2.5 billion barrels a day by 1990.

**1980 Law.** Finally cleared in June 1980, the Energy Security Act set a goal of producing the equivalent of at least 500,000 barrels of crude oil a day by 1987, increasing to two million barrels a day by 1992.

The law established the quasi-governmental Synthetic Fuels Corporation and directed its seven-member board to offer loans, loan guarantees, purchase agreements or price guarantees to nudge private industry to design and build a synthetic fuels conversion industry. In setting up the program, Congress provided for federal funding that ultimately could reach $88 billion over the following decade.

The law authorized an initial $14.9 billion for the corporation through fiscal 1984. At that point SFC was to submit a detailed report to Congress on its future strategy. Thereafter Congress could make additional authorizations, subject to annual appropriations, up to another $68 billion by 1990.

Carter in September 1980 named John C. Sawhill, a deputy secretary of energy and former energy adviser to President Ford, as SFC board chairman and chief operating officer.

### Ebbing Synfuels Prospects

From the start the federal synthetic fuels program disappointed its congressional backers. Reagan in 1981 fired Carter's synfuels corporation directors, and political maneuvering slowed the process of selecting their replacements. And, as the corporation geared up to go into operation, the turnaround in world oil markets dampened short previous enthusiasm for developing synthetic fuel technologies. Many potential synfuel sponsors backed off.

In January 1982 SFC accepted 11 synfuel projects for possible federal support. But in May, with synthetic fuel prospects ebbing, Exxon Corp. abruptly abandoned its huge oil shale project in western Colorado. Construction continued on a Union Oil Co. oil shale plant in Colorado and on a Great Plains coal gasification project in North Dakota, but private backers of other projects lost interest. By early 1984 SFC had found only one small project to support and had committed just $120 million of the nearly $15 billion Congress made available four years before. House Majority Leader Jim Wright, D-Texas, a prime backer of the 1980 legislation, and other supporters complained that the SFC board was moving too slowly.

**SFC Internal Problems.** A series of embarrassing revelations of internal problems at the SFC fueled congressional doubts and left the board for a time without a quorum to make decisions. In August 1983 SFC President Victor A. Schroeder resigned amid conflict-of-interest charges. On April 26, 1984, his successor to the $135,000-a-year post, Victor M. Thompson, also resigned under fire for failing to disclose, when he was appointed, that his actions as head of a Tulsa, Okla., bank were being investigated by the Securities and Exchange Commission.

Just before Thompson quit, the board approved $1.4 billion in subsidies for two controversial projects. His departure, followed by another 1984 resignation, left the board with just two members. By year's end Reagan had made three recess appointments to the board — thus allowing it to resume operations.

**Reagan Cutback Request.** As the White House in May 1984 announced that Reagan would fill the SFC board vacancies, the president proposed substantially scaling back the corporation's spending authority. He asked Congress to cancel $9 billion in SFC spending authority and restrict the remaining funds to projects that met a "market test."

By limiting SFC support to projects that could produce fuels at costs not significantly higher than competing fuels, the White House plan would have ruled out most proposed facilities then under SFC consideration.

Reagan's proposal effectively preempted congressional attempts to scale back or even kill the SFC. Even so, his plan did not go far enough for some congressional critics of the synfuels program. Sen. William Proxmire, D-Wis., complained that Reagan "should have gone all the way and shut it down."

## Rescissions

Just two days after Reagan asked for a $9 billion cutback, the Senate voted to rescind $2 billion in SFC funding as part of a deficit-cutting package that the House previously had passed. Senate Republican leaders persuaded five moderate Republicans to go along with the spending cut measure by agreeing to channel the $2 billion from synfuels program savings to non-defense discretionary programs. Although the House had provided for no SFC rescission, conferees accepted the $2 billion cut in the final budget-cutting legislation that Congress cleared June 27.

Despite strong opposition from Wright, Congress used continuing appropriations legislation in October to cut another $5.375 billion from previously approved synfuels funding.

SFC critics argued during House debate that the nation could ill afford to spend billions promoting synthetic fuels projects that could damage the environment while cutting domestic programs. SFC backers contended that the government should push ahead, despite falling oil prices, with technologies that ultimately would reduce U.S. dependence on foreign energy supplies from volatile regions such as the Persian Gulf nations. "How shall we expect the United States ever really to be taken seriously in the world," Wright asked during debate, "if, only five years after the second Arab oil embargo brought our nation to its economic knees for the second time in a decade, we abandon the goal of energy independence by doing away with the one long-term program . . . to achieve that goal?"

## 1985 Action

The House July 31, 1985, voted in effect to kill the SFC by rescinding most of its remaining funds as part of the fiscal 1986 Interior Department appropriations

bill. A month earlier, the Energy Department had cancelled the Great Plains coal
gasification plant in North Dakota.

The fate of the agency was to be
decided in the Senate when the appropriations bill was considered. Meanwhile, the
SFC announced in August approval of $744
million in subsidies for three synthetic fuel
projects. In response to congressional criticism of the contracts, SFC Vice Chairman

Tom Corcoran explained that the projects
had been under way for several years.

The funds included $184.3 million in
subsidies for the Seep Ridge oil shale
project in Utah, $60 million for the Forest
Hill "heavy oil" project in Texas and $500
million for Union Oil Co.'s oil shale project
in Colorado. This plant already had received $400 million in federal subsidies but
had produced no oil.

# 3

# Mineral Leasing

When James G. Watt became secretary of the Interior Department in 1981, he brought with him a determination to open federal lands to development by private industry. But in a series of politically charged confrontations, Congress whittled back Watt's ambitious leasing plans by declaring federal wilderness areas and some pristine coastal waters off limits to oil and gas exploration.

Watt proposed no changes in the basic federal laws that authorized his department to lease minerals beneath public lands and the federally controlled Outer Continental Shelf (OCS) for drilling and mining by private companies. As Watt's plans became clear, however, Congress acted, usually through riders to Interior Department appropriations bills, to overrule him.

In 1981 and again in 1982 Congress ruled out oil and gas leasing in federal wilderness areas, thwarting Watt's efforts to encourage exploration before a 1984 deadline would close those lands. In both years Congress also prohibited Interior from leasing rights to explore off the central and northern California coasts for federally owned oil and gas resources.

Under vigorous lobbying by environmental groups, members concluded that Watt's leasing plans risked damage to wildlife and ecosystems in federal wilderness and ocean basins. They also heeded charges

by conservation professionals and economists that Interior would be selling valuable public resources, including federally owned coal, at bargain prices by leasing them while world energy demand was depressed.

Even as it questioned Watt's leasing goals, Congress in 1982 approved the administration's request to tighten management of federal oil and gas resources. To prevent outright oil theft and to improve collection of federal oil and gas royalties, Congress approved legislation that strengthened Interior Department procedures for enforcing lease terms and accounting for royalty payments.

## Wilderness Leasing

The House Interior and Insular Affairs Committee in 1981 forced Secretary Watt to delay Interior Department decisions on leasing rights to explore wilderness areas within the U.S. national forests for oil and gas deposits. Congress followed up in 1982 by passing a fiscal 1983 Interior appropriations bill that barred leasing in those primitive federal lands through Sept. 30, 1983.

Three months later, on Jan. 1, 1984, a provision in the Wilderness Act of 1964 permanently closed federal lands within the national wilderness system to further mineral leasing. Congress meanwhile resisted Watt's demand that it act quickly to release for development additional national forest lands that were being considered as possible wilderness areas.

In creating the federal wilderness system in 1964, Congress kept wilderness areas within national forests — but not national parks — open to mineral leasing for 20 years. After the Reagan administration took office in 1981, Watt began prodding U.S. Bureau of Land Management (BLM) officials to grant pending oil company requests for rights to explore wilderness regions. But Congress, led by the House Interior and Appropriations committees, took legislative steps that stalled BLM approval of those leases as the deadline approached.

In addition to designated wilderness preserves, Congress forbade leasing in lands that the U.S. Forest Service had recommended for protection or for further study of their wild character. Suspicious of Watt's motives, members and their environmental group allies ignored the secretary's 1982 offer to bar mining and drilling in wilderness areas until the year 2000 while the government surveyed them for valuable mineral deposits.

By heading off Watt's wilderness leasing plans, Congress heeded environmentalists and sportsmen who were fighting the Reagan administration's plans to accelerate resource development in Western states. The outcome frustrated oil company officials and Western businessmen who contended that the government should permit the industry to study promising public lands — especially near the Rocky Mountain Overthrust Belt — before "locking them up." Starting in the late 1970s "wildcat" drilling in Wyoming and Utah had discovered huge natural gas reserves along the Overthrust Belt, a geologic formation that follows the Rocky Mountain chain. The discoveries whetted industry interest in leasing rights to explore national forests and range lands, including some wild lands that lie above or close to promising formations.

As the controversy mounted, however, even Western Republicans who backed Watt's philosophy turned against wilderness leasing plans. Rep. Manuel Lujan Jr., N.M., the Interior Committee's top-ranking Republican, supported efforts to ban wilderness leasing after Interior in September 1981 granted three leases allowing exploratory drilling beneath the Capitan Wilderness in New Mexico. Senate Energy and Natural Resources Committee Chairman James A. McClure, R-Idaho, who also chaired the Senate Appropriations Subcommittee on Interior, bottled up initial House anti-leasing bills but eventually accepted the 1982 appropriations bill rider.

Watt bowed to congressional sentiment after the fiscal 1983 prohibition was approved. On the day President Reagan signed the bill, Watt promised that the department would not "try to slip things through" by granting leases in wilderness areas during the 90 days between Sept. 30, 1983, when the fiscal 1983 ban expired, and Jan. 1, 1984, when the permanent prohibition went into effect. As events turned out, Watt resigned the Interior post on Oct. 9, 1983.

### Background

In the Mineral Leasing Act of 1920, Congress gave the interior secretary the authority to lease at his discretion the rights to find and produce coal, oil and gas and other minerals beneath federally owned public lands. That authority applied to all public domain lands, largely in Western states, that were managed by the Interior Department and by the U.S. Forest Service. But through legislative and administrative actions, the government in subsequent years restricted oil and gas exploration on millions of acres to protect scenic views, natural ecosystems, archeological sites and other non-consumptive values.

In creating most national parks from the public lands, Congress prohibited mineral leasing within their boundaries. Interior and Forest Service officials barred exploration on other lands through administrative "withdrawals" from availability under leasing programs. Starting in the 1920s, Forest Service officials designated large roadless regions within the national forests for protection in their wild state.

**1964 Wilderness Act.** In the 1964 wilderness law, Congress gave those still-wild lands protection by statute. Timber companies, mining firms, ranchers and other commercial interests in Western states with large expanses of national forest objected that a permanent wilderness system would deny access to commercial resources that might be needed in the future.

The Wilderness Act declared that the government should preserve its wild lands as "an area where the earth and its community of life are untrammeled by man, where man himself is a visitor who does not remain." To keep wilderness that way, the law prohibited logging, commercial ventures, construction of roads or buildings or the use of motor transportation within wilderness boundaries.

But at the insistence of Rep. Wayne N. Aspinall, D-Colo. (1949-73), who was the House Interior Committee chairman, Congress accepted compromise provisions that protected some commercial interests in wilderness areas. The law permitted ranchers to continue grazing livestock on wilderness forests, and it honored previously filed mining claims on those lands. For 20 years, until Dec. 31, 1983, the law allowed prospectors to stake mining claims to hard-rock minerals in wilderness areas under the Mining Law of 1872. For the same period, the law also continued the interior secretary's authority to lease coal, oil and gas, and other resources beneath those lands under the Mineral Leasing Act of 1920.

Congress initially set aside 9.1 million acres in wilderness areas established by the 1964 law. By 1983 it had expanded the national forest wilderness system to 25 million acres through subsequent legislation. Congress also created 35 million acres of wilderness in national parks, where mining and leasing were prohibited, and another 19 million acres in national wildlife refuges. In the early 1980s Congress was reviewing, through state-by-state bills, Forest Service proposals drawn up during the Carter administration to expand the national forest wilderness system to 33 million acres. Meanwhile, BLM was studying 24 million acres that it had identified on Interior Department lands for possible wilderness status. *(Wilderness legislation, p. 171)*

While wilderness remained technically open for leasing, the government in practice permitted little actual activity in those areas. Concentrating their drilling programs in areas with proven potential, oil and gas companies indicated little interest in exploring rugged mountain wilderness terrain where drilling would be costly. In managing its wilderness, the Forest Service also discouraged mineral development by severely restricting activity that might alter natural landscapes.

BLM, an Interior agency, issued oil and gas leases on national forests as well as its own lands. But the bureau in practice required exploration crews to obtain Forest Service consent to operate on forest lands. Between 1964 and 1982 the government granted only 50 oil and gas leases on existing Forest Service wilderness or candidate wilderness areas.

**New Leasing Demands.** Starting in the late 1970s deep wildcat wells discovered huge new petroleum fields, chiefly producing natural gas, along the Rocky Mountain Overthrust Belt formation in Wyoming, Utah and Idaho. Oil and gas companies eagerly sought leases to explore national

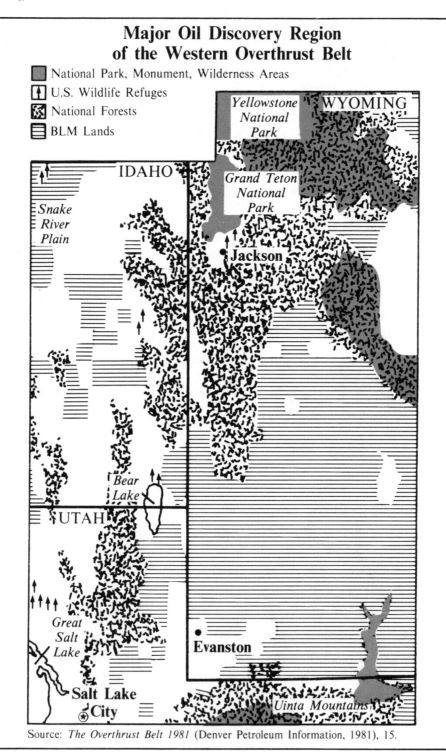

## Major Oil Discovery Region of the Western Overthrust Belt

National Park, Monument, Wilderness Areas

U.S. Wildlife Refuges

National Forests

BLM Lands

WYOMING

Yellowstone National Park

Grand Teton National Park

IDAHO

Snake River Plain

• Jackson

Bear Lake

UTAH

Great Salt Lake

Evanston

Salt Lake City ⊛

Uinta Mountains

Source: *The Overthrust Belt 1981* (Denver Petroleum Information, 1981), 15.

forests and Interior lands that made up most of the region, including several designated wilderness areas, proposed additions, candidate wilderness study areas and lands surrounding national parks. Company officials contended that advances in seismic exploration technology, using helicopters and lightweight equipment to monitor underground formations, made it practical to study rugged mountains and forests with no permanent environmental damage. Slant drilling techniques also made it possible to extract oil or gas from beneath a wilderness area with wells drilled from outside its boundaries.

During the same period, both the Forest Service and BLM were studying millions of acres for possible wilderness protection. After identifying roadless areas for possible designation, the agencies restricted access until Congress decided whether or not to include them in the wilderness system. Some regions that the agencies proposed for preservation or for further study lay over promising formations near the Overthrust Belt discoveries. In Wyoming alone, a 1981 General Accounting Office (GAO) study for Congress estimated that 483,000 acres of BLM wilderness study areas and 1.3 million acres of recommended national forest wilderness had oil and gas potential.

As of early 1982 BLM had granted about 5,000 oil and gas leases covering 26 percent of the 24 million acres it was studying for possible wilderness recommendation. The government had issued at least 337 leases on 19.5 million acres in national forests that were being reviewed by Congress or studied by the Forest Service for preservation. In addition, 891 lease applications were pending on Forest Service wilderness and wilderness candidate areas, with another 745 applications pending for leases on Forest Service wilderness study areas.

After taking charge of the Interior Department in 1981, Watt backed the industry's demand for a chance to explore both designated and potential wilderness areas to assess their oil and gas potential before the Wilderness Act barred leasing. "If we are to put much of this area off limits to exploration and potential development, it should be done so consciously and with full recognition of the values to be forgone," Watt maintained in a 1982 letter to Sen. Malcolm Wallop, R-Wyo., chairman of the Senate Energy and Natural Resources Subcommittee on Public Lands and Reserved Water.

But environmentalists contested industry assessments of wilderness areas' oil and gas potential. A 1982 Wilderness Society study, updated in 1983, calculated that wilderness regions might hold 3.9 percent of the nation's undiscovered oil reserves and 3.4 percent of its undiscovered gas, not counting offshore petroleum deposits. Conservation groups contended that oil companies should first explore less fragile lands, keeping wilderness areas as a last resort for development only in event of a severe energy emergency. "What we're talking about are supplies that can be measured in a few days of national petroleum consumption," Brant Calkin, the Sierra Club's Southwest representative, argued in 1981. "That's not adequate promise to put in roads [into wilderness areas] that are going to last a lot longer than the oil will."

## 1981 Interior Committee Stance

Twice in 1981 the House Interior Committee challenged Watt's leasing plans in Montana and New Mexico. Watt complied with the committee's stand reluctantly, agreeing to shelve wilderness leasing actions until mid-1982.

**Montana Wilderness Test.** In the first test of congressional opposition to wilderness leasing, the Interior panel May 21 voted 23-18 to order Watt to close three areas, located south of Glacier National Park in Montana, to oil and gas leasing. In its vote, the panel approved a resolution ordering Watt to withdraw the entire 1.5 million acres of the Bob Marshall, Scapegoat and Great Bear wilderness areas of Montana national forest lands.

The committee's resolution was based on a little-used provision of the Federal Land Policy and Management Act of 1976 (FLPMA). The act allowed the secretary to order the immediate withdrawal of specific land if either the secretary or the House Interior or Senate Energy committees determined that an emergency existed requiring the land to be protected from development. At the time the 1976 law was being considered, the attorney general said the provision might be unconstitutional.

The provision had been used by the committee once before, when it voted in 1979 to protect water wells in Ventura, Calif., from uranium mine tailings. In addition, Carter administration Interior Secretary Cecil D. Andrus used it Nov. 16, 1978, to withdraw 110 million acres of Alaskan land after the 95th Congress failed to pass legislation to protect them.

The Montana wilderness areas, which form the headwaters of the Missouri and Columbia rivers, lie along the Overthrust Belt. When the committee acted, 343 lease applications from oil companies seeking to explore the region were pending before the Forest Service. The resolution's backers said they intervened because they feared the Forest Service would grant a request by a Denver-based geophysical exploration firm that wanted permission to detonate 5,400 separate seismic charges in and around the wilderness to test the oil and gas potential of underlying rock formations.

The committee resolution left the three areas off-limits for leasing until the 1984 cutoff went into effect. Although Watt bowed to the panel's wishes, the Reagan administration joined in a court challenge to the resolution. Mountain States Legal Foun-

dation, a conservative public interest law group that Watt had headed before taking the Interior post, filed a lawsuit contending that the FLPMA provision under which the committee acted was unconstitutional. In an Aug. 6 letter to House Speaker Thomas P. O'Neill Jr., D-Mass., Attorney General William French Smith announced that the Justice Department, instead of defending the land withdrawal, would side with the plaintiffs in the case. Smith contended that the FLPMA provision amounted to a one-house veto of the sort that the Justice Department consistently opposed as a congressional intrusion on executive branch powers. (In a subsequent decision on a separate dispute, the U.S. Supreme Court ruled that one-house veto provisions were unconstitutional.)

**Six-Month Moratorium.** In a second 1981 showdown the Interior panel voted 41-1 Nov. 20 to ask the administration to hold up action on any oil and gas leases in wilderness areas until June 1, 1982. Watt agreed to go along with the moratorium under pressure from committee Republicans.

The committee acted after Interior officials leased 700 acres in the Capitan Mountain Wilderness Area, in Lujan's state, without conducting environmental studies or notifying Congress. Lujan responded by introducing a resolution that would have prevented the department from issuing oil and gas leases on the 23.4 million acres of wilderness in the lower 48 states. After a Nov. 19 meeting with Lujan and Interior Committee Republicans Dick Cheney, Wyo., and Don Young, Alaska, Watt promised that the department would complete environmental studies and notify Congress and the public before granting wilderness leases. The next day, however, the panel requested the six-month moratorium to give Congress time to consider legislation

**Caterpillar tractor near Wyoming's Grand Teton mountains. Western states are torn between developing mineral resources and protecting their region's natural beauty.**

to protect wilderness from leasing.

## 1982 Appropriations Rider

With congressional displeasure more evident, Watt agreed to hold off oil and gas leasing in all wilderness areas and proposed preserves until the 97th Congress adjourned at the end of 1982. That still left a one-year "window" for leasing until the permanent ban went into effect. The entire Congress moved to close it in 1982.

As the controversy continued, Watt threw Congress and environmentalists off balance by proposing a plan that appeared to reverse his 1981 stance on wilderness. In a Feb. 21 network television interview, Watt suggested legislation to close wilderness areas to oil and gas leasing until the year 2000.

Environmental group leaders initially hailed Watt's announcement but attacked it after Interior officials leaked draft legislation. Watt proposed closing wilderness areas while the government surveyed them and reported to Congress every five years on what minerals it was finding. After the year 2000 Congress could vote to open some areas to development if it determined such a step was needed.

Because the measure was silent on what would become of all wilderness acreage after the year 2000, it caused consternation among some in Congress and the environmental community who feared it would lift wilderness protections after that date. Another provision raising some hackles set deadlines for Congress to act on pending wilderness proposals or they would be "released" for non-wilderness uses such as logging.

Under Watt's plan, no drilling or mining would be allowed in the wilderness areas unless ordered by the president because of an urgent national need — such as an energy or strategic-mineral shortage. Congress would have 60 days in which to pass legislation blocking such presidential action, but that bill would have to be signed by the president.

John F. Seiberling, D-Ohio, the House Public Lands Subcommittee chairman, dismissed Watt's plan as "the most sweeping and devastating *anti*-wilderness bill I have ever seen." Seiberling's subcommittee responded in June by drafting legislation to ban wilderness leasing that the full House approved overwhelmingly. But the Senate Energy panel bottled up the measure, forcing leasing opponents to act through the annual appropriations process.

**Interior Committee Bill.** The Public Lands Subcommittee bill, approved by the full Interior panel on a 34-7 vote June 24, covered 33 million acres in the lower 48 states that were already designated as wilderness, recommended for protection by the Forest Service or under study for wilderness status.

The measure allowed energy and mineral prospecting and inventories that were "compatible with the preservation of the wilderness environment," but it barred seismic surveys conducted with explosives. It gave the president authority to ask Congress to approve mineral development on a specific tract of withdrawn land in cases of "urgent national need." The House passed its bill by a 340-58 vote Aug. 12. In urging the House to act, leasing opponents said Watt had been completing paperwork on pending lease applications so the department could grant them quickly when the previous moratorium expired.

But McClure and other senators

wanted to trade off an extended leasing ban for "release" language that would force Congress to resolve quickly the status of proposed additions to the wilderness system. The Senate panel bottled up the House-passed bill.

**Appropriations Riders.** Fearful that the Interior legislation would be held up too long for action by the 97th Congress, backers of the leasing ban shifted tactics in September. Over the following months Congress amended legislation funding Interior operations to block the department from processing and granting wilderness lease applications.

Congress first wrote an amendment barring the department from spending money to process wilderness lease applications into a continuing resolution appropriating funds for government operations after fiscal 1983 began Oct. 1. Watt himself, in a letter to Senate Appropriations Committee Chairman Mark O. Hatfield, R-Ore., urged the panel to approve the freeze to relieve congressional doubts about whether he was observing the moratorium.

Congress subsequently extended the moratorium through fiscal 1983 with an amendment to the regular Interior appropriations measure cleared in December. The ban extended until Congress had made a final determination of the status of lands not already formally designated as wilderness.

The committee noted its prohibition did not extend to BLM lands under study for possible wilderness designation, but it said the Interior Department "should take whatever action is necessary to ensure the Congress' prerogative to designate BLM wilderness study areas as wilderness is not foreclosed by leasing or mineral survey activities."

The full House passed the bill Dec. 3 without discussing the leasing ban. Before passing the bill Dec. 14, the Senate approved an amendment, offered by John Melcher, D-Mont., that contained the key points sought by leasing opponents. Melcher's proposal barred leasing in designated wilderness, areas recommended for wilderness and areas under study for wilderness. It also banned seismic studies using explosives.

The conference version, cleared Dec. 19, included the Senate wilderness language. President Reagan signed the bill on Dec 30.

# Oil and Gas Royalties

Congress in 1982 tightened Interior Department procedures for collecting royalties on oil and gas produced from federal lands. Responding to charges of chronic mismanagement, lawmakers Dec. 21 cleared legislation giving the secretary of the interior stronger authority to make sure that companies leasing the right to extract oil and gas from public lands paid the government all the royalties they owed.

In January a special commission appointed by Secretary Watt had charged that the federal government was losing $200 million to $500 million in revenues a year from underpaid royalties and outright theft of oil from wells on public lands. Watt had ordered the study in response to complaints from Western state governments and Indian tribes that lax Interior Department enforcement was costing them millions of dollars in lost revenues from oil and gas production within their borders.

Watt responded by setting up a new Interior agency, the U.S. Minerals Management Service (MMS), to handle revenues from federal energy leasing programs. Congress followed up by approving the commission's recommendations for improving lease operator record-keeping, tightening well-site security and toughening Interior enforcement of the financial terms of federal oil and gas leases.

## Background

In the Mineral Leasing Act of 1920, Congress set up a system for leasing oil and gas beneath federally owned lands for discovery and production by private companies. The law charged leaseholders annual rentals for access to public lands and required them to pay the federal government a royalty of 12.5 percent of the value of the oil and gas they extracted.

The 1920 law required competitive bidding for leases on lands known to hold oil and gas but allowed the Interior Department to grant leases without competition to companies that wanted to explore for unknown deposits. To win competitive leases companies offered the government a bonus payment through sealed bids. Although annual rentals had been revised over the years, in 1982 they were still only $2 an acre for most non-competitive exploratory leases. Competitive leases ran for five years and non-competitive leases for 10 years, or as long as production continued.

Royalty payments produced the most revenue from federal energy leasing programs. In 1982 royalties on most federal land leases remained at 12.5 percent, although the department charged 16 2/3 percent royalties for leasing oil and gas reserves in the federally owned Outer Continental Shelf and in the National Petroleum Reserve on Alaska's North Slope.

Federal leasing revenues surged in the 1970s with the rise in oil and gas prices. Before 1973 a 12.5 percent royalty brought the government around 25 cents per barrel of oil. The federal share jumped to approximately $3 per barrel with decontrol of U.S. crude oil prices. In 1982 the government collected $874 million in royalties and other revenues from oil and gas leases on federal lands, along with another $146 million in oil and gas revenues from leases on Indian reservations, according to MMS figures. In the same year the government took in $3.8

billion in royalties and rents from offshore oil and gas production. Oil and gas companies also paid nearly $4 billion in bonus bids for offshore leases that year and another $95.3 million in bonuses for competitive onshore leases.

With the growth in royalties, federal oil and gas leases became an important source of revenues for the U.S. Treasury. Indian tribes and state governments with oil-producing federal lands within their borders also reaped financial benefits. Interior passed along all mineral leasing revenues from Indian lands to tribal governments or individual Native American landowners. And under the Mineral Leasing Act the federal government shared half of its royalties from onshore mineral production with state governments. In a 1976 law revising Interior coal-leasing procedures, Congress increased the state share of all mineral leasing revenues to 50 percent from 37.5 percent. In Alaska, state and local governments received more than 75 percent of federal oil and gas royalties.

Three Interior Department agencies shared authority over federal oil and gas leases: the Bureau of Land Management, the U.S. Geological Survey's (USGS) Conservation Division and U.S. Bureau of Indian Affairs (BIA).

## Mismanagement Charges

Those agencies supervised drilling and production from federal oil and gas leases that were scattered over vast expanses of public mountains and deserts. Despite long-standing complaints of thefts and underpaid royalties, Interior officials had never come up with procedures to keep track of how much oil and gas was being produced from federal leases and how much well operators owed in royalties. USGS collected royalties on an honor system without independently verifying the production that leaseholders reported to the government.

Since 1979, studies by Congress, state governments, tribal leaders, the GAO and the Interior Department itself had found federal lease supervision too lax to detect and prevent irregularities. Concern increased in the early 1980s after oil prices rose and Watt announced plans to expand oil and gas exploration on public lands. State and tribal leaders in 1981 demanded that Watt take strong action to improve royalty collection.

In Wyoming, Watt's native state, Arapahoe and Shoshone tribal leaders on the Wind River Reservation urged Interior to cancel existing oil and gas leases after allegations of theft and underpaid royalties. California and 10 other states filed suit against the federal government to demand that Interior account for royalties back to 1920.

In response to those pressures, Watt in July 1981 appointed a Commission on Fiscal Accountability of the Nation's Energy Resources, chaired by David F. Linowes, a University of Illinois professor, to investigate such charges. In a scathing report issued Jan. 21, 1982, the commission charged that the federal government was losing $200 million to $500 million annually due to oil thefts and royalty underpayments by oil companies.

The commission found that accounting and collection procedures were outmoded, enforcement was weak, penalties were insufficient and security on well sites was lax. The report said oil company royalties, which should reach $14 billion a year by 1990, were collected almost totally on the honor system.

## MMS Established

After the Linowes commission issued its report, Watt overhauled the Interior Department's royalty collection system. Under a department reorganization completed in 1983, Watt shifted the Conservation Division out of the scientifically oriented USGS to form the Minerals Management Service. The new agency was responsible for collecting federal mineral royalties. It also took over the authority to lease offshore oil and gas reserves, a function previously performed by BLM.

Watt announced that the department would impose tighter internal controls on the leasing process and hire and train new field inspectors to supervise drilling and pumping operations. Watt also called for new legislation to tighten royalty collection and management procedures. Congress responded by passing legislation, which became law Jan. 12, 1983, to implement procedures proposed by the commission.

# Offshore Leasing

Three months after taking office, Secretary Watt announced plans to accelerate the Carter administration's program for leasing oil and gas drilling rights on the federal Outer Continental Shelf. A year later, Watt approved leasing schedule that aimed at offering by 1987 more than one billion acres of the coastal sea floor for exploration by oil and gas companies.

The Interior Department had been leasing offshore oil and gas since 1954, but exploration and discoveries had been confined to the Gulf of Mexico and the Southern California coastlines. By speeding up lease sales and condensing environmental reviews, Watt maintained, the government could give the industry a chance to select and explore other promising regions, especially off the Alaska coast, to inventory their oil and gas potential. In the process, the Reagan administration hoped that the Interior Department would take in between $40 billion and $80 billion for the U.S. Treasury.

But the 97th Congress stepped in with legislation that ruled out leasing in environ-

mentally sensitive waters off the northern California and New Jersey coastlines. Environmental groups and coastal state governors meanwhile mounted legal and political challenges that forced the Interior Department to postpone planned lease sales in unexplored California and Alaska offshore basins.

With a 1969 offshore well blowout off the Santa Barbara, Calif., coast still much on members' minds, Congress responded to environmentalists' protests that accelerated leasing would raise the risk of destructive oil spills that would threaten pristine waters and important fishing grounds. Watt's critics also charged that the government would sacrifice potentially larger revenues by leasing offshore oil and gas reserves while world energy demand was depressed.

### Background

In 1953 Congress asserted federal govon about 1.1 billion acres of submerged sea floor three miles or more off the nation's coastlines. Settling rival state and federal claims, Congress in the Submerged Lands Act of 1953 recognized coastal state governments' authority to manage the sea bed and its resources within three miles of their coasts. In the Outer Continental Shelf Lands Act, passed the same year, Congress established federal authority over the OCS beyond the three-mile limit and gave the interior secretary authority to lease its oil and gas resources for exploration and development by private companies.

In the following 25 years the Bureau of Land Management offered 12 million acres, roughly 1 percent of the OCS, for oil and gas development. BLM actually sold leases for 5.3 million acres off the Texas and Louisiana coasts in the Gulf of Mexico and another 1.3 million acres along the Pacific Coast in Southern California. Between 1953 and 1983 industry produced 6.3 billion barrels of oil and 62.1 trillion cubic feet of natural gas from federal OCS leases. During that 30-year period the federal government earned $47.1 billion in bonus bidding for leases and $20.7 billion in rents and royalties on oil and gas production at a rate of 16 2/3 percent.

By the early 1980s federal OCS leases produced roughly 10 percent of U.S. domestic oil output and 25 percent of its natural gas. Geologists generally agreed that unexplored OCS regions held the nation's best prospects for discovering new oil and gas resources. When world oil prices began climbing in the mid-1970s, oil companies became more eager to explore promising offshore frontiers off the Pacific Coast of northern California, the Atlantic Coast of New England and the Mid-Atlantic states, and along Alaska's deeply indented bays and peninsulas.

The Nixon and Ford administrations drew up plans in the 1970s for expanding OCS leasing into frontier regions. But since the 1969 oil well blowout in the Santa Barbara Channel blackened beaches north of Los Angeles, killing thousands of fish and waterfowl, opposition had been mounting to offshore drilling. State governors, local officials, the fishing and tourist industries and environmental activists in coastal states feared that scenic beaches and productive marine resources could be ruined.

Congress in 1978 revised the 1953 OCS law in an effort to meet environmental concerns while encouraging offshore petroleum development. In Outer Continental Shelf Lands Act Amendments, enacted with President Carter's support, Congress tightened environmental controls on drilling operations, directed Interior to consider recommendations from state governors in scheduling lease sales and specified procedures to foster competition among oil companies in bidding for OCS leases.

The law directed the interior secretary to draw up a five-year schedule for planned OCS lease sales, taking into account the relative environmental sensitivity and marine productivity of areas under consideration for exploration. In scheduling sales, the secretary also was directed to assure that the government received "fair market value" for its OCS resources.

Operating under the new standards, Secretary Andrus in 1980 scheduled 36 OCS sales to offer about 27.5 million acres to the industry by 1985. The Andrus program envisioned an average of seven lease sales a year, double the leasing pace in the 1970s. It targeted the Gulf of Mexico as the primary leasing area but included 10 sales in Alaskan waters. It excluded four areas — the Florida Straits, the Washington and Oregon coasts, Alaska's Bristol Bay and southern Aleutian Shelf — that had once been considered for leasing.

The Andrus program encountered stiff resistance from state officials and environmental groups. Massachusetts filed suit against leasing in the Georges Bank fishing grounds off the North Atlantic coast, and Alaska urged Interior to delay three of the 10 planned sales near its shores. California Gov. Edmund G. Brown Jr., D, urged the department to exclude 33 tracts in the northern reaches of the Santa Maria Basin off his state from a proposed 1981 sale, arguing that oil spills could threaten marine mammals. A week before the 1980 presidential election, Andrus deleted four untouched offshore basins off northern California from the 1981 lease offering.

### Watt Leasing Plan

After replacing Andrus, Watt determined that Interior should open as much OCS acreage as possible for exploration, giving industry a chance to assess the oil and gas potential of all remaining untapped offshore regions within 10 to 15 years.

In February 1981 Watt stunned California officials and angered the state's congressional delegation by announcing that he was reconsidering Andrus' decision the previous year to bar leasing in the four Pacific basins. Controversy over OCS leasing grew in the following two years as Interior put together a five-year plan that was much more ambitious than the Carter administration's schedule.

Watt outlined his goals in April, announcing an accelerated program that scheduled 41 sales, an average of more than eight a year, through 1986. Watt also revised Interior leasing procedures to expedite environmental and economic reviews — and let the industry identify for leasing the offshore regions it considered most promising.

In the past Interior officials had put limited OCS areas up for bidding after studying their geologic and environmental characteristics. Before offering to lease drilling rights, the department estimated a fair bonus bid for each price as a standard for judging whether the bids oil companies made would pay the government fair market value.

Watt's program, put into final form in July 1982, essentially reversed the procedure. After companies had selected regions where they wanted to drill through competitive bids, Interior officials would conduct site-specific environmental studies on the tracts. The department also determined the fair market value of OCS leases only after taking bids to gauge demand for tracts.

"The market will select lease tracts instead of the government," Watt said in defending the five-year program. Interior officials contended that the program would speed up the leasing process by eliminating extensive environmental and economic studies on tracts that drew no interest. Except for the Santa Barbara spill, Watt maintained, offshore drilling had been conducted with little environmental damage. Drilling rig operations were much less risky, admin-

istration spokesmen argued, than the threat of spills from tankers carrying imported oil to U.S. refineries. While the government would open virtually the entire OCS for bidding, they pointed out, whether the amount of acreage leased would actually rise above previous levels depended on market demand for offshore oil.

## Critics' Challenges

State officials, environmental groups and some economists challenged Watt's reasoning. They argued that drilling posed unacceptable risks to fishing and marine life in pristine offshore waters. Friends of the Earth, an environmental organization, called Watt's accelerated leasing program "overly ambitious" and worried that "environmental concerns will be downplayed or disregarded."

Watt's critics also challenged the proposed sales on economic grounds. With world oil demand lagging, they contended, the government was likely to receive bids far below long-term value if Watt insisted on leasing so much OCS acreage in five years. While Watt maintained that his program would promote competition within the oil industry, critics said that intense bidding for OCS tracts was unlikely. In 13 previous sales, Interior received two or fewer bids on 58 percent of the tracts it leased, and only a single bid on 38 percent of the tracts, according to department figures.

Critics also charged that the industry had neither the interest nor the equipment to explore so much acreage in five years. Even some oil executives worried that Watt, by moving so fast, would stir political opposition and invite legal challenges that would stall leasing for years.

Throughout 1981-82, state and local governments in coastal states joined with environmental groups to press lawsuits to block specific OCS lease sales. In July 1981 a U.S. District Court judge blocked Interior from accepting bids for 29 tracts in the northern reaches of the Santa Maria Basin off central California. Gov. Brown had urged Watt to withhold the tracts from bidding to protect migrating whales and endangered sea otters. The judge ruled that leasing the Santa Maria tracts would be inconsistent with the state's coastal management plan.

In the following years legal challenges held up planned sales off Alaska and Massachusetts. After negotiations Watt dropped plans to open two sensitive Alaskan basins. Watt also delayed controversial California lease sales while the government appealed the district judge's decision. *(Supreme Court decision, p. 54)*

Although exploratory drilling in the OCS off Alaska and the Atlantic coastline during the late 1970s and early 1980s produced no major discoveries, oil industry executives and geologists remained convinced that federal offshore waters offered the best prospects for finding new domestic oil and gas reserves. During 1981-82 expanded OCS leasing paid off with successful drilling that suggested major reserves beneath the Santa Maria Basin, just 40 miles from the Santa Barbara well that blew in 1969 and south of the disputed tracts where Congress and California state officials held up leasing plans.

### Congressional Response

From the start, Watt's plans for all-out OCS leasing drew heated opposition from Congress. Neither the House nor the Senate tried to thwart the entire five-year plan, but Congress blocked leasing in untouched California and New Jersey waters through amendments to the Interior Department appropriations bills for fiscal 1982 and 1983.

The administration underestimated fears among environmentalists and coastal state residents that oil spills would damage pristine waters and beaches. Watt's announcement that he would consider leasing in the four California offshore basins that Andrus decided to keep off-limits turned out to be a political blunder. "I don't think any of us recognized the emotional fervor that surrounded that [leasing] issue," Stanley H. Hulett, Watt's director of congressional and legislative affairs, acknowledged in 1981.

Watt was personally convinced that the national interest required exploring the California basins, one House member later recalled, and was surprised when California Republicans refused to rally behind the plan. But with political sentiment in the state running strongly against leasing, most of the state's Republican and Democratic members joined to oppose reconsideration of Andrus' ruling. The delegation held stormy meetings with Watt, wrote angry letters to President Reagan and maneuvered for House Appropriations Committee action to deny funding for opening the disputed basins.

In 1983-84 Congress continued temporary bans on federal oil and gas leasing off the California, Florida and Massachusetts coastlines. Through amendments to fiscal 1984-85 Interior Department appropriations bills, Congress renewed the riders that prohibited the department from issuing drilling leases in specified OCS regions. After banning OCS leases for the fourth year in a row, House and Senate conferees on the fiscal 1985 Interior funding measure expressed hope that Congress no longer would need to impose these moratoriums if Interior officials took steps to protect marine resources in future offshore leasing decisions.

In drafting fiscal 1984 Interior appropriations legislation, the House Appropriations Committee in 1983 accepted proposals by Interior Subcommittee Chairman Sidney R. Yates, D-Ill., to protect California,

Florida and Massachusetts coastal waters. The Yates proposals prompted intense committee debate before they were approved, in modified form, by voice vote. The panel softened the bans slightly to allow preparation for lease sales but not the sales themselves.

The California ban applied to waters off Southern California, from the U.S.-Mexico border north through San Diego County and some of Orange County, starting three miles out at the limit of state-controlled waters and reaching to about 20 miles offshore. It also included buffer zones around the Channel Islands and in the Santa Barbara Channel.

The one-year ban was requested in a June 6 letter to Yates signed by 23 of the 45 House members from California. That division within the state delegation, heightened by the pressure to develop a reportedly rich new petroleum find in the area, made the ban hotly controversial.

House and Senate conferees reduced the number of Gulf of Mexico tracts off Florida where leasing was barred and substituted more complex provisions to cover Southern California coastal tracts up to 12 miles offshore.

In 1984 Congress again renewed leasing prohibitions off California and in the Georges Bank fishing grounds off New England. Unable to finish work on regular Interior appropriations, the House and Senate wrote those riders into a yearlong fiscal 1985 omnibus continuing appropriations resolution that funded Interior programs.

## Offshore Revenue Sharing

At the same time coastal states were joining environmentalists in challenging leasing in unexplored ares, they were also demanding that the federal government turn over some of its OCS leasing revenues. The state governments claimed more money was needed to protect shorelines against damaging development, cope with the side effects of OCS drilling, and manage fisheries and marine life.

In proposing legislation in the House, members from coastal states pointed out that the federal government since 1920 had been sharing its mineral leasing revenues from onshore public lands with the states, mostly with the West, where federally owned lands were located. Under the Mineral Leasing Act of 1920, subsequently amended in 1976, Congress directed the U.S. Interior Department to turn over 50 percent of revenues from leasing coal, oil and gas, and other minerals on public lands to state governments.

By granting the states a share of its OCS revenues, the federal government could give them more incentive to cooperate with OCS development, some members argued. "If the states cannot act as partners in this process, they are going to act to obstruct the process through litigious means," said Norman E. D'Amours, D-N.H., chairman of the Merchant Marine Subcommittee on Oceanography. If that happened, he went on, the federal Treasury could lose billions of dollars in offshore revenues.

Interior Department leases for oil and gas exploration and production from the OCS were expected to produce $6 billion in fiscal 1985 revenues for the deficit-ridden U.S. Treasury. Administration officials, led by OMB Director David A. Stockman, strongly opposed coastal state demands to share in the funds.

The House in both 1982 and 1983 passed legislation to share up to $300 million a year with coastal and Great Lakes state governments, but these measures died in the Senate. A similar proposal made it all the way to House approval of a conference report in 1984. Under the threat of a presidential veto, however, the Senate refused to consider the conference report, and the measure died.

### State Powers

The Supreme Court ruled Jan. 11, 1984, against California's legal challenge to Secretary Watt's 1981 decision to lease 115 federal tracts in the Santa Maria Basin off that state's coast for oil and gas exploration. By a 5-4 vote, the high court ruled in *Secretary of the Interior v. California* that states could not block federal offshore lease sales by arguing that the sales were inconsistent with state plans for protecting their coastal areas. Congress was unable to pass legislation to overturn the decision.

In its ruling the Supreme Court rejected California's contention that Interior Department decisions to lease OCS tracts for exploration could be blocked if development were inconsistent with state coastal zone management plans.

The decision sharply limited potential state government control over federal government decisions on managing its extensive offshore oil and gas deposits. Major petroleum-producing states such as Texas and Louisiana, and to some extent Alaska, generally welcomed drilling off their shores, both in federal waters and in state waters less than three miles from the coastline. But some heavily populated coastal states — including California, Oregon, Florida and Massachusetts — resisted federal offshore development. Environmentalist sentiment generally was stronger in those states and OCS development was viewed as threatening economically important fishing and recreation industries.

The court case involved a clash between two federal laws. The 1972 Coastal Zone Management Act (CZMA) assured states that once they won federal approval for plans for managing and protecting their coastal areas, any federal action "directly affecting" those coastal zones would have to be consistent with the state plans as far as possible.

Six years later Congress amended the Outer Continental Shelf Lands Act to overhaul federal programs for leasing OCS lands for development of oil and gas resources. But the 1978 amendments did not end the frequent conflict between the federal interest in producing more energy and the state interest in protecting fishing and recreation industries along local shores.

While he did not start the conflict, Watt fueled the flames with his proposal to offer nearly the entire OCS for oil and gas leasing. Although the Supreme Court ruled against California's stand, Interior Secretary William P. Clark, who had replaced Watt in 1983, backed off from the administration's ambitious offshore leasing plans, slowing the pace of lease sales and smoothing relations with state officials.

## Watershed Leasing

Congress in 1982 ruled out federal oil and gas leasing on national forest lands that supplied drinking water to Seattle and Tacoma, Wash. Over U.S. Forest Service objections, the Interior Department early in the year granted leases for oil and gas exploration in a national forest in mountains that serve as a watershed for the two cities. The city governments protested, and the state's entire congressional delegation joined to force officials to cancel the leases.

Washington senators Henry M. Jackson, D, (1953-1983) and Slade Gorton, R, contended the leases demonstrated that the Reagan administration was opening federal lands throughout the West without taking sufficient account of their value for other purposes. The Washington delegation's response demonstrated growing concern, even in Western states, about Watt's efforts to step up federal energy leasing. The issue also illustrated conflicting demands on national forests and federal rangelands that held potential energy reserves but also provided water and recreation opportunities for the residents of large Western cities.

BLM eventually canceled the leases under pressure from the Washington congressional delegation. But Gorton and Jackson decided to make sure Interior could not reinstate them, and the Senate June 14 approved such an amendment to the Council of Environmental Quality authorization legislation. The House accepted the amendment, and President Reagan signed the measure Oct. 18.

During Senate floor debate, the sponsors suggested that the administration's failure to recognize the natural values that public lands provide was undermining public support for developing federal energy resources. In floor remarks June 14, Gorton charged that the administration's environmental policy "is that oil and gas exploration, even where there is no known oil and gas reserves, outweighs the protection of the natural forested areas in which the population of two large American cities draws its drinking water. I do not believe that this is a good policy."

Jackson criticized the Interior Department's "helter-skelter approach" to oil and gas leasing on public lands. The Washington Democrat said the department's "act first and think later" policy "is bound to stimulate widespread opposition to development, even in circumstances where development would be appropriate."

## Coal Leasing

At Secretary Watt's direction, the Interior Department accelerated a federal coal leasing program that the Carter administration had set in motion. In clearing the fiscal 1983 Interior appropriations bill Dec. 19, 1982, Congress granted the Reagan administration's full $15.79 million request for coal leasing efforts by BLM. But the Republican-controlled Senate took note of a growing coal leasing controversy when it defeated, by only one vote, a proposal by Sen. Dale Bumpers, D-Ark., to cut BLM's budget by $2.13 million.

Bumpers and other critics of administration coal policy said the Treasury was not receiving fair market value for coal lands Watts leased, because BLM had set minimum bids too low and was quickly selling large amounts of coal at a time when coal company reserves were high.

In an agreement reached a few days before the vote, House and Senate conferees agreed to fund the coal leasing program but voted to delay two sales planned during fiscal 1983 for at least three months, deferring one of them until fiscal 1984. The dispute foreshadowed a controversy that erupted in 1983, prodding the 98th Congress to clamp a moratorium on coal lease sales while Interior reassessed BLM's program. The moratorium eventually was extended to 1985.

Lawmakers imposed the moratorium while a blue-ribbon commission studied the department's coal leasing program. Congress earlier in the year had ordered Watt to set up the commission to investigate charges that Interior in 1982 had sold rights to mine federal coal at "firesale prices" in the coal-rich Powder River Basin of Wyoming and Montana.

The dispute over coal leases led to Watt's resignation. William Clark, Watt's successor, overhauled coal leasing procedures and scaled back the department's ambitious plans for oil and gas leasing in federal offshore waters. Clark's conciliatory approach tempered congressional, environmental group and state government protests against the administration's plans to bolster U.S. energy supplies by expanding federal mineral leasing. *(Watt resignation, p. 61; background, p. 89)*

### Moratorium

The moratorium frustrated the administration's plans to open billions of tons of federal low-sulfur coal in six Western states for development by private mining companies. The furor deepened divisions among Western state governors, environmental groups and the U.S. energy industry over whether the government should resume large-scale leasing of its Western coal reserves to supply future U.S. demand for fuel.

By offering large coal reserves, while at the same time curtailing federal strip-mining controls, Watt undermined political support for an Interior coal leasing program revived by the Carter administration. A previous 10-year moratorium had lasted through the 1970s. In the process "Watt introduced a lot of uncertainty into a [coal leasing] system that was nearing a point of stability," Frank Gregg, who directed BLM during the Carter administration, contended in 1983.

Shifting Interior coal leasing policies revealed the difficult judgments facing Congress and executive branch officials concerning management of the government's vast mineral resources. The U.S. government owned 60 percent of the West's low-sulfur coal reserves, resources that the nation eventually would need to develop synthetic liquid fuels and generate electric power throughout the country. But the spectacular swings in U.S. energy markets from the early 1970s to the early 1980s made it difficult to predict how soon those reserves should be developed.

It took coal companies an average of seven years to put new mines into operation. Federal coal leased in the early 1980s would be available for production only in the following decade. If Interior officials leased more coal than mining companies demanded, they risked falling short of the "fair market value" that Congress demanded for federal coal resources. But if the department leased too little coal, the government risked future shortages that could drive fuel prices upward and leave the

nation dependent on foreign oil imports.

During the Carter administration the department had fashioned a comprehensive coal management program that tried to match leasing levels to predicted electric power and synthetic fuel demand. Watt and Garrey E. Carruthers, the assistant interior secretary for land and water resources, substantially boosted the preliminary targets for the tonnage of federally owned coal that Interior planned to put up for bidding. In line with the Reagan administration's free market philosophy, Watt and Carruthers contended that the government should bolster private mining companies' coal reserves, then let energy demand determine how quickly federal coal would be mined.

Just as Interior expanded its leasing goals, however, a worldwide oil glut and lagging electric power demand curtailed expected markets for coal. By early 1982 congressional investigators were questioning whether the procedures that Interior followed in offering federal coal violated the department's obligation to obtain fair prices for public resources.

Congress responded in July 1983 by ordering Watt to appoint a five-member commission to review Interior coal leasing procedures. In September Congress approved the temporary moratorium after the department defied a House Interior and Insular Affairs Committee demand that it cancel a scheduled lease auction for federal coal in the Fort Union Basin of Montana and North Dakota. At the height of the controversy Watt resigned under congressional fire after publicly joking about the composition of the coal leasing commission.

That commission, led by David Linowes, in February 1984 proposed significant changes in the way Interior conducted its coal leasing program. Clark accepted most of the group's recommendations, but Interior was still revising its program when Clark resigned as secretary in 1985. In the meantime members of Congress, Western state governments, environmental groups, economists and the coal industry continued to debate how rapidly the government should offer its vast Western coal reserves for development.

### Background

The U.S. government assumed ownership of vast coal and other mineral deposits beneath Western lands it acquired on behalf of the nation through 19th century territorial expansion. As settlement pushed west, the government sold or granted some of its coal-bearing lands to state governments, homesteaders and railroads. In the early decades of the 20th century the government began holding onto increasingly valuable mineral resources. Even when the government turned surface title over to ranchers and other private owners, it reserved title to minerals beneath the ground for the public benefit.

The Mineral Leasing Act of 1920 gave the secretary of the interior discretionary power to lease federally owned coal, oil and gas and other minerals for development by private companies. The 1920 law directed the department to collect royalties from the leaseholders based on the value of resources they extracted. It required Interior officials to auction rights to mine known federal coal deposits to companies that bid the highest bonus payment to win leases. But it granted companies a "preference right" to lease previously unknown coal reserves that they discovered on public lands without bidding against competing firms.

The federal government owned roughly 200 billion tons of coal, including some Southern coalfields. But most federal coal lay in six Western states — Montana, Wyoming, North Dakota, Colorado, Utah and New Mexico — in thick seams lying close to the surface. Before the 1960s there was little demand for Western coal deposits that

were far from the nation's population and industrial centers. As demand for electric power demand grew, however, mining companies began eyeing the West's largely untapped coal reserves that could be extracted cheaply through strip-mining methods.

The federal Clean Air Act of 1970 also increased interest in Western coal because this coal is low in sulfur content. By burning low-sulfur fuel, power plants and factories could meet federal sulfur emission standards without installing expensive equipment to cleanse the smokestack gases. During the 1960s and early 1970s electric utilities built huge coal-fired power plants at Rock Springs, Wyo.; Colstrip, Mont.; Craig, Colo.; and the Four Corners region of New Mexico to generate power for fast-growing Western cities. Utilities in Texas, the Midwest and other distant regions began purchasing coal from Western fields to fuel their power plants.

By 1970 Interior had issued more than 500 leases for federal coal, and mining companies had filed more than 170 preference right lease applications. Yet BLM, the agency that handled the mineral leasing system, in 1970 reported that federal coal production in the six Western coal states actually had fallen since World War II, suggesting that leaseholders were keeping federal deposits in the ground — speculating that its value would rise — in the knowledge that Interior had never enforced stipulations that the coal be mined in timely fashion.

Interior Secretary Rogers C. B. Morton responded in 1971 by halting most new leasing while officials drafted a new leasing program. The moratorium eventually was extended for 10 years, until 1981.

### Revised Coal Leasing System

Congress meanwhile replaced 1920 Mineral Leasing Act provisions with an updated leasing law for federal coal depos-

**Secretary of the Interior James G. Watt, who resigned Oct. 9, 1983, after several years of conflicts with Congress and environmentalists.**

its. In the Federal Coal Leasing Amendments Act of 1976, enacted over President Ford's veto, Congress abolished future preference right leasing and instead directed that all federal coal be leased through competitive bidding. The 1976 law also required that all accepted bonus bids for coal leases provide the government with "fair market value." It raised federal coal royalties, previously assessed at 5 cents per ton of production, to at least 12½ percent of the value of surface-mined coal at the mine. It gave the interior secretary authority to charge a lower royalty rate — 8 percent in 1983 — for deep federal coal veins that had to be extracted through underground mining tunnels.

To combat speculation, the 1976 law imposed a "diligent development" provision that required companies to start mining federal coal within 10 years or forfeit their leases. It set the term of federal coal leases at 20 years, with extensions for so long as coal could be mined in commercial quantities. Another provision increased, to 50 percent from 37½ percent, the portion of revenues from leasing federal minerals that the Interior Department shared with state governments where the resources were extracted. The U.S. coal industry opposed the revised system, and Ford, in vetoing the measure, objected to "rigidities, complications and burdensome regulations" that he contended would inhibit federal coal production. But a strongly Democratic House and Senate overrode the veto by substantial margins.

Congress the same year cleared the Federal Land Policy and Management Act of 1976, giving BLM specific authority to regulate coal leasing as well as other uses of public lands it administered. In 1977, after President Carter took office, Congress also cleared the Surface Mining Control and Reclamation Act, imposing federal regulation of coal strip-mining operations on both private and federally owned lands.

In combination with the 1976 coal leasing amendments, those measures substantially expanded Interior Department control over the way mining companies managed and extracted the coal they leased on federal lands.

**Carter Coal Program.** The Carter administration spent two years redrafting Interior's coal leasing program. Unveiled in 1979, the Carter program attempted to set Interior coal leasing levels to match Department of Energy (DOE) computer forecasts of expected coal demand. After DOE determined coal production goals and calculated expected output from existing mines, Interior officials would set targets for leasing additional federal coal to make up anticipated shortfalls in national production. BLM in the meantime began studying federal coal tracts to screen out lands where poor coal, critical wildlife habitat or other conflicting values made strip mining undesirable. Secretary Andrus formed regional coal teams, composed of BLM state office directors and governors from states within the six Western coal regions, to review Interior's leasing goals, rank which tracts should be made available for leasing first and draw up lease sale schedules for the interior secretary to consider.

Andrus in 1979 scheduled sales to offer nearly 1.5 billion tons of coal, half of that in the Powder River Basin, for leasing during 1981-82. BLM continued to process pending preference right lease applications, filed before Congress revised the leasing system in 1976, for as much as 5.8 billion tons of federal coal. In setting its preliminary leasing targets BLM allowed a 25 percent "fudge factor" to match unexpectedly high demand. Under the Carter program "we could lease and produce far more coal than the market could possibly absorb," Gregg, Carter's BLM director, maintained in 1983.

Western coal-state governors, environmental groups and the coal industry by and large backed the Andrus program as a way to meet national energy needs while protecting the region's interests. But critics argued that the government's efforts to plan its leasing goals on the basis of computer forecasts of energy demand could not keep up with shifting market conditions. DOE in fact sharply revised its regional coal production goals as 1979 foreign oil price increases, reduced electric power demand and rising natural gas prices altered the nation's energy supply and demand outlook.

**Watt Leasing Speedup.** After the 10-year moratorium the Interior Department resumed coal leasing in January 1981 with a sale in the Green River-Ham's Fork region of Wyoming and Colorado that had been scheduled under the Andrus program. Watt took office the same month and began revising the coal program to fit the administration's free market philosophy. At Watt's

direction Interior accelerated its lease sale schedule and streamlined the Andrus leasing regulations. Scrapping DOE's formal production goals, Interior adopted a policy of setting leasing goals to meet the mining industry's demand for coal reserves. The Reagan administration's goal was to increase coal market competition by providing many companies with ample reserves of federal coal, then let market supply and demand determine where and how fast those resources would be produced.

## 1982 Powder River Sale

Interior officials viewed the 1982 Powder River sale as an opportunity to prove that the government could offer large amounts of coal for lease without the disruptions that caused the 1970s moratorium. The Powder River Basin is the West's richest coal region, with 146 billion tons of recoverable reserves; the federal government owns about 80 percent of that total. In scheduling the sale in 1979, Andrus had set a preliminary target of 776 million tons. With the regional coal team's consent, BLM in 1981 doubled the final target to a range of 1.4 billion to 1.5 billion tons. In February 1982, two months before the sale, Watt himself raised the Powder River leasing goal again, to 2.2 billion tons. During the intervening three years, however, world oil prices had started to fall and demand for Western coal reserves plunged far below expectations in the late 1970s. Although those trends became evident during the winter of 1981-82, Interior officials went ahead with what they termed the largest coal lease sale in U.S. history.

In the April 1982 Powder River sale, Interior received bids totaling $54.7 million on 11 tracts holding 1.6 billion tons of coal. No bids were received on some tracts and others were dropped from the offering because Interior officials were unable to obtain consent from private owners of surface lands above federal coal deposits. Although the sale received little national attention at the time, during the following year controversy broke out in Congress over whether the administration had driven bonus bids below fair market value by offering so much coal on depressed markets.

A year after the Powder River sale was held, the House Appropriations Committee and GAO criticized the way Interior had handled the bidding. In a report released April 20 the House committee investigations staff contended that Watt's leasing policies had reduced the federal government's dollar return for public resources. "Such large-scale leasing under poor economic conditions distorts the market by flooding it with leased coal," the report said. "It temporarily reduces fair market value and allows the industry to acquire coal at firesale prices." In a May 11 report GAO found that Interior received far less than fair market value for the Powder River leases and recommended that Congress revise coal leasing law to prevent such underpayment.

Charges of mismanagement and even possible impropriety in the sale centered on a last-minute change in the system for making bonus bids. Until a few weeks before the Powder River sale, the system called for Interior officials to calculate "minimum acceptable bids" representing "fair market value" before the sale. But shortly after field officials sent their calculations to Washington, D.C., top headquarters officials decided to change the bidding system.

The new system replaced minimum acceptable bids with what were called "entry level bids." These were intended to be the point, well below fair market value, at which bidding could open, with an assumption that auction-like competition would bid up the price.

Critics of Watt's coal leasing program

also charged that Interior officials had leaked the minimum acceptable bids for the Powder River sale to coal companies before the sale was announced.

Bidding for the Powder River coal demonstrated flaws in the government's competitive leasing procedures. Of 11 tracts that Interior actually leased in the April 1982 sale, only eight received more than one bid and the other three received only two bids. The results failed to bear out the administration's belief that competitive bidding would produce a fair price for federal coal reserves.

## Legislative Action

Watt's coal leasing plans had drawn congressional fire long before the critical reports on the Powder River sale were issued. Efforts to slow or block the coal program began in 1982, when the House Appropriations Subcommittee on Interior tried to cut BLM funding for coal leasing activities by $2.1 million. Although the House accepted the cutback, the Senate restored the funds.

In May 1983 House Interior and Insular Affairs Committee Chairman Udall introduced legislation to impose a leasing moratorium for at least one year while Interior developed new leasing procedures. There was no action on Udall's bill, but House coal leasing critics, led by Rep. Yates again attacked the program through riders to appropriations bills.

When the House passed a fiscal 1983 supplemental appropriations bill, the measure included a ban on further coal leasing through Sept. 30, 1983. But the Senate, after heavy administration and coal industry lobbying, defeated, 48-51, margin an amendment supporting the moratorium.

Although conferees also dropped the House moratorium, they wrote into the final version a provision ordering Watt to set up the commission to study coal pricing issues.

Watt Aug. 4 appointed David Linowes to head the Commission on Fair Market Policy for Federal Coal Leasing. Linowes previously chaired a separate commission appointed by Watt to study the government's oil and gas royalty program.

**Moratorium Proposal.** Even as the Linowes commission was being formed, House critics pressed efforts to halt Watt's coal program. On June 7 Yates' subcommittee had approved the fiscal 1984 Interior appropriations measure with another coal leasing moratorium attached. The provision, accepted by the full Appropriations Committee when it reported its bill on June 21, kept the moratorium in effect while Interior's coal leasing program was studied by the independent commission.

The full House passed the appropriations bill, with its leasing bans intact, on June 28. The Senate Appropriations Subcommittee on Interior again stripped coal leasing restrictions from the measure before sending it to the full committee, which reported it without the moratorium provision. By the time the Senate took up the coal leasing issue on Sept. 20, Watt had angered congressional leaders by ordering Interior to conduct a Sept. 14 coal lease sale in the Fort Union region of North Dakota and Montana despite a House Interior Committee resolution directing that the sale be postponed.

With the Fort Union dispute fresh in senators' minds, Bumpers offered a leasing moratorium amendment on Sept. 20. This time the Senate approved it 63-33, with 16 members who had opposed an earlier moratorium proposal in June switching to support it. Bumpers said the moratorium was needed to keep Watt from "trying to give away our national heritage to whoever happens to show up."

Bumpers' amendment barred spending for new coal leasing, with certain exceptions, until 90 days after the Linowes commission reported to Congress on the Interior Department's coal leasing policies.

**Watt Resignation.** Stung by the Senate's stand, Watt accused Congress of ignoring U.S. energy needs that he contended were threatened by conflicts in the Middle East and Central America. "The world is ready to ignite and your secretary of the interior has to deal with 535 members of Congress that don't seem to be concerned about the future supply of energy in America," Watt complained in a Sept. 21 breakfast speech to the U.S. Chamber of Commerce.

In that same speech Watt touched off a new round of criticism on Capitol Hill and elsewhere with a remark about the makeup of the Linowes commission. "We have every kind of mix you can have. I have a black, I have a woman, two Jews and a cripple. And we have talent," said Watt. He later described his comments as "unfortunate" and apologized for them, but the political uproar continued. On Oct. 9 Watt resigned.

## Linowes Commission Report

In a report submitted to Clark in February 1984, the Linowes commission urged Interior to establish a predictable and stable coal leasing schedule to supply fuel for U.S. consumption. But the commission, faulting the department for offering so much Powder River coal on depressed markets, also proposed that the government maintain "the flexibility to change the timing of lease sales and the quantity of coal offered based on its assessment of market conditions."

Since the federal government held potential monopoly power in Western coal markets, the commission suggested that Interior's inability to respond quickly to shifting demand could exaggerate coal price fluctuations. "Indeed, in the 1979-80 boom period, the unavailability of new federal coal leases due to the moratorium [during the 1970s] probably drove coal reserve prices higher in an already inflated market for Western coal reserves," the report noted. "In 1982 the leasing of more coal, planned in response to 1979-80 circumstances, may have further lowered prices in a new depressed market for coal reserves."

Reviewing the 1982 Powder River sale, the commission concluded "that the Interior Department probably offered excessive amounts of federal coal in a declining market and that this, in turn, probably lessened the prospect of receiving fair market value. At the very least, the Interior Department made serious errors in judgment in its procedures for conducting the 1982 Powder River lease sale and failed to provide a sound rationale for many of its actions."

**Commission Recommendations.** For future lease sales the commission recommended that the government continue to rely on competitive bonus bidding to obtain fair market value for most federal coal deposits. But it offered 36 proposals, including six requiring legislation by Congress, to improve the department's coal management program.

Among its major recommendations the commission urged Interior rapidly to finish processing pending preference right lease applications for non-competitive federal coal tracts, then take those reserves into account before leasing additional reserves. In selecting tracts for future sales, the commission maintained, Interior should first offer reserves that were likely to attract bids from more than one company. In leasing tracts where no competition was expected — such as reserves that could be developed only as part of an existing adjacent mine — the commission suggested that Interior officials have authority to negotiate a fair price directly with existing mine operators without going through the bidding process.

The report urged Interior to restore public support for the coal leasing program in Western states by giving Regional Coal Teams composed of BLM officials and state governors a significant role "both in establishing leasing levels and in setting leasing schedules."

**Diligent Development Law.** The commission proposed congressional action to deal with other coal leasing problems, including the effect of the 10-year diligent development requirement and surface owner rights on the value of federally owned coal. By forcing companies to start mining federally owned coal within 10 years or lose their leases, the report noted, the diligent development standard in the 1976 coal leasing law might stimulate excessive production even if market conditions provided an incentive to keep the coal in the ground. In addition, coal market economists told the commission that mining companies reduced the prices they bid for federal coal leases to take account of the risk that unexpected problems could keep them from beginning production in time to meet the 10-year deadline.

The commission recommended retaining the 10-year diligent development requirement to prevent speculation in federal coal leases. But it suggested that Congress should revise the law to allow companies to hold onto leases for another 10 years without starting production if they paid the government advance royalties, on an escalating schedule, for the coal they expected eventually to mine and sell.

### Clark Response

The congressionally imposed coal leasing moratorium expired on May 17, 1984, 90 days after the Linowes commission filed its report. But Clark successfully steered clear of renewed controversy over the program by voluntarily suspending further leasing until 1985.

After receiving the Linowes report,

Clark told the Senate Energy and Natural Resources Committee in April that he would adopt all but one of the group's 30 administrative recommendations. An Interior spokesman said Clark also supported the commission's proposals for congressional legislation revising coal leasing laws. The secretary refused to agree to the commission's proposal that Interior require coal companies to turn over information on private coal transactions for officials to use in analyzing market pricing.

At least initially Clark's promise to revamp the coal leasing procedures failed to satisfy House Democratic critics of Watt's policies. Yates' Appropriations Subcommittee on Interior at first recommended extending the leasing moratorium. But after the subcommittee grilled Clark about coal leasing revisions during June 13-14 hearings, Yates withdrew the moratorium extension before the subcommittee approved a fiscal 1985 Interior appropriations measure.

Interior coal leasing plans remained on hold after Donald P. Hodel, former secretary of energy, replaced Clark in the Interior post in 1985. The department continued to draft an environmental impact statement on a revised coal leasing program. Except for occasional emergency sales to keep existing mines in operation, Interior officials predicted it would be late 1986 before the department was ready to resume large-scale leasing.

# 4

# Nuclear Power

More than 80 nuclear power plants were operating in the United States at the beginning of 1984, and nearly 50 more were under construction. But utility companies had placed no new orders for reactors since 1978, and, in just over a decade, more than 100 orders had been cancelled. By 1983-84 nuclear power projects were being abandoned at advanced stages of construction even after billions of dollars had been invested in them. In one instance, which involved the Shoreham plant on Long Island, a bitter political debate erupted over whether to start up a plant that was already completely finished. Meanwhile, the utility was paying more than $1 million a day in interest on the money it had borrowed to build the facility, which cost about 10 times more than had been estimated when the project was launched in the early 1970s.

Added to these problems is an even more serious issue — nuclear waste disposal. Critics of the industry have considered it scandalous that hundreds of nuclear power plants were built in the United States and abroad before anybody knew how spent fuel from the reactors could be safely stored. In the mid-1970s West Germany and Sweden enacted laws that barred construction of additional nuclear power plants until the waste disposal problem was solved. Even in those countries, however, it was not anticipated that permanent underground disposal sites would be available until well into the 21st century.

Spent reactor fuels contain highly radioactive materials that must be kept completely isolated for thousands of years. They also contain plutonium, which can be used as the explosive material in atomic bombs. In the mid-1970s, when the industry assumed that plutonium would be extracted from spent fuels and used as fresh fuel for reactors, experts warned that it would soon be much easier for governments, terrorists, or even criminal groups to obtain material for bombs. Even if the United States decided not to recycle plutonium, the threat still exists because Japan and several European countries continue the practice.

All this adds up to disenchantment with an industry that showed much promise, and with the technology that was supposed to free the United States from dependence on non-renewable fossil fuels.

During President Reagan's first term, the same feelings were evident in Congress, which underwent a change of heart concerning the U.S. commercial nuclear power industry. While the 97th Congress took major steps in 1981-82 to clear away obstacles facing the industry, the 98th Congress offered it little help with financial and environmental troubles.

After deliberating through most of its two yearly sessions, the 97th Congress dealt with two of the industry's most troublesome problems: long delays in nuclear plant construction and the lack of safe methods for permanently disposing of radioactive reactor wastes. But members' lingering doubts about the economic health and fundamental safety of nuclear power generation technology was revealed in eroding House and Senate support for the costly Clinch River breeder reactor project.

Near the end of its 1982 post-election session, Congress cleared legislation that permitted electric utilities to obtain temporary licenses to start up newly built reactors before all licensing hearings had been completed. The lame-duck Congress also wrapped up a long-debated plan directing the federal government to develop and operate nuclear waste storage facilities to keep reactor byproducts isolated from the human environment.

But during 1983-84 lawmakers in fact abandoned the federal government's previous support for promoting nuclear breeder technologies. Concerned by rising costs and safety doubts, both the House and Senate in 1983 voted decisively to scrap the controversial Clinch River breeder reactor, a joint government-industry project that experts once had hailed as a solution to U.S. energy problems.

With members growing more skeptical about nuclear power prospects, Congress resisted the Reagan administration's plans to expedite nuclear power plant construction. It refused to renew authority for temporary licenses to operate new reactors before formal safety hearings had been completed.

Electric power industry plans for building new nuclear plants continued to be plagued by cost overruns, high interest rates and construction problems. In the Pacific Northwest, the Washington Public Power Supply System, nicknamed "Whoops" by nuclear critics, in 1983 defaulted on $2.25 billion in bonds for nuclear plant construction, but Congress showed little interest in stepping in to solve the industry's fiscal difficulties.

# Radioactive Wastes

As the 1982 post-election session drew to a close, lawmakers forged an agreement on comprehensive nuclear waste legislation that the House and Senate had been considering for four years. President Reagan and the nuclear power industry had pushed hard for a congressional decision on what to do with spent reactor fuel that had been piling up at the nation's commercial nuclear plants.

The measure, signed into law by Reagan Jan. 7, 1983, spelled out timetables for the federal government to open an underground facility for storing spent fuel rods and other commercial wastes in perpetual isolation from the human environment. But to win the bill's passage, Congress exempted radioactive wastes from nuclear weapons production from most of the law's regulations.

The law directed the president to select an underground site by 1987 for a permanent waste repository to be ready by the mid-1990s. For the meantime, the legislation authorized the Department of Energy (DOE) to provide temporary storage for spent civilian reactor fuel from power plants that ran out of space to hold it.

In addition to a permanent repository, Congress ordered DOE to draft experimental plans for storing nuclear wastes in manmade vaults where they could be monitored and eventually removed. The government could keep wastes there for 50 to 100 years, then retrieve them for permanent disposal or for reprocessing to remove plutonium.

Before the mid-1970s the nuclear in-

Up to 1,300,000 gallons of high-level radioactive waste can be stored in tanks such as these in South Carolina. The carbon steel tanks are surrounded by two to three feet of concrete before being buried 40 feet underground.

dustry generally had assumed that spent commercial power plant fuel would be reprocessed to yield plutonium that could be recycled into more reactor fuel. President Carter, concerned that recycled plutonium could be diverted to make nuclear bombs, in 1977 withdrew federal support for a commercial reprocessing plant then being built at Barnwell, S.C. Since then the government and industry had stepped up their search for alternative ways to store reactor wastes as spent fuel without further reprocessing.

The Reagan administration favored reprocessing as the ultimate solution to nuclear waste disposal. No commercial reprocessing industry operated in the United States during the early 1980s. But Congress kept that option open for future years by directing that government repositories store spent fuel in ways that would permit its

later removal for reprocessing.

Congress had been trying to put together a comprehensive nuclear waste measure since 1978. But action was slowed by debate over whether military and civilian wastes should be stored together and subjected to the same regulatory restrictions. And various members delayed consideration as they tried to make sure that DOE would not put a nuclear waste dump within their states or districts. After four years of maneuvering, Congress exempted military wastes and gave a state's governor or legislature power to veto a federal disposal site within its borders. But Congress retained authority to overturn the state's stand through action by both the House and Senate.

Environmental groups opposed the final bill, arguing that tight deadlines could force the government to make hasty choices

# Low-Level Nuclear Waste...

Some low-level radioactive waste — gloves and boots worn by workers at nuclear power plants or glass vials used to hold radioactive pharmaceuticals — would barely elicit a tick from a Geiger counter. Other materials, including filters that collect sludges of radioactive elements such as cobalt 60 and strontium 90 from the cooling water at nuclear power plants, would start the instrument chattering rapidly.

Though called "low-level waste," in its more potent forms it is capable of causing fatal radiation sickness in anyone exposed to it. Moreover, if significant concentrations of radioactivity from such waste were to get into drinking water or food, it could pose a threat of cancer or genetic damage.

Low-level nuclear waste is a broad category, defined principally by what it is *not*. It is any radioactive waste material that is not:

—Spent reactor fuel or radioactive liquids produced by reprocessing that fuel (high-level waste),

—Rock and sand from which uranium has been extracted (uranium tailings),

—11 man-made radioactive elements from the production of nuclear weapons and from fuel reprocessing (transuranic waste).

Most low-level waste has a relatively short half-life (the length of time it takes half the unstable radioactive atoms to decay into stable elements), measured in decades or hundreds of years. High-level and transuranic wastes have half-lives of thousands of years.

According to a 1983 survey by the Department of Energy (DOE), 64 percent of low-level wastes came from nuclear reactors, 28 percent from industrial uses such as testing welds and instrument manufacturing, 3 percent from research and 3 percent from medical uses.

Low-level waste is usually measured by volume, not by radioactivity. Approximately three million cubic feet are produced each year from commercial sources. A

in evaluating repository sites and designing storage arrangements. They objected that temporary storage for spent reactor fuel would bail out nuclear utilities that had failed to develop safe methods for handling dangerous wastes created by their own plants. And they warned that shipping spent fuel around the country to federal waste repositories would risk thefts, sabotage and accidents that could threaten public health and safety.

## Background

The U.S. government and electric utility corporations had been generating dangerous nuclear waste since the atomic bomb was developed during World War II. But 40 years later the nation had yet to come up with a national policy for disposing of spent reactor fuel and other nuclear fission byproducts that would remain highly radioactive for thousands of years.

U.S. government reactors at Hanford, Wash., and Savannah River, S.C., that manufactured plutonium for nuclear weapons also produced intensely radioactive liquid wastes. Since 1957, when the nation's first commercial nuclear power plant began operations at Shippingsport, Pa., private utility reactors had been generating elec-

## ... Buried in Trenches

typical nuclear reactor will produce 15 truckloads in a year; a large hospital one truckload.

From the 1940s to 1970, much low-level waste was put in steel drums and dumped into the ocean. But gradually, the Atomic Energy Commission, which later became part of DOE, began to bury them. DOE maintains 13 sites for disposal of defense-related low-level wastes.

The first commercial facility for the disposal of low-level wastes was opened in Beatty, Nev., in 1962. The site at Hanford, Wash., opened in 1965, and the site at Barnwell, S.C., in 1971.

Three other sites were opened in the 1960s and closed between 1975 and 1979: West Valley, N.Y.; Maxey Flats, Ky.; and Sheffield, Ill. The first two were shut because poor storage conditions led to radiation leakage; the Sheffield site was filled to capacity.

The three currently operating sites are run by private firms, under state and federal regulations. Disposal charges average $20 to $25 per cubic foot.

The materials are transported to disposal sites in steel drums or wooden boxes. Most liquid wastes are solidified by mixing them with concrete. At all three sites, the waste is buried in trenches, 50 feet deep and several hundred feet long. The wastes are covered with several feet of earth. The most dangerous wastes are buried deepest, and a concrete shield is put over them to keep future generations from digging into them.

When filled, the sites are monitored to make sure there is no leakage. State and local officials are sensitive to the word "dump," maintaining that the sites are carefully controlled.

In Europe, several countries keep the waste in above-ground storage chambers or isolate it deep underground, rather than allowing it to decay near the surface as the United States does.

---

tricity from heat produced by chain reactions in fuel rods holding enriched uranium. Once the fuel was used up, the spent rods still held radioactive "high-level" wastes after they were removed from reactor cores. Both military and commercial nuclear operations, along with radiopharmaceutical manufacturing plants, medical and research centers, also produced large volumes of slightly contaminated "low-level" radioactive wastes.

Since the 1940s federal government military weapons plants and research facilities had produced more than 77 million gallons of liquid high-level wastes. The gov-

ernment had stored the military program wastes temporarily in steel tanks at the Washington and South Carolina plants and at the government's nuclear research center at Idaho Falls, Idaho. Between 1956 and 1976, about 500,000 gallons had leaked into the ground at the Hanford plant from tanks that had corroded faster than expected.

In the private sector, 82 nuclear power plants were in operation in 1984 in the United States. By 1980, the commercial industry had accumulated about 25,000 spent fuel assemblies that had been removed when reactors were refueled with fresh enriched uranium. In the absence of permanent disposal arrangements, nuclear plant operators had been storing spent fuel rods in pools of water at plant sites. But many utility operators said their plants were running out of storage space, and DOE in 1981 estimated that capacity at reactor sites would no longer be adequate by 1986.

For several years, federal officials had been studying underground formations as possible waste-storage sites. The government in 1972 abandoned the first site examined — a salt dome at Lyons, Kan. — after experts concluded that water might leak into the formation from old mining boreholes. In the mid-1970s the Energy Research and Development Administration, DOE's predecessor agency, developed plans to build a Waste Isolation Pilot Plant (WIPP) in underground salt beds near Carlsbad, N.M. Congress authorized WIPP as a demonstration project for disposing of both high-level and low-level military wastes. DOE in 1979 proposed expanding the plant to include an experimental facility for storing spent commercial fuel rods, subject to Nuclear Regulatory Commission (NRC) licensing. But Congress, through an amendment to fiscal 1980 nuclear weapons authorization legislation, restricted the project to its original purpose of storing wastes from weapons production. Carter in 1980 attempted to cancel the WIPP program, proposing instead that the government build depositories, subject to NRC regulation, to handle military as well as high-level commercial wastes. But Congress continued to fund construction of a separate unlicensed WIPP project for handling military wastes.

DOE meanwhile surveyed other potential sites for storing nuclear wastes below ground in mined-out geologic formations. The NRC had ruled that, before selecting a permanent repository site, the government must consider at least three different sites in at least two different kinds of geologic formations.

The sites considered the leading contenders for a permanent repository were basalt formations at the government's Hanford, Wash., Nuclear Reservation; volcanic tuff formations at its Nevada nuclear test site, and several salt formations in Utah, Texas, Louisiana and Mississippi. Salt and granite formations in other states also had been surveyed, but not explored in great detail. In December 1984 the Energy Department listed three sites that officials wanted to consider for the permanent underground repository. They included the Hanford facility, near Richland in southeastern Washington state; Yucca Mountain, on the Nevada nuclear testing reservation 100 miles northwest of Las Vegas; and Deaf Smith County, in the Texas Panhandle 30 miles west of Amarillo. In announcing the three candidate sites, Secretary of Energy Donald P. Hodel conceded that none of the states was eager to have a repository within its borders.

In the same period, nuclear utilities pressed the government to provide some kind of interim "away-from-reactor" (AFR) storage for the spent fuel rods that the companies were keeping at power plants.

The most likely sites for AFR storage of spent fuel were considered to be defunct or never-used privately owned reprocessing facilities at Morris, Ill., Barnwell, S.C., and West Valley, N.Y.

Congress in 1980 established a national policy for handling low-level radioactive wastes — including slightly contaminated gloves, clothing, equipment and other materials — generated by commercial uses of nuclear energy. Through legislation passed that year, Congress gave state governments the responsibility to establish dumps where private low-level wastes could be buried. The law authorized states to form regional compacts among neighboring state governments to set up a regional facility to handle low-level wastes from a wider area. *(Low-level wastes, p. 68)*

The Senate in 1980 approved a bill directing the government to build above-ground storage vaults to temporarily store high-level wastes from defense as well as civilian facilities. But the House substituted a different measure setting a timetable for opening a permanent underground repository. Efforts to draft compromise legislation were blocked by Senate Energy Committee Chairman Henry M. Jackson's, D-Wash. (1953-83), objection to provisions allowing states to veto plans to store military wastes within their borders.

## 1981-82 Issues

The 97th Congress still faced some formidable technical and political questions when it took up nuclear waste legislation in 1981. Nuclear industry spokesmen maintained that the nation possessed the technology to safely dispose of nuclear wastes in sealed containers that would keep radioactive materials isolated for as long as they remained dangerous. Joined by the Reagan administration, the industry urged Congress to move ahead with waste disposal plans to help restore sagging public confidence in nuclear power's safety.

Environmentalists and anti-nuclear activists, on the other hand, claimed that many unresolved technical questions left it doubtful that nuclear waste could be safely buried. They contended that no government plan could assure that buried waste would remain undisturbed for centuries in the future. They warned that earthquakes, groundwater intrusion, other geologic processes or even inadvertent drilling by men could pierce underground storage chambers and bring contaminated wastes into contact with human air and water supplies. Industry critics cautioned that transporting reactor byproducts to temporary and permanent storage sites would increase the risk of accident, theft or sabotage. And they opposed any legislation that would set tight deadlines for selecting depository locations,

accelerate environmental impact reviews or short-circuit NRC procedures for licensing nuclear waste storage facilities.

With those fears in mind, state governments and Indian tribal leaders were reluctant to accept nuclear-storage facilities. Thirty states had potential depository sites, but none was happy about the possibility that the federal government might build a nuclear dump within its borders. As a result, senators and representatives from those 30 states maneuvered throughout 1981-82 to write the nuclear waste legislation in ways that would preclude selection of disposal sites within the regions they represented.

Among the issues Congress had to consider were the following:

—Permanent Disposal Facility. The Carter administration and environmental groups proposed that the government place high-level wastes in deep underground formations, where they could be permanently removed from the surface environment. But some members of Congress, notably from the Gulf Coast states, proposed that the government first build experimental man-made vaults, where waste could be held and monitored for a long period. They contended that man-made "monitored, retrievable storage" (MRS) would prove safer than underground disposal, thus making below-ground facilities unnecessary.

—AFR Disposal. The Carter administration had proposed building a federal "away-from-reactor" facility to store spent fuel rods from commercial power plants until a permanent repository was ready. Several bills proposed a federal facility that would be funded by nuclear utilities. But the Reagan administration maintained that private industry, not the government, should provide AFR storage. And environmental groups opposed a temporary facility as an industry bailout. They also warned that the AFR plan would risk dangerous accidents as utilities began shipping spent fuel rods from around the country to the temporary federal facility.

—State Role. State officials and nuclear critics urged Congress to allow state governments and Indian tribes to veto a depository site within their borders. Most proposed legislation allowed state or tribal governments to object to the federal government's decision to proceed with a repository, then let the veto stand if either the House or the Senate passed a resolution to uphold it. The industry preferred an alternative "two-house" procedure that required that both the House and the Senate, not just one chamber, uphold a state veto to let it stand.

—Military Waste. Carter proposed canceling WIPP and burying military waste along with spent commercial fuel rods in a permanent underground facility licensed by NRC. Environmental groups, citing leaks from high-level military wastes at Hanford, contended that the NRC should regulate disposal of military as well as commercial wastes. But some members of Congress, including House and Senate Armed Services Committee leaders, argued that NRC regulation could interfere with weapons production. They also said it would be a bad precedent to allow states to object to the siting of defense facilities — including nuclear storage facilities — within their borders. The 1980 nuclear waste bill died when some members refused to agree to let states object to storage within their borders of waste from the production of nuclear weapons.

—Funding. Most nuclear waste proposals required that nuclear power consumers, not the federal government, pay for storing commercial wastes. Most bills imposed a mandatory surcharge on electricity generated by nuclear plants to cover the government's waste management costs.

### Senate, House Action

In both the Senate and House, the leaders of the principal environment and energy committees maneuvered throughout 1981 and 1982 to put together comprehensive nuclear waste legislation. In the fall of 1981 Senate Energy and Natural Resources Committee Chairman James A. McClure, R-Idaho, began pushing efforts to work out compromise legislation with other Senate panels. A year later, House Interior and Insular Affairs Committee Chairman Morris K. Udall, D-Ariz., spurred backstage negotiations with other House committee chairmen that finally produced a nuclear waste measure that could win House approval.

Since Congress had abolished its once powerful Joint Atomic Energy Committee in 1977, three Senate committees and seven House panels shared jurisdiction over nuclear waste legislation. While the joint committee had been protective toward nuclear industry interests, the fragmentation of responsibility among other standing House and Senate committees gave industry critics more opportunities to influence subcommittee and full committee deliberations. During the nuclear waste debate, the shared jurisdiction slowed and complicated the process of drafting disposal plans that both the House and Senate could support. It also produced a number of compromise bills that committee chairmen and staff members devised behind the scenes to reconcile conflicting committee positions.

Through months of such negotiations, congressional leaders finally settled on a nuclear waste plan directing the government to move ahead to build a permanent below-ground waste repository. Congress also authorized temporary away-from-reactor storage for spent fuel rods and experimental plans for a retrievable storage facility. But the House and Senate Armed Services committees intervened to preserve the option of developing a separate disposal system for nuclear waste from weapons production. And in a last-minute compromise, demanded by Sen. William Proxmire, D-Wis., Congress agreed to strengthen state government authority to refuse to bury nuclear wastes within its borders.

# Nuclear Plant Licensing

After two years of controversy, Congress in 1982 approved a measure that enabled the NRC to allow electric utility companies to start up newly built nuclear plants before public hearings on licensing the facilities were completed. The Reagan administration had backed giving NRC this authority as part of its campaign to streamline federal regulation of the troubled nuclear power industry. In October 1981 the president said that hopes to expand electric power production by nuclear reactors had been "strangled in a morass of regulations that do not enhance safety, but that do cause extensive licensing delays and economic uncertainties."

To help correct that problem, the bill gave NRC power through the end of 1983 to issue temporary licenses to operate new nuclear reactors. When Congress began debating the interim licensing proposal in 1981, NRC licensing delays were expected to hold up power production from 13 nuclear plants scheduled to be completed in the following two years. Electric utilities that were building nuclear units complained bitterly that lengthy NRC hearings on granting operating licenses raised electricity rates for consumers by keeping new plants out of service for months after construction had been finished.

Environmental groups opposed interim licensing, contending that full-scale NRC hearings should be completed to assure that public safety would be protected before reactors began producing power. Congressional critics of the nuclear industry cited the 1979 accident at the Three Mile Island (TMI) nuclear plant in Pennsylvania in opposing any shortcuts in NRC procedures for determining whether reactors could be operated safely.

By the time Congress cleared the legislation, concern about long delays in licensing nuclear plants was ebbing. NRC received no applications for temporary licenses in 1983, and Congress let the commission's authority to issue them expire on schedule at the end of the year. But NRC officials warned again in 1983 that temporary licenses might be necessary to prevent start-up delays in five plants nearing completion.

In October 1984 Congress reauthorized NRC programs, but not the temporary operating licensing provision. Before approving reauthorization, the House and Senate had to reach accord on how to handle the evacuation of people in the event of a nuclear accident. In its final form the measure allowed NRC to approve evacuation plans even if state and local governments refused to take part in drafting them.

Senate Environment and Public Works Committee action on NRC reauthorizations had been stalled for several months by differences over evacuation planning requirements. The issue was of particular concern to New York, where the Long Island Lighting Company had been prevented from opening its Shoreham nuclear power plant in part because Suffolk County authorities refused to draw up an emergency evacuation plan. Suffolk County argued that population density on Long Island made evacuation impossible.

### Background

Congress established the five-member Nuclear Regulatory Commission in 1974. As part of a general reorganization of federal energy research and regulation functions, Congress that year enacted legislation that abolished the federal Atomic Energy Commission (AEC), an agency created in 1946 to promote nuclear power development and regulate civilian nuclear plants. The 1974 law transferred the AEC's research programs to a new Energy Research and Development Administration, which was absorbed by the Energy Department in 1977. It also created the NRC, composed of five members appointed by the president, to take over AEC responsibility to regulate the construction and operation of nuclear reactors for generating electricity. Ever since, NRC had been caught in the middle of continuing disputes over the safety of nuclear power plants.

NRC procedure followed a two-step system for giving private utilities approval to build and then operate reactors. NRC first granted a construction permit approving plans to build a nuclear plant. When the facility was ready, the commission subsequently granted an operating license allowing the utility to start the reactor and generate electricity. Before approving both steps, NRC officials conducted public hearings and drawn-out investigations. NRC officials reviewed license applications to determine whether proposed plants could be built and operated without unduly risking public health and safety or damaging the environment. They also investigated whether utilities planning to operate nuclear plants were properly insured against accidents.

After a utility decided to build a nuclear plant, it usually took 10 to 12 years to obtain an NRC construction permit, build the facility and obtain an NRC operating license. Utilities and reactor manufacturing companies contended that time-consuming NRC procedures and hearings were the primary cause of construction delays and cost overruns that vastly inflated the cost of bringing nuclear plants into operation. By the late 1970s lagging electric power demand and rising construction costs forced U.S. utilities to cancel more than 30 planned reactors and defer construction of

dozens more.

In 1978, at the urging of Secretary of Energy James R. Schlesinger, the Carter administration proposed that Congress revise the nuclear licensing system to reduce construction time. The Carter plan would have authorized the NRC to approve joint construction permits and operating licenses, eliminating the need for two separate hearings. It also would have empowered the commission to approve nuclear plant sites and standard reactor designs before construction permits were filed. Schlesinger contended that the changes would cut the time required to design, build and license a new plant to 6.5 years.

Congress paid little attention to Carter's 1978 licensing plan. Environmental groups and other nuclear industry critics continued to challenge existing NRC regulation as too lax to ensure that nuclear plants could operate safely. After the 1979 Three Mile Island mishap, Congress focused attention on tightening NRC controls instead of speeding plant licensing. A commission appointed by Carter to investigate the accident recommended that the NRC be abolished and replaced by an executive branch agency headed by a single administrator. Carter instead reorganized the NRC in 1980 to give its chairman more authority.

In 1979 and again in 1980 congressional debates over how to respond to the nuclear power problems delayed action on NRC funding authorizations. Congress did not pass a fiscal 1980 NRC authorization until that year was more than half over, and it never approved an authorization bill at all for fiscal 1981.

## 1984 Emergency Planning

After temporary licensing authority expired at the end of 1983, congressional debate on NRC authorizations shifted toward the controversy over emergency evacuation planning.

NRC policy adopted after the Three Mile Island accident accepted emergency evacuation plans drafted by utility companies only if planning by state and local officials was under way but had been delayed. In June 1983 planning problems nearly led to the shutdown of the already-operating Indian Point nuclear plant in New York. The planning dispute delayed Senate Environment Committee action on NRC legislation in 1984 while Alan K. Simpson, R-Wyo., chairman of the panel's Nuclear Regulation Subcommittee, and Daniel Patrick Moynihan, D-N.Y., tried to resolve New York officials' concerns.

Simpson and Moynihan finally reached a compromise that specified that even if state or local officials refused to take part in developing an emergency preparedness plan, the NRC could issue an operating license for a nuclear power plant if it determined that the utility itself had prepared an acceptable emergency preparedness plan. The NRC was required to evaluate whether a plan submitted by a utility would work. Previously the NRC had accepted utility emergency plans only when state or local officials were working on an emergency plan but it was delayed. This bill cleared Congress Oct. 11.

# Three Mile Island Cleanup

Congress in 1982 sidetracked Pennsylvania members' plan to force nuclear utilities throughout the nation to share the cost of cleaning up the damaged Three Mile Island power plant reactor in their state.

General Public Utilities Corp. (GPU), the TMI plant's owner, was seeking financial help with the estimated $1 billion cost of decontaminating the reactor and building that were damaged in a 1979 accident. The TMI mishap, the nuclear industry's worst accident, had reinforced doubts throughout the nation about whether nuclear power plants could be operated safely.

Financially troubled GPU had slowed its TMI cleanup operations as it exhausted $300 million in insurance payments. Pennsylvania officials, fearing that the plant might leak radioactivity as time went by, drew up cost-sharing plans in an effort to decontaminate the TMI plant as soon as possible. The Senate Energy and Natural Resources Committee in March approved one cost-sharing measure, but Congress took no action.

## Background

The accident at Three Mile Island occurred March 28, 1979. A valve stuck open on TMI-2, one of two reactors at the island in the Susquehanna River near Harrisburg, Pa., causing a loss of cooling water. The nuclear fuel core overheated and, at least partially, melted. Area residents were evacuated when it was feared a hydrogen explosion might rip the reactor building apart.

Most of the radioactive water was removed from the reactor building and the building adjoining it. But the toughest part of the cleanup remained: decontaminating the reactor building and then dealing with the reactor core.

State officials and congressional delegations from Pennsylvania and New Jersey, the regions served by GPU, contended that completing the cleanup was a national responsibility that would benefit all utilities. Gov. Richard L. Thornburgh, R-Pa., proposed a cost-sharing plan under which the federal government, the nation's utilities and nuclear manufacturers would pay about half the cost of the cleanup, with the other half coming from payments by GPU, its customers and the states of Pennsylvania and New Jersey.

Rep. Allen E. Ertel, D-Pa., who represented the district where the TMI plant lay, and Sen. John Heinz, R-Pa., pushed different plans to set up a quasi-public insurance corporation to insure nuclear plants and make a retroactive payment to cover three-fourths of the TMI cleanup costs. In September 1982 the Edison Electric Institute (EEI), an association of stockholder-owned utilities, proposed raising $192 million over six years for the TMI cleanup by imposing an annual fee on all electric utilities, plus a surcharge on those that operated nuclear-power plants.

### Congressional Inaction

Those proposals foundered because of opposition to requiring ratepayers and shareholders of all nuclear utilities to share in the cost, and because of fears that it would set a precedent for future federal "bailouts" for financially troubled utilities.

The American Public Power Association (APPA) opposed efforts to spread TMI cleanup costs to the nation's electricity users, saying it would set a bad precedent. APPA officials said GPU could raise its rates enough to finance the entire cleanup and still not have the highest electric rates in the region.

The Union of Concerned Scientists also opposed legislation that would allow utilities to pass their share of cleanup costs through to electricity consumers, in effect creating a "national tax" on electricity to help repair Three Mile Island. Electricity rates already had risen more than 80 percent over the past year in some areas of the country, a spokesman for the group noted.

The Senate Energy Committee March 31 voted 12-8 to report one cleanup measure drafted by Heinz and Bill Bradley, D-N.J. The bill charged nuclear utilities a fee of 28 cents per kilowatt hour on nuclear generating capacity, up to a maximum of $1.6 million a year for each company, over a six-year period. The bill never reached the Senate floor. The House Interior and Energy and Commerce committees held 1982 hearings on TMI cleanup proposals but reported no legislation.

# Clinch River Reactor

Congress in 1983 ended federal government support for building the Clinch River breeder reactor, a project that once promised the nation an almost limitless source of electrical power.

Both the House and Senate voted decisively to deny more funds for the decade-old breeder project. That action scrapped joint government-industry plans to demonstrate "fast breeder" nuclear technology that would produce more fuel than it burned. In the process of generating electric power, a breeder would convert uranium into plutonium that could be removed to provide abundant nuclear fuel. *(Breeder technology, p. 79)*

Congress first authorized the Clinch River project in 1970 and funded the breeder program throughout the following decade as a solution to the nation's long-term energy problems. By the 1980s, however, congressional support was being eroded by long delays, sharply rising costs, flattening electric power demand and concern about the safety of nuclear technology. Although the government had spent $1.5 billion on planning the project, construction never got under way at the site near Oak Ridge, Tenn.

In the late 1970s President Carter had tried to cancel the Clinch River program, arguing that breeder reactors producing plutonium, a key ingredient in atomic bombs, would encourage the spread of nuclear weapons. Congress nearly killed the project in 1981-82, despite President Reagan's support and powerful backing from Senate Majority Leader Howard H. Baker Jr., R-Tenn.

By 1983, after the 98th Congress convened, most members concluded that the potential energy yield no longer justified the project's escalating costs or the technology's risks. Both the House and Senate voted to scrap the Clinch River project by decisive

**Architectural rendering of the Clinch River breeder reactor plant, which was to be built in Oak Ridge, Tenn. Congress killed the project in 1983.**

margins. The House in May voted 388-1 to repeal existing law authorizing funds for the program. The Senate in October refused, 56-40, to spend any more money for the project.

Congress included no money for the Clinch River breeder in its fiscal 1984 energy and water development appropriations bill. The House and Senate ignored the Reagan administration's plea to salvage the project through a new plan for sharing the cost with private industry.

### Background

Congress approved the breeder project as the nation entered a decade of uncertainty about how to develop and produce reliable supplies of energy. Because the technology could produce more fuel than it burned — hence the name "breeder" — the program showed promise of providing a

nearly inexhaustible source of power for generating electricity for industrial and residential use. "The breeder could extend the life of our natural uranium fuel supply from decades to centuries," President Nixon told the nation in 1971.

By building the Clinch River plant, the government intended to demonstrate that breeder reactors could generate electricity on a commercial scale even as they produced plutonium for additional nuclear fuel. The government also hoped that the plant's construction would spur private companies to develop an industrial base for building additional privately financed breeders. As initially authorized, the Clinch River breeder was expected to cost $700 million, of which private industry agreed to pay $250 million, about one third of the total.

From the start environmental groups

and anti-nuclear activists opposed the breeder program. Environmentalists feared the possibility of a horrendous accident — a meltdown of the reactor core, which, if secondary safety measures did not go as planned, could release clouds of lethal radioactive gases into the air. Others said the breeder would promote the spread of nuclear weapons. Unlike normal "light water" nuclear reactors, breeder reactors used and bred plutonium, a key ingredient of atomic bombs.

Congress insisted on funding the Clinch River program throughout the 1970s despite environmental and anti-nuclear groups' opposition. Concerned about potential nuclear weapons proliferation, Carter renounced plans for burning plutonium as nuclear fuel in the United States and asked Congress to terminate the demonstration breeder. But Congress repeatedly overrode Carter's policy, refusing in a series of 1977-79 votes to end Clinch River funding.

Research, development and design of the Clinch River reactor continued throughout the 1970s, incorporating innovations into the project. Breeder engineers dismissed press reports that Clinch River was technologically obsolete; they said the design of the reactor core was unique and far more efficient than the core design being used overseas.

Licensing procedures for the plant proceeded as planned. The NRC issued a final environmental statement in October 1982, and the major court challenges had been dealt with.

## Economics

But as work proceeded, the initial $700 million projected cost of the project soared to $4 billion. Meanwhile energy conservation efforts and slowing economic growth held electric power demand well below levels that U.S. energy planners predicted when the Clinch River project was conceived. With national energy independence no longer the obsession that it was in the early 1970s, the economic justification for the breeder program was called into question. Even the TVA, which had promised to purchase the power from the Clinch River breeder, had no real need for it.

Clinch River designers originally planned to complete the plant by 1980, but that target had slipped by a decade. Congress by 1983 had appropriated $1.5 billion for the project as its total cost rose to $4 billion. Private industry, however, still was committed to pay only $250 million, by then only one-sixteenth of the total.

Not until September 1982 was any work done on the Clinch River site near Oak Ridge. Then, however, site clearing began, and a year later a 100-foot-deep hole the size of a football field was almost ready for concrete pouring.

Half of the $1.5 billion spent on the project had been used for research, development and design, all complete by 1983. In addition, some $749 million in component parts had been ordered.

## Eroding Congressional Support

As costs shot up and the construction date slipped, fiscal conservatives in Congress turned against the Clinch River program. These members supported nuclear power in general and gave little weight to traditional arguments that the breeder was environmentally unsafe or a threat to world peace. Their concern was money. Given the current budget squeeze, they said, funneling $200 million to $300 million a year into a research and development project that would not pay off for decades — or possibly ever — was unconscionable.

Among the most active of these conservative Clinch River opponents were Sen. Gordon J. Humphrey, R-N.H., and Rep. Vin Weber, R-Minn. Both helped lead the campaign against the breeder in Congress.

# Breeder Technology

The technology of the breeder reactor dated back to World War II, when scientists were working to develop the atomic bomb. The first prototype breeder, the Experimental Breeder No. 1, went into operation in 1951 in Arco, Idaho. By 1970 several breeder plants were in operation, but the electric power industry still was not convinced of their commercial viability.

The nuclear power plants in operation in the United States in 1983 were light water reactors, which did not breed fuel. The difference between those reactors and breeder reactors had to do with the nature of nuclear reactions.

A nuclear reaction occurs when a "fissionable" element — either uranium-235 or man-made plutonium-239 — is packed in concentrated form. Tiny neutrons, which are thrown off at random by the atoms of these elements, will then strike other atoms. This causes the release of more neutrons, and a chain reaction begins. The reaction generates tremendous heat, which converts water into the steam that powers the turbines of an electrical generator.

In light water plants water is used both to cool the reactor core and to slow down the free neutrons, making the chain reaction easier to control.

In the liquid metal fast breeder reactor, however, the neutrons are allowed to travel at much faster speeds, quickening the chain reaction. The reactor core is surrounded with a "blanket" of non-fissionable uranium-238, which absorbs the stray neutrons from the reaction. After absorption the uranium becomes a new element, plutonium-239, which can then be removed and used as new fuel.

In uranium ore found in nature the non-fissionable uranium-238 element is much more plentiful than fissionable uranium-235. Before it can be used in a reactor, the uranium must be "enriched" to increase the concentration of uranium-235. The byproduct of this enrichment is uranium-238, which is stored in large canisters at Energy Department installations.

Without a breeder reactor that uranium-238 is of little value. With a breeder, however, it can be converted to plutonium and can provide an abundant energy source.

The nation's current supplies of uranium-238 could, with a breeder reactor, provide 700 times more energy than all the coal used in the United States in a year, and 400 times more energy than all the oil used in a year, the Department of Energy said.

Their opposition swayed other key conservatives who previously had supported the breeder, such as Reps. Trent Lott, R-Miss., and Phil Gramm, R-Texas.

Backing the efforts of these members was a group of conservative lobbying groups including the National Taxpayers Union and the Heritage Foundation.

In 1981-82 Baker and the rest of the Tennessee congressional delegation fought hard to keep the Clinch River project going. Baker helped convince the Reagan administration to support funding for the program over the objections of Office of Management and Budget (OMB) Director David A. Stockman. In lobbying fellow members, the Tennessee delegation pointed out that the project employed more than 3,500 workers, with preliminary work spread throughout the country, giving members in 32 states political incentive to support continued funding.

**1981-82 Debates.** During the Carter administration, the House Science and Technology Committee had provided key support for the program. But the panel reversed its stand in 1981, after the Reagan administration came to power and backed Clinch River. The committee in 1981 voted 22-18 to kill the project, but its action was overturned in the budget reconciliation bill.

In 1982 the full House voted to kill Clinch River, but the Senate upheld the project by one vote. Conferees on a continuing appropriations resolution finally provided $181 million to keep work going through Sept. 30, 1983, but they prohibited any permanent construction work at the site and directed DOE to explore alternative sources of financing.

**Reagan Cost-Sharing Plan.** Responding to that directive, the administration in 1983 sent Congress a plan for raising additional private funds to build the Clinch River plant. The plan proposed raising $1 billion from private sources, $150 million through the sale of stock and the rest from the sale of bonds in 1990 and from funds already committed by utilities and other investors. But opponents pointed out that private industry would assume no more risk under the plan than under previous financing arrangements. By the time the administration sent the plan to Capitol Hill on Aug. 1, moreover, the House already had voted to kill the project and Senate support was dwindling.

**1983 Congressional Action.** In the House the Science and Technology panel

led the effort to scuttle the Clinch River program. The committee voted 24-16 in April 1983 to halt all work on the project by Sept. 30 unless the government approved a new plan for sharing costs with private industry by that date. It attached that provision to legislation authorizing funds for DOE civilian research and development programs for fiscal 1984. The House passed the legislation, but the Senate took no action.

The Senate, which had kept Clinch River alive by a single vote in 1982, sealed its fate in October by refusing to provide $1.5 billion to complete the plant. The Senate Appropriations Committee Oct. 19 had approved an amendment, offered by Energy and Natural Resources Committee Chairman McClure to appropriate $1.5 billion for Clinch River as part of a fiscal 1984 supplemental appropriations bill. But the full Senate Oct. 26 killed the McClure amendment by 56-40.

The margin of defeat was wider than either side of the Clinch River debate had expected.

# Power Plant Construction Costs

The Senate in 1984 killed a House proposal to limit federally regulated electric utilities' ability to charge customers for the cost of building new power plants that still were under construction.

The House Feb. 8 passed legislation that its Energy and Commerce Committee drafted in response to a 1983 Federal Energy Regulatory Commission (FERC) ruling. The Senate did not act on the measure, which the House passed by a 288-113 vote.

The commission, which regulated about 10 percent of the nation's electric power sales, permitted utilities to recover through immediate rate increases up to 50 percent of the interest they paid to borrow funds for ongoing plant construction.

The FERC rule, which went into effect July 1, 1983, followed similar decisions by many state regulatory agencies to permit interest costs for construction work in progress (CWIP) to be included in utility rate bases. Under standard rate-setting procedures, utilities could recover the direct costs of building power plants through a depreciation component in utility rates after the facilities went into service.

The House legislation would have restricted the use of CWIP charges to finan-cially pressed utilities unable to borrow construction funds except at above-average rates. Its advocates maintained that restricting CWIP charges would hold consumer electricity rates lower and encourage utilities to consider alternatives to building costly plants. But the measure's opponents, mostly Republicans, replied that the restrictions would discourage needed investments in future generating capacity — and expose consumers to future "rate shocks" when new plants were completed.

# Part II

---

# Environment

# 5

# Environment: New Challenges

President Reagan came into office in 1981 committed to reversing the growth of federal government programs and regulation. This policy reflected Reagan's view that excessive regulation was responsible for many of the nation's economic woes. Environmental regulations were among the primary targets, despite their popular support.

Although many important environmental laws were due to expire and, therefore, to be reconsidered in Congress, the Reagan administration decided to pursue its deregulatory policy primarily through administrative means — by appointing like-minded officials to key positions, by cutting budgets, and by expanding executive oversight authority.

The Reagan policy created an expanded role for the Office of Management and Budget (OMB) — that of reviewing rules made by government agencies before the rules were published in the *Federal Register*. In 1985 a new executive order extended OMB's supervision to agency activities, such as research projects, that preceded the formulation of rules.

Congress reacted to the Reagan policies, not with new legislation, but with its power to investigate. In a probe of the Environmental Protection Agency (EPA), for example, congressional investigators uncovered abuses that lead to the resignation of EPA administrator Anne M. Burford and most of her top staffers. Later investigations focused more explicitly on OMB's role.

At the Department of the Interior the president's policies emphasized conflicting responsibilities of protecting natural resources while fostering the nation's economic growth.

## Interior's Dual Role

Congress created the Department of the Interior in 1849 and assigned it the task of managing the vast public lands that the national government acquired with the nation's western territories. Throughout the 19th century the department's principal goal was to transfer federally owned lands to homesteaders, ranchers, newly formed state governments, railroads and other owners to encourage settlement of the West. Over the years, however, Congress complicated the department's missions by assigning it responsibility for developing water resources, leasing federal minerals, preserving national parks, protecting wildlife habitat and supervising American Indian reservations.

As James G. Watt, President Reagan's first interior secretary, put it in a 1982 television interview, "The secretary of the interior is sitting on a department filled with

# Nine Environmental Protection Laws...

Nine major environmental laws must be acted upon by Congress because their funding authorizations have expired or will do so in 1985:

**Superfund.** This 1980 law, officially the Comprehensive Environmental Response, Compensation and Liability Act, set up a $1.6 billion fund to pay for prompt cleanup of abandoned hazardous-waste dumps and toxic spills. It also made dumpers and dump owners legally responsible for paying cleanup costs. The Environmental Protection Agency (EPA) could use the fund for immediate cleanup and then go to court for the slower process of recovering costs. A tax on petrochemicals that paid for most of the superfund was due to expire Sept. 30, 1985.

**Toxic Substances Control Act.** Enacted in 1976 after five years of debate, this law expanded federal regulation of industrial and commercial chemicals and for the first time required pre-market testing for those considered potentially dangerous. The act was renewed for two years (1982-83) in a 1981 law with no substantive changes.

**Clean Air Act.** The nation's principal air pollution control law, the Clean Air Act was enacted in 1970 and substantially amended in 1977. Its funding authorization expired in 1981, as Congress found itself buffeted by conflicting pressures. The Reagan administration and several industries sought to relax the law, while environmentalists wanted new controls on acid rain and toxic air pollutants. Unwilling to pay the high political price needed to settle the quarrel, Congress opted for inaction. It imposed a moratorium on moves by the EPA to punish cities that failed to meet legal deadlines for cleaning up their air, and it pushed the problem of reauthorization under the rug.

**Clean Water Act.** Funding authorization for the regulatory part of this law, which controls water pollution by requiring permits for any discharge into a waterway, expired Sept. 30, 1982. Authorization for politically popular sewage-plant construction grants expired Sept. 30, 1985.

conflict." The department's National Park Service struggles to preserve scenic vistas in national parks while hosting millions of visitors each year who come to view them. Its U.S. Fish and Wildlife Service designates endangered species for protection and manages national wildlife refuges for waterfowl and animals, but it also traps and hunts coyotes and other predators to keep them from damaging farmers' crops and ranchers' livestock. The Bureau of Land Management (BLM) manages more than 300 million acres of public lands, largely in Western states, for multiple uses that include mining, oil and gas drilling, livestock grazing, hiking, hunting, archeological digs and other, often irreconcilable, activities.

In addition, Interior's Bureau of Reclamation has built and operates dams, reservoirs and irrigation systems throughout 17 predominantly arid Western states. Its U.S. Geological Survey studies the nation's geologic characteristics and maps the extent of valuable mineral deposits beneath federal

# ...To Be Reauthorized by Congress

**Federal Insecticide, Fungicide and Rodenticide Act (FIFRA).** The main law regulating the registration, labeling and use of pesticides, FIFRA was due for reauthorization in 1981. The last major overhaul of the act came in 1978. Congress cleared a simple one-year reauthorization of the pesticide control law in 1983.

**Safe Drinking Water Act.** This 1974 law gave EPA the power to set maximum allowable levels for chemical and bacteriological contaminants in drinking water systems serving more than 25 customers. Congress enacted a three-year reauthorization in 1979, which expired at the end of fiscal 1982.

**Ocean Dumping Act.** This law, which is Title I of the Marine Protection, Research and Sanctuaries Act of 1972, set up a program to regulate the dumping of industrial waste, municipal sewage sludge and other materials in the ocean. Funding authorization expired in 1982.

**Coastal Zone Management Act.** This 1972 law established a federal-state planning program to balance preservation of coastal natural resources such as fishing grounds with economic development efforts such as offshore oil and gas drilling. The act was amended in 1976 to authorize a $1.2 billion program of federal aid to coastal states to help them offset the effects of energy development. Congress drastically cut authorization levels for the program, however, in 1980. Most authorizations under the act were due to expire at the end of fiscal 1985.

**Endangered Species Act.** Originally enacted in 1973, this law made it a federal offense to buy, sell, possess, export or import any species listed as endangered or threatened. It also prohibited federal projects from jeopardizing listed species or their habitat. Congress enacted a three-year reauthorization of the act in 1982, reaffirming the basic outlines of the program, but streamlining its enforcement. Lawmakers rejected Reagan administration proposals for greater consideration of economic costs of listing species and set tightened deadlines in an effort to force the administration to speed up listing decisions.

lands and forests. Its Bureau of Mines studies mining techniques, while its Office of Surface Mining enforces a 1977 federal law limiting damage from strip-mining coal on private as well as public lands. Its Bureau of Indian Affairs acts as trustee for Native American tribes in managing reservation lands and resources. Its Minerals Management Service, an agency that Watt set up in 1982, collects royalties from federal mineral leases and also manages the government's Outer Continental Shelf oil

and gas leasing program in federally controlled coastal waters.

In addition to valuable coal, oil and gas, oil shale and other minerals, BLM administers some productive federal timber stands in Washington and Oregon. But the U.S. Forest Service, a separate agency within the Agriculture Department, manages most federal timberlands as part of the 187-million-acre national forest system.

For years Congress generally was content to set broad goals for federal resource management, leaving the interior secretary discretion to administer the lands and resources the department controlled. Most interior secretaries came from Western states, and the department staff was largely drawn from Westerners. Politically powerful public land users, notably ranchers, loggers, miners and farmers who relied on federal irrigation water, wielded strong influence over decision making by Interior officials who viewed the department's primary task as making federal resources available for economic production.

During the late 1960s and 1970s the National Environmental Protection Act, Endangered Species Act and other new laws forced Interior agencies to consider how public land resource development affected wildlife, air and water quality, and undisturbed wild country. In 1976 Congress through the Federal Land Policy and Management Act gave BLM a permanent mandate for managing remaining public lands for multiple uses, including natural values as well as resource production. Conservation groups also began questioning the way Interior managed BLM lands, planned Bureau of Reclamation water projects and handled its mineral leasing efforts.

Meanwhile national energy problems increased pressure on the department to step up production of federally owned coal, onshore oil and gas and offshore petroleum deposits.

It fell to President Carter, a Democrat elected in 1976 with strong environmentalist backing, to implement the more balanced resource management policies that Congress mandated in the early 1970s.

While initially viewed as acceptable to Western interests, Carter's interior secretary, former Idaho Gov. Cecil D. Andrus, angered advocates of resource development by appointing environmental activists to key Interior posts and by expanding funding and manpower for BLM's conservation ef-

forts. In its first weeks in office the administration also offended Western congressional delegations by releasing a "hit list" of authorized water projects that officials planned to cancel. Carter's resource policies sparked a "Sagebrush Rebellion" in Western states among miners, ranchers, state legislators and other interests that previously had dominated Interior policy making. In selecting Watt as his interior secretary in 1981, President Reagan signaled his intention to overhaul Carter's preservationist approach.

## Watt's Stewardship

From the start James Watt emerged as the most combative and controversial proponent of the Reagan administration's strategy for encouraging natural resource production to fuel U.S. economic recovery. Through budget cutbacks and widespread staff changes, Watt steered Interior's resource-managing agencies away from the conservationist goals that congressional environmental laws and Secretary Andrus had set during the Carter administration.

In keeping with the administration's faith in free market economic forces, Watt prodded the department back toward its once traditional mission of promoting rapid development of federally owned energy, timber, water projects and other resources by private business for consumption by the American public. And, as chairman of Reagan's Cabinet Council on Natural Resources and the Environment, Watt influenced policies followed by the Energy Department, EPA, U.S. Forest Service and other federal agencies.

In the Senate, with a Republican majority elected in 1980, Western senators who assumed leadership positions backed Watt's efforts to spur resource development on federally owned lands that made up the bulk of the 11-state region.

But Watt's aggressive leadership style, combined with a penchant for jokes and ideological statements that offended many groups, embroiled the secretary in a series of political controversies that eventually forced him to resign in October 1983.

## Watt's Background

Born in Wyoming, Watt brought a Westerner's pro-development perspective to the Interior post. But through extensive service in Washington, D.C., both on the Senate staff and in various natural resource agencies, Watt also developed an insider's knowledge and political skills for dealing with the Interior bureaucracy.

Watt worked on the staff of Sen. Milward L. Simpson, R-Wyo. (1962-67), then held several posts during the Nixon and Ford administrations. After serving as deputy assistant secretary of the interior for water and power resources, Watt in 1972 was named head of the department's Bureau of Outdoor Recreation.

President Ford in 1975 appointed Watt to the Federal Power Commission, an energy regulatory agency that the Carter administration in 1977 merged into the newly formed Department of Energy.

After leaving the commission, Watt moved to Denver, Colo., as president of the Mountain States Legal Foundation, a conservative public interest legal group founded by Joseph Coors, a Colorado brewing heir, and other businessmen. In that position, Watt challenged many of the environmental protection policies that Interior adopted under Andrus, in the process developing a reputation among Western interests as an enemy of environmental groups. In the foundation's 1979-80 report, Watt vowed to "move to check the power of the federal government wherever possible in issues pertaining to the use of federal lands and the development of the West."

Despite environmentalists' misgivings

about Watt's views, the Senate confirmed his appointment by an 83-12 margin on Jan. 22, 1981. Reagan later named Watt chairman of the President's Cabinet Council on Natural Resources and the Environment.

## Controversial Programs

After taking over the Interior Department, Watt moved forcefully to "swing the pendulum back to center" from the preservationist tack that Carter administration officials had taken in managing federal resources. Watt sought no major legislation from Congress but instead shifted the department's priorities through budget cuts and personnel changes. Watt fired or demoted career Interior employees and relied heavily on advisers he brought into the department. Through budget decisions he strengthened Interior programs for promoting resource development while curtailing conservation efforts.

The secretary deeply angered environmentalist leaders by refusing to meet with them and by reducing their access, both in Washington and at the local level, to Interior decision-making procedures. Only a few months after Watt took office, the Sierra Club, Wilderness Society, National Audubon Society and other environmental groups demanded his ouster. Even the National Wildlife Federation, considered the most conservative of major conservation organizations, joined in calling for Watt's resignation.

Watt maintained that the government could protect its scenic wild lands and manage other public lands for resource production. In speeches and other public statements, the secretary invoked the once-traditional definition of conservation as requiring wise *use* of public resources for public benefits. "The key to conservation is management," he told the North American Wildlife and Natural Resources Conference in 1981. "Conservation is not the blind

locking away of huge areas and their resources because of emotional appeals."

Following up on that philosophy, Watt
accelerated Interior plans for leasing coal,
offshore oil and gas, and onshore petroleum
deposits beneath federal lands. He also tried
to open national forest wilderness lands,
especially along the petroleum-rich
Overthrust Belt region in Wyoming, Utah
and Idaho, for mineral exploration. He
slowed national park land purchases, although Congress rejected his plan to divert
Land and Water Conservation Fund money
from park expansion to repairing existing
park facilities. As part of the Reagan administration plan to reduce the national
debt, Watt also drew up proposals to sell off
small, hard-to-manage federal tracts to private owners.

## Growing Controversy

The Common Cause lobbying group
issued a report in 1981 claiming that Watt's
new leadership team had "a disproportion-
ately industry-oriented perspective." The
report — entitled "Who's Minding the
Store?" — said 11 of the top 16 Interior
officials had been employed by or served
clients in the five industries — oil, mining,
timber, livestock and utilities — whose activities on public lands were regulated by
Interior.

Watt's ambitious agenda and abrasive
manner quickly stirred stiff opposition from
Congress, environmental groups and state
governments. Watt clashed frequently with
the Democratic leaders of House committees that authorized and appropriated funds
for Interior programs. The secretary frequently dismissed environmental group
leaders, and House Democratic critics, as
an elite who were more interested in preserving wild lands for enjoyment by a privi-
leged few than in providing sufficient energy, timber, water and other resources for
the benefit of all Americans. Watt barred

Interior officials from consulting leading
environmental groups in developing plans
for managing public lands. Nearly all environmental groups — even the 1.5-million-
member National Wildlife Federation, a
generally conservative organization representing hunters and fishermen — responded
early on by calling for Watt's dismissal.

Although he had vowed to make the
Interior Department a "good neighbor" to
the West, Watt alienated even some Western governors with his plans to accelerate
energy development on public lands in their
states. California and Oregon sued to halt
Watt's plans to expand offshore drilling
along their coastlines and governors in other
Western states opposed the way Watt
wanted to speed up coal production in their
states.

Watt's admirers contended that the
secretary's controversial methods were essential to push his programs through a
reluctant Interior bureaucracy and overcome resistance from members of Congress,
congressional committee staffs and environmental groups who had supported the Carter policies. Sen. Malcolm Wallop, R-Wyo.,
chairman of the Senate Energy and Natural
Resources Subcommittee on Public Lands,
in 1981 called Watt "hands-down the first
real secretary of the interior that the country has had in a couple of decades."

But environmentalists, economists and
some resource professionals contended that
Watt's campaign to promote rapid federal
resource production went far beyond wise
stewardship of public lands. In leasing vast
coal and oil reserves to private companies
while world energy markets were slack, they
argued, the secretary violated his obligation
as trustee of public lands to obtain fair
market value for them. Critics suggested
that Watt's ambitious leasing plans
stemmed from his philosophical distaste for
federal government control over valuable
land and resources.

## Watt's Resignation

Watt met his downfall in 1983. There was growing criticism of his policies, with charges that Watt was engaged in a massive "giveaway" of public resources to private interests. But Watt's abrasive personality proved a greater liability than his policies. Bitter and personal feuding between Watt and key members of the House Interior Committee had broken out as early as 1981. That year Watt said: "I never use the words Democrats and Republicans. It's liberals and Americans."

After Republican losses in the 1982 congressional elections, Watt's political standing eroded. During his term in office Watt's combative speeches and sometimes inflammatory phrases offended important national political interests. He angered American Indian leaders by calling reservations a dramatic example of the "failures of socialism." He frequently went out of his way to dismiss environmental group leaders as elitists who pursued selfish interests at the expense of other Americans.

In 1983 Watt continued his string of public relations disasters — for example, banning the popular Beach Boys singing group from the capital's 1983 Fourth of July celebration, saying they attracted "the wrong element." Among their staunchest fans was first lady Nancy Reagan. Watt instead invited Las Vegas singer Wayne Newton to provide the afternoon's entertainment.

On Sept. 21, 1983, Watt offended four major voting groups in as many seconds by calling members of a coal leasing advisory commission "a black . . . a woman, two Jews and a cripple." It proved to be the last gaffe.

Republican senators, worried that Watt might prove to be a millstone around their own necks as well as Reagan's in 1984, deserted him in droves. Facing a Senate "no confidence" vote, Watt resigned Oct. 9.

# Clark's Calming Effect

President Reagan in October 1983 picked William P. Clark, his national security adviser, to succeed Watt as head of the Interior Department. Clark never disavowed Watt's policies, but his low-key management style and political skills quieted House Democrats' and environmental groups' anger.

Clark stayed in the job for a little more than a year, but in that time he returned Interior to "the humdrum agency it used to be," in the words of one longtime department staffer. Defusing bitter controversies over Watt's policies, Clark resumed buying lands for national parks, slowed plans for leasing federal offshore oil and gas and halted federal coal lease sales while Interior officials overhauled leasing procedures. Softening Watt's hard-line rhetoric, Clark opened ties to House Democrats whom Watt had defied and consulted environmental group leaders whom Watt had excluded from the Interior policy-making process.

Although environmental groups welcomed Clark's conciliatory style, they found little change in the administration's basic pro-development goals during his brief Interior tenure. Clark on Jan. 1, 1985, announced that he was resigning the Interior post to return to his ranch in California. Reagan named Secretary of Energy Donald P. Hodel, who previously had served as Interior under secretary under Watt, to replace Clark.

# Congressional Action

In 1981 the president proposed drastic cutbacks in the politically popular federal program of grants for construction of local sewage systems. Congress voted those reductions, along with cuts in the budget of the EPA that were part of broader domestic spending cuts. But environmentalists and their legislative allies dug in their heels on other issues before Congress. With surprising ease they managed to stave off administration proposals to relax both the Clean Air Act and the regulatory provisions of the Clean Water Act.

Congress feuded with Watt throughout 1981-82 over his ambitious energy leasing plans. Early in 1981, Watt vowed to open federal wilderness areas for oil and gas leasing so industry could explore promising formations. Existing law permitted mineral leasing in designated wilderness areas until the end of 1983 and Watt pressed Interior officials to grant leases in those regions before a permanent ban took effect.

But those wilderness leasing plans angered many members of Congress, including Republicans who were embarrassed by Interior decisions to open wilderness regions in their states and districts for possible development. The House Interior Committee in 1981 invoked an obscure provision in a 1976 public land law to declare a Montana wilderness off limits to oil and gas leasing.

Watt subsequently agreed to put off wilderness leasing until the 97th Congress adjourned in 1982. Congress, still suspicious of Watt's plans, amended the fiscal 1983 Interior appropriations bill to extend the moratorium until the end of 1983, when the permanent leasing prohibition went into effect.

With environmentalists raising an alarm over Watt's plans for developing federal lands, Congress also stepped in to block some controversial decisions. Western senators, led by Senate Energy and Natural Resources Committee Chairman James A. McClure, R-Idaho, welcomed Watt's efforts to reverse public land policies adopted by Secretary Andrus.

But House Democratic leaders on environmental legislation — notably Interior and Insular Affairs Committee Chairman

Morris K. Udall, D-Ariz.; Appropriations Subcommittee on Interior Chairman Sidney R. Yates, D-Ill.; and Henry A. Waxman, D-Calif., chairman of the Energy and Commerce Subcommittee on Health and Environment — led a series of fights to preserve Interior and EPA programs that they had helped launch during the previous decade.

On many issues, Watt and Burford stirred angry congressional resistance by taking hard-line stands without consulting members or listening to environmental groups' positions. Congress responded through legislative riders, oversight hearings and angry exchanges in the press that forced the administration to back off from some controversial initiatives.

Through language that the House wrote into Interior Department appropriations bills, Congress kept national forest wilderness areas and sensitive California offshore waters off limits to Watt's plans to expand oil and gas exploration. To Watt's dismay, California's entire congressional delegation united to oppose development of environmentally pristine ocean basins off that state's coastline. Congress also halted Watt's ambitious coal leasing plans by imposing a temporary moratorium after Interior sold millions of tons of federal coal on depressed national coal markets.

Through politically charged hearings and protracted committee debate, House critics of Burford's policies forced EPA to abandon proposed Clean Air Act revisions and prodded the agency to move more quickly to implement the "superfund" program for cleaning up abandoned toxic waste dumps. Congress had created the superfund the year before Reagan took office.

In response to the scandals at EPA, Congress in 1984 tightened federal controls on handling and disposing of toxic wastes, taking away EPA administrative discretion that members contended the agency had abused in enforcing previous law.

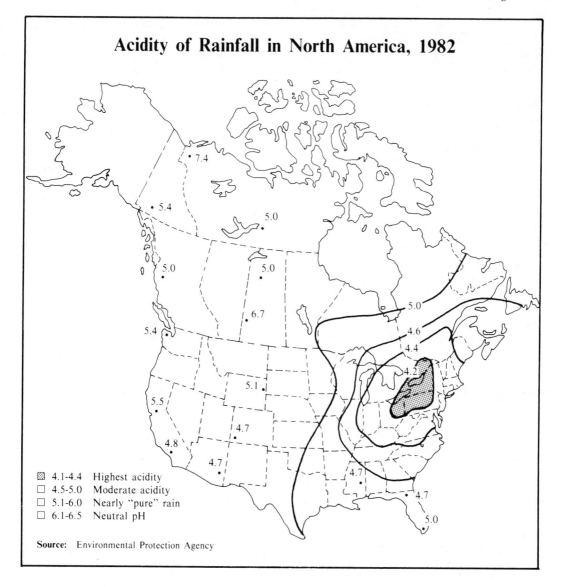

## Acidity of Rainfall in North America, 1982

▨ 4.1-4.4  Highest acidity
☐ 4.5-5.0  Moderate acidity
☐ 5.1-6.0  Nearly "pure" rain
☐ 6.1-6.5  Neutral pH

**Source:**  Environmental Protection Agency

And, under a compromise worked out by Senate Republicans and House Democrats, Congress in 1984 passed and the president signed a series of laws that began settling the long-raging debate over how much of the lands in the U.S. national forests should be preserved as permanent wilderness and how much should be kept open for logging and other development.

But White House resistance and re-gional divisions within Congress prevented revision of federal clean air and clean water laws. Concerned by potential economic costs, the administration and Congress took a go-slow approach toward environmentalists' demand that the federal government curb Midwestern power plant emissions. Studies had found that these emissions produced "acid rain," which damaged Eastern lakes and forests.

After the resignations of Watt and Burford in 1983, their successors improved environmental enforcement, opened communications with environmental groups and shifted controversial agendas to the back burner as the 1984 presidential election approached. During the campaign Reagan proclaimed the administration's environmental record the "best-kept secret" of his first White House term.

But environmental groups remained skeptical at best, and they continued to attack Interior's mineral leasing goals and EPA's reluctance to propose strict controls on acid rain drifting over the Northeast from Midwestern coal-fired power plant smokestacks. Taking unprecedented stands, the Sierra Club and Friends of the Earth, two major environmental groups, endorsed Walter F. Mondale, Carter's vice president, in his unsuccessful 1984 Democratic campaign to defeat Reagan.

## Struggle Over EPA

Like Watt, EPA Administrator Burford was considered more sympathetic than her predecessors to the industries the agency dealt with. Although Congress refused to ease pollution control standards by revising environmental laws, the EPA during Burford's tenure took steps to grant regulatory relief through budget and administrative decisions.

Under Burford's leadership EPA took a less adversarial approach toward industry. Burford gleaned most of her top administrators from the ranks of major corporations. In the regulatory area, she abolished the agency's office of enforcement, preferring to rely on negotiating agreements for voluntary industry compliance with federal pollution standards. She cut back the number of enforcement cases that EPA took to court and reviewed pollution regulations to ease industry burdens. The administration simultaneously slashed the EPA budget, from $1.3 billion in fiscal 1981 to $1.09 billion in fiscal 1982, including deep cuts in research and development.

From the start House members questioned whether EPA relations with industry were growing too friendly. In 1981 Rep. Toby Moffett, D-Conn., chairman of the Government Operations Subcommittee on the Environment, criticized the administrator and other top agency officials during oversight hearings to investigate meetings EPA had held with chemical industry representatives to discuss proposed regulatory actions affecting that industry.

Three other congressional panels joined Moffett's in holding oversight hearings to determine whether EPA was using deep budget cuts and regulatory "reforms" to retreat from its congressionally mandated pollution control duties.

Using leaked EPA budget documents, a group comprised largely of former EPA officials formed the "Save EPA Committee." The group kept Congress and the press up to date on the administration's 1983 budget proposals, which it claimed would "demolish" the agency.

"Unable to repeal the country's environmental laws because the public would never stand for it," said William Drayton, former EPA assistant administrator for planning and management and a member of Save EPA, "Reagan is gutting them through the personnel and budgetary back doors."

When it disagreed with agency actions, Congress could rarely do much more than raise a fuss. But in some cases that was enough. After noisy congressional protests, for example, EPA backed off from a decision to suspend an existing ban on dumping toxic liquid wastes into unlined landfills and from plans to consider relaxing or repealing restrictions on lead in gasoline.

The struggle over EPA came to a head

in 1983, when Burford resigned in the midst of a series of congressional investigations into the agency's conduct. She resigned March 9. *(EPA scandals, p. 157)*

To replace Burford, the president called the first EPA administrator, William D. Ruckelshaus, back into service. Under Ruckelshaus EPA began enforcing environmental laws with more vigor. After several years of decline, EPA's operating budget expanded in fiscal 1984 but still fell short of where the agency's funding stood at the end of the Carter administration. By most accounts Ruckelshaus restored public confidence in EPA's integrity by taking aggressive actions against several polluting industries. Ruckelshaus, who had earned a favorable reputation among environmentalists during his first stint at EPA (1970-73), succeeded in pushing tougher restrictions on lead in gasoline and imposed mandatory controls on use of the pesticide EDB. But Reagan refused to accept Ruckelshaus' proposal for immediate action against acid rain, insisting instead on more research.

Environmentalists remained unconvinced that the White House had given Ruckelshaus the leeway to pursue environmental goals over objections by the Office of Management and Budget (OMB), which exercised final control over many EPA decisions. They contended that Reagan needed a strong environmental advocate within the White House staff to counter OMB Director David A. Stockman's pressure for budget cutbacks in environmental programs. Those doubts increased after Ruckelshaus abruptly resigned the EPA post Nov. 28, 1984. Reagan named Lee M. Thomas to replace Ruckelshaus.

## Clean Air Act Stalemate

While Congress forced EPA to move more aggressively to control pollution, the House and Senate were unable to forge legislative agreements on revising existing environmental laws. During Reagan's first term, House and Senate committees tried, without success, to rewrite the federal Clean Air Act of 1970, the nation's flagship environmental protection measure.

After Reagan's election, industry leaders had hoped (and environmental groups had feared) that his administration would push a major relaxation of the law through the 97th Congress. Industry complained that the law saddled it — and ultimately consumers — with billions of dollars in cleanup costs. Environmentalists countered that air pollution, left unchecked, cost as much or more in damage to human health, crops and property. The act affected a wide range of industries, especially steel, coal, autos, chemicals, petroleum and electric utilities. Clean air legislation excited intense regional rivalries, because one region's economic mainstay was often another's major polluter. *(Acid rain map, p. 93)*

But after a year-long struggle in 1982, neither House nor Senate committees could come up with Clean Air Act revisions that congressional leaders were willing to take to the floor.

The Senate Environment and Public Works Committee, chaired by Robert T. Stafford, R-Vt., reported out a carefully constructed "fine-tuning" of the existing law. But even though that bill represented a virtual consensus of the committee, it faced a bruising battle on the floor and Senate leaders never called it up.

In the House Energy and Commerce Committee, Chairman John D. Dingell, D-Mich., took a different approach, attempting to settle some issues by tests of raw voting power. Dingell led a faction supporting major relaxations of the existing law, while Health and Environment Subcommittee Chairman Waxman fought to strengthen it. Neither side was able to gain a lasting advantage and the panel finally abandoned all attempts at a markup.

Despite its inconclusive nature, the 1982 clean air maneuvering did much to pinpoint the issues that needed to be settled before a bill could pass. These included acid rain, toxic air pollutants, auto and truck emission controls and programs to prevent deterioration of air that was cleaner than required by the national standards.

By 1984, in the wake of Watt's resignation and EPA scandals, environmentalists held the high ground in congressional debates. Waxman went on the offensive, pressing his subcommittee to report a clean air bill that actually strengthened the existing law by imposing controls on acid rain. But Waxman shelved the measure after the subcommittee voted, 10-9, to strip out the acid rain provisions. In the Senate the Environment panel approved a clean air bill with acid rain controls, but the measure again never reached the floor. *(Clean air, p. 105)*

## Toxic Waste Measures

Environmental advocates were more successful in pressing legislation to tighten federal controls on toxic wastes. The EPA superfund scandal and public fears that were spurred by widespread publicity about dangerous waste dumps across the nation spurred congressional action.

Taking the most significant pollution control action during Reagan's first term, Congress in 1984 reauthorized the Resource Conservation and Recovery Act (RCRA) of 1976, the law ordering EPA to regulate how business handled, stored and disposed of hazardous waste chemicals. In the 1984 revisions Congress banned disposal of hazardous liquids in landfills, from which they might seep into groundwater supplies, and extended EPA regulations for disposing of hazardous materials to tens of thousands of small businesses, from dry cleaners to gasoline filling stations.

The bill's enactment demonstrated how potent toxic wastes had become as a political issue. The House passed the measure in November 1983, but the Senate acted only after Democrats made clear at their July 1984 convention that they intended to use Reagan's record on the control and cleanup of such wastes against him. The logjam of objections that had stalled the bill short of the Senate floor finally broke after the Democratic convention, when the administration signaled it wanted an environmental bill to sign.

Aware that Reagan would be reluctant to veto a strong bill before the election, Rep. James J. Florio, D-N.J., chief sponsor of the 1980 superfund law, decided to seek renewal of the $1.6 billion program a year before it was due to expire. Although the House approved the extension, in the process boosting funds for the five-year cleanup program to $10.2 billion, a more modest $7.5 billion Senate version was stalled by the Senate Finance Committee, which held jurisdiction on the tax on petrochemicals that provided most of the cleanup funds. *(Hazardous wastes, p. 157)*

## Federal Water Policy

Congress struggled for four years, with few results, to reconcile costly federal water pollution and development programs with Reagan's budget-cutting demands.

Spurred by Reagan's refusal to request new funding for sewer construction grants unless spiraling costs were curtailed, lawmakers in 1981 cut annual authorizations for the program from $5 billion to $2.5 billion. But Congress made little progress in revising federal water pollution control laws that gave EPA power to regulate industrial and municipal wastewater discharges. The House in 1984 passed legislation revamping the Clean Water Act and the Safe Drinking Water Act, but the Senate took no action.

Budget problems and regional rivalries thwarted congressional efforts to fund new water development projects by the Army Corps of Engineers and Interior's Bureau of Reclamation. Watt came into office pledging to back water projects that Carter's environment-minded administration tried to kill, but internal administration debate over "cost-sharing" arrangements requiring state and local governments to pay part of construction costs delayed agreement on launching new projects. Meanwhile congressional delegations from Eastern states jockeyed for more funding for sewer repairs in their region as the price of supporting Western reclamation and flood control projects.

Just before the Democratic convention, the House approved an omnibus $18 billion water development bill authorizing more than 300 projects, mainly in the East. But the Senate never took up its own $11 billion version, in part because Western senators objected to proposals to create a national water policy board, replacing one that Congress abolished at Reagan's request in 1982. The board could have put the Reclamation Bureau, which served the West, and the Corps of Engineers under one policy-making mechanism.

Western water interests accomplished more in Congress than Eastern ones. The Reclamation Bureau once again increased its share of the total available water appropriations at the expense of the Corps of Engineers. Westerners also got a $650 million dam safety bill and a reaffirmation of below-market pricing for federal hydroelectric power from the Hoover Dam. *(Water development, p. 121)*

# National Forest Policy

During Reagan's first three years in office Congress resisted administration attempts to accelerate logging in national forests and to resolve the status of roadless lands that the Forest Service had identified as potential wilderness.

Assistant Secretary of Agriculture John B. Crowell, Jr., former general counsel of the Louisiana-Pacific Corp., the nation's second-largest timber company, prodded Forest Service planners to abandon conservative timber harvest schedules. These plans restricted logging in "old-growth" Pacific Northwest forests that industry was eager to cut. Backed by McClure and other Republican senators from Western states, the administration urged Congress to move to designate wilderness areas and open other forest lands for timber production.

The wilderness debate had been building since President Carter in 1977 sent Congress his recommendations for expanding wilderness areas in the national forest system, based on the Forest Service's RARE II survey of remaining roadless regions. Congress ever since had been slowly working its way through those proposals in state-by-state bills, usually offered by congressional delegations from the state involved. The state-by-state process meant that in most cases loggers, miners and environmentalists had to reach consensus on which lands deserved protection, then win support from most members of a state's delegation.

As the designation process dragged on, McClure and other senators demanded that Congress "release" roadless lands for multiple-use development that the Forest Service had left out of its RARE II proposals. But environmentalists opposed the release procedure, preferring to keep the lands undeveloped for possible inclusion in an expanded wilderness system. McClure finally negotiated a compromise in 1984 with Rep. John F. Seiberling, D-Ohio, chairman of the House Interior Subcommittee on Public Lands, clearing the way for an outpouring of wilderness legislation. The bills set aside for protection more than 8.3 million acres in

20 states while releasing more than 14.6 million acres for possible development. *(Land management, p. 167)*

# Regulatory Power Clash

The Office of Management and Budget played a key role in the regulatory reform campaign that began in the first days of the Reagan administration. Through a series of executive orders, the president gave OMB authority to review agency rules before they were issued and to block them if it decided they were not worthwhile. Using that power, OMB functioned as the operating arm of the President's Task Force on Regulatory Relief, which was established Jan. 22, 1981, under the chairmanship of Vice President George Bush.

Reagan's program was more than just a pragmatic solution to excesses in regulation that even his critics conceded have occurred at times. It was an expression of a philosophy that disapproved of government regulation of business generally. That philosophy was stated in the Aug. 11, 1983, report of the Bush task force.

"Government regulation of private economic activity, as traditionally designed and implemented, has certain general characteristics that lead to inefficient or counter-productive policies in a wide variety of substantive areas," the report stated.

The task force reported that the administration had "rationalized the rulemaking process and slowed the growth of new federal rules, revised or eliminated hundreds of unjustifiable inherited rules (including hundreds of millions of hours in paperwork requirements), and commenced the revision of a number of regulatory statutes." The task force claimed savings to the U.S. economy of more than $150 billion over 10 years.

With its report, the task force went out of business. But it left behind a new rulemaking process, with OMB firmly in control. The main instrument of that control was Executive Order 12291, issued Feb. 17, 1981, which required agencies not to publish regulations in the *Federal Register* (thereby putting them into effect) until OMB had reviewed them.

The order required agencies to submit to OMB along with any major rule a "Regulatory Impact Analysis" describing its costs and benefits. OMB was to ensure that benefits exceeded costs. The order allowed OMB to extend its review time for as long as it considered necessary — in effect allowing indefinite postponement of regulations.

OMB could use these powers only "to the extent permitted by law," meaning, among other things, that it could not require compliance by "independent" regulatory agencies such as the Federal Communications Commission, whose actions are legally shielded from review by other executive branch agencies. Bush asked those agencies to comply voluntarily.

## 1985 Executive Order

On Jan. 4, 1985, shortly before his second inauguration, Reagan issued a new executive order (No. 12498) that further strengthened OMB's grip on the regulatory process. The new order concentrated on controlling regulations much earlier in their development than the one issued in 1981.

The 1985 order extended OMB's supervision to "pre-rulemaking actions" by the agencies. Those are defined as "any important action taken to consider whether to initiate, or in contemplation of, rulemaking, publication of advance notices of proposed rulemaking and all similar notices, publications and requests for public comment; and development or dissemination of ... documents that may influence, anticipate, or could lead to the commencement of rulemaking proceedings at a later date."

The 1985 order also required most other civilian government agencies to submit to OMB annually a "Draft Regulatory Program" listing all significant regulatory actions, including pre-rulemaking actions, they plan to take during the coming year. OMB could ask agencies to redo their proposals. Agencies could appeal disagreements with OMB to a Cabinet-level body named by the president. But once OMB published the plans for all agencies as the "Administration's Regulatory Program," the agencies could take no actions not included in it unless they are legally required to or have obtained OMB's approval.

## Administrative Procedure Act

Federal agencies were not permitted to make rules according to mere whim. An elaborate body of law specified what they could do and how they could do it. Procedures varied, but almost all civilian agencies were bound by the Administrative Procedure Act (APA), enacted in 1946 and amended frequently since then. The act set procedural safeguards aimed at promoting fair regulatory decisions.

Independent and executive agencies were also subject to related laws, including the Freedom of Information Act, giving citizens a right of access to most government records, and the Government in the Sunshine Act, requiring most formal government meetings to be open to the public.

Basic procedural requirements of the APA included public notice of a proposed rulemaking in the *Federal Register,* the opportunity for comment by interested or affected parties, the creation of a record documenting the reasons for issuing a rule, and the right of parties who feel aggrieved to seek court review of agency decisions.

The courts could overturn an agency rule if it violated the Constitution or federal law, if it was "arbitrary or capricious," if it was not reached by legally required proce-

dures, or if it was unwarranted by the evidence accumulated in the record by the agency.

Different procedures applied to "formal" and "informal" rulemaking. One key difference was that in formal proceedings, rulemaking officials had to avoid contact with some of the interested parties without notice to the others. In informal rulemaking, however, such contacts were not clearly forbidden. Many agencies, seeking to avoid court challenges, recorded such contacts in a public docket anyway.

## Congressional Backlash

Early in Reagan's first term, Congress appeared sympathetic to regulatory reforms like those sought by the president. In 1981 committees in both the Senate and the House approved bills to rein in rulemaking agencies.

By 1983, however, a backlash had developed. Rep. Dingell and other critics charged that OMB acted improperly in contacts with industries affected by federal regulations and in contacts with the rulemaking agencies themselves. OMB denied that it did anything improper. The basic charge of Dingell and others was that OMB encouraged industries to explain privately what regulations they want relaxed or stopped, that OMB then directed rulemaking agencies to comply with industry wishes, and that it obscured any record of these contacts. Dingell argued that the whole legal structure for ensuring that rules were developed fairly was bypassed when OMB overturned a proposed rule based on what he called "Star Chamber" proceedings.

One specific controversy concerned OMB's effort to thwart EPA regulation of asbestos, a cancer-causing material widely used to insulate buildings. *(Asbestos regulation, p. 100)*

Dingell presided over a committee with

# Asbestos Regulation and the Value of a Life...

The Office of Management and Budget (OMB) prevented the Environmental Protection Agency (EPA) from issuing rules to ban asbestos because it felt EPA was placing too high a value on human life, Democratic members of a congressional investigating committee charged April 16, 1985.

The OMB-EPA debate over the dollar value of human life came out in testimony and documents at a hearing held by the House Energy and Commerce Subcommittee on Oversight and Investigations, chaired by John D. Dingell, D-Mich. The derailing of asbestos regulations is only one in a series of OMB regulatory actions Dingell has examined and criticized.

EPA in 1984 planned to issue rules phasing out almost all use of asbestos, a fibrous mineral that was widely used as a building material because it does not burn. The EPA proposal, like most federal regulations, was subject to OMB review under Executive Order 12291 to make sure its benefits exceeded its costs.

For much of 1984, EPA sought to justify its plans to OMB. On Feb. 1, 1985, under pressure from OMB, EPA abruptly announced it was required by law to turn the regulatory job over to the Consumer Product Safety Commission (CPSC) and the Occupational Safety and Health Administration (OSHA). The asbestos industry had urged just such a referral.

Dingell objected, and on March 8, EPA flip-flopped again, saying it would not yet turn over asbestos regulation.

Asbestos was politically important because of the large number of people exposed to it. For years it was commonly used in ceiling tiles, pipe insulation and floor coverings. If it crumbles, dust-like particles float through the air, and they can cause lung cancer, asbestosis and other diseases. In schools alone, some 15 million children were estimated to be exposed to asbestos.

Evidence of the health threat posed by asbestos had been accumulating for decades. EPA already had legal authority, under the Clean Air Act of 1970 and the Toxic Substances Control Act (TSCA) of 1976, to do something. The agency had been contemplating action against asbestos since at least October 1979, when it issued a public notice that it would try to develop regulations on the commercial and industrial use of asbestos. EPA toxics chief John A. Moore commented, "If we can't regulate asbestos, we can't regulate anything." But until 1983, EPA had only studied the problem.

When William D. Ruckelshaus replaced Anne M. Burford as administrator of EPA in 1983, things started to move. EPA planned to ban use of asbestos in certain building products and to phase out remaining uses of the fiber over several years. On May 14, 1984, EPA sent one of its proposed rules, a ban on asbestos in cement pipe and roofing and flooring materials, to OMB for review.

On Aug. 15, 1984, EPA sent a 10-year phase-out rule. "EPA is proposing to substantially eliminate rather than control asbestos," Ruckelshaus wrote in a letter to Dingell, "because we believe that the risks from the life cycle of asbestos (i.e., mining, milling, manufacturing, use, removal and disposal) are unreasonable even when asbestos is controlled...."

# ... EPA-OMB Fight Exposed on the Hill

EPA's proposed rules never emerged from OMB's review. At hearings held by Dingell's subcommittee April 16, staff investigators for the panel detailed a lengthy chronology showing how OMB stopped the asbestos plan.

One OMB objection involved the way EPA's cost-benefit analysis valued the benefit of preventing a cancer death. OMB had raised this issue as early as the summer of 1984, but in a March 27, 1985, letter to EPA's Acting Deputy Administrator A. James Barnes, OMB's deputy administrator for information and regulatory affairs, Robert P. Bedell, stated that EPA had flunked OMB's cost-benefit test.

EPA's "monetized benefits" for a cancer case avoided under the 10-year phase-down were about $1 million. OMB objected, however, that EPA should have "discounted" the value of a life saved, because lung cancer often did not appear until 30 or 40 years after a person was exposed to asbestos. The cost-benefit analysis discounted costs, and OMB argued benefits also should be discounted for the comparison to be valid.

"Discounting," in economic terms, is a calculation of the "present value" of a long-term investment, in light of the shrinkage caused by interest rates. An IOU promising to pay $1 a year hence would be worth just over 94 cents, if going interest rates were 6 percent — because 94 cents invested at 6 percent would bring the same return. The higher the discount rate and the longer the time period, the more the present value of an item shrinks. Thus, the value of a life would have appeared smaller under OMB's analysis, and less expense would be justified to save it.

Barnes and other EPA officials said at the April 16 hearing that while the agency had sometimes put dollar values on human life in policy analyses, it was agency policy not to use such analyses as the sole basis for regulatory action. Various EPA officials also said the technique of discounting lives had not been used before at EPA and that it was "wrong," "inappropriate" and "misguided."

As OMB and EPA staff haggled over asbestos rules, they focused mainly on cost-benefit issues, but remained at an impasse. By the end of the year, the debate escalated to higher officials in both agencies, and EPA was telling OMB it was frustrated at OMB's inaction on asbestos and other rules EPA had proposed. Then OMB suggested EPA lacked legal authority to regulate asbestos at all.

"When it became clear to the OMB folks that EPA was prepared to fight, and fight hard, for the value of a life and over discounting, they had to come up with something else, if they were going to torpedo the regulations," said subcommittee member Ron Wyden, D-Ore.

What OMB came up with was Section 9 of the TSCA, a never-used procedure for EPA to "refer" a regulatory issue to another agency when EPA finds that a chemical presents a health risk and that the other agency has legal authority sufficient to control it. Ruckelshaus had asserted in writing when he sent the rules to OMB that referral would not bring adequate protection.

EPA was expected to go forward with its ban on asbestos and to issue its rules in the fall of 1985. The referral of the issue to another agency was put on hold.

oversight of a substantial portion of the federal rulemaking bureaucracy. He chaired not only the Energy and Commerce Committee, but also its Subcommittee on Oversight and Investigations. That panel's subpoenas for EPA documents led in 1983 to a constitutional clash that toppled Burford and the top rank of EPA officials. Charges of closed-door meetings between EPA rulemakers and the corporate officials they regulate were what led to the EPA investigations.

"I will inform you that OMB is constantly fiddling around with the regulatory process through the back-door mechanism," Dingell said at a 1983 hearing. "They are not to be trusted. They regard themselves as above the law. They withhold documents. They refuse to cooperate. Their interpretation of statute and their behavior under law are often at variance with the law," he said.

During the 97th and 98th Congresses, several subcommittees held hearings to scrutinize how OMB used its power to supervise rulemaking. Among them were the House and Senate Judiciary subcommittees on administrative practice, which were considering regulatory reform bills.

Another interested panel was the House Government Operations Subcommittee on Manpower and Housing, chaired by Barney Frank, D-Mass. After March 1982 hearings by that panel, the Government Operations Committee adopted a report concluding: "In practice, the executive order [No. 12291] has been used as a back-door, unpublicized channel of access to the highest levels of political authority in the administration for industry alone."

Members based that conclusion on their examination of OMB's contacts with industries regulated under the Occupational Safety and Health Administration's rules for industrial toxic chemicals and commercial underwater diving operations and subsequent OMB intervention in OSHA rulemaking.

Dingell's subcommittee, in an Aug. 30, 1984, report, adopted two main findings on OMB's role at EPA:

"The OMB has compromised the fairness and openness of EPA's regulatory process by acting as a conduit for affected industries commenting on draft EPA regulations, by providing copies of proposed regulations to affected parties in advance of publication in the *Federal Register,* and by attempting, on occasion, to displace the decision-making authority of the EPA administrator," the report said.

"The OMB has acted contrary to the public interest by overemphasizing costs in its cost-benefit analyses, by causing extensive delays in the promulgation of certain EPA regulations, and by requesting EPA officials to take certain regulatory actions which such officials construed as contrary to specific statutory mandate," the subcommittee said.

The panel recommended that OMB and rulemaking agencies put all communications involving OMB reviews into writing, for inclusion in a rulemaking file open to the public.

The subcommittee findings were based in part on testimony by former EPA Administrator Anne M. Burford and her chief of staff, John E. Daniel. "I think it is appropriate for the president of the United States to have an office which can overview regulations," Burford said, "but I think that there were some serious abuses."

Burford and Daniel cited, among other cases, instances where OMB tried to hold up rules that EPA was under court order to issue by a certain date. Executive Order 12291 explicitly denies OMB authority to delay rules when to do so would conflict with judicial or statutory deadlines.

In one case, after Burford had waited in vain for OMB approval before a court-ordered deadline, she went ahead with the rule in question. "Late that evening," Daniel testified, "I received a call from an OMB official in which ... he said to me words to this effect: that there was a price to pay for doing what we had done, and that we hadn't begun to pay it."

## OMB: One-Sided Contacts?

Dingell and others stepped up their requests that OMB and the agencies document their outside contacts and give the information to Congress and the public. OMB complied with those requests to some degree, but congressional investigators were not satisfied with the quality or quantity of the information given to them by either OMB or the agencies.

OMB denied charges that it meets only with industry, but admitted it did not meet with everyone who asked. In the asbestos case Dingell examined April 16, OMB met frequently with the asbestos industry and did not meet at all with environmental groups or those representing exposed workers. Frank's panel reported it had found a similar pattern relating to OSHA rulemaking.

In written answers to written congressional questions on its private conversations with business representatives, OMB in 1983 stated: "OMB officials have met with countless numbers of groups over the past two years, but we do not compile records of meetings or of the subjects discussed. OMB is not required by law to make available its comments ... or to provide information to the public concerning its decision to return

a regulation."

Some legislative proposals during the 1981-83 debate over regulatory reform would have required OMB to keep records of its contacts in exchange for congressional recognition of its oversight power.

The budget office, according to its spokesman Edwin L. Dale, opposed any requirement that it record and put in the public docket its meetings and phone calls with outside parties and agencies. Agency officials testified that OMB rarely put into writing its instructions to agencies on how to set rules. OMB said such requirements would be "unworkable" and "a paperwork nightmare," and would create a basis for "pointless" challenges to OMB decisions in court.

The entire issue may be decided in court. The Environmental Defense Fund has filed a suit alleging that an EPA rule to control underground storage of toxic waste was delayed for months, causing the statutory deadline to be missed. EPA said that the rule went to OMB two weeks before the deadline.

The Justice Department pointed out that agency heads were legally free to ignore the president's executive order and to issue regulations without OMB's review. In response, an EPA attorney said that Justice's argument "comes as a surprise to those who have watched [the system] operate as a practical matter." Another official remarked that, as presidential appointees, agency heads who do not comply may not keep their jobs.

# 6

# Clean Air

Perhaps no issue better illustrates the tension between industry and environmentalists than air quality. Ronald Reagan became president in 1981 after campaigning against clean air regulations that he maintained were curtailing industrial expansion in the United States. During the president's first two years in office, industry and some labor union leaders pressed Congress to revise the 1970 law and its 1977 amendments to defer deadlines and ease Environmental Protection Agency (EPA) regulations for complying with national air quality standards.

But environmental groups and their allies in the U.S. Congress regarded the Clean Air Act as the cornerstone of the movement to protect public health and safety. And, despite Reagan's landslide victory in 1980, public support for the law was still vigorous.

With sharp divisions between pro-environment and pro-industry positions, neither the House Energy and Commerce Committee nor the Senate Environment and Public Works Committee could revise clean air laws in a way that could win full congressional approval. The lack of agreement left the 1970 Clean Air Act and its 1977 amendments intact, ensuring continuing debate over the economic costs of removing pollutants from the air.

## The Politics of Air

In his 1980 presidential campaign Reagan pledged to revise federal clean air laws as part of an overall policy of reducing government regulation of U.S. industry. Critics of EPA clean air rules viewed Reagan's landslide victory over President Jimmy Carter as a mandate for major changes in the law.

Before Reagan's inauguration, David A. Stockman, a Republican member of Congress from Michigan whom Reagan nominated as Office of Management and Budget (OMB) director, released a planning document that identified the Clean Air Act as the incoming administration's prime target for deregulating industry. Stockman termed the 1977 amendments to the law "staggering excess built upon dubious scientific and economic premises." EPA funding authorizations for enforcing the Clean Air Act were due to expire on Sept. 30, 1981, and administration officials expected to push for far-reaching changes in the law during the 1981 congressional session.

On Capitol Hill the mood in favor of clean air laws appeared to have shifted since 1977. Some of the architects of the 1977 law were no longer in Congress to defend their handiwork. Republicans had captured control of the Senate in the 1980 elections, giving the president's party a majority on the Environment Committee, the panel that held jurisdiction over the clean air law. In the Democratic House, moreover, Energy Committee Chairman John Dingell, D-Mich., who represented a Detroit district encompassing Ford Motor Co. headquarters and more than a dozen automobile manufacturing plants, was backing the troubled industry's requests that Congress ease auto emission standards to make U.S. cars more competitive with foreign imports.

But the administration and industry evidently had misread public opinion on environmental protection and congressional willingness to tackle a major revision of clean air standards. In March 1981 the bipartisan National Commission on Air Quality, set up by Congress in 1977, released a report contending that the Clean Air Act was sound and needed only some refinements. The *Harris Survey* in June 1981 disclosed that 38 percent of respondents believed the law should be stricter, 48 percent thought it was fine as it was and only 12 percent thought it should be weakened.

As environmental groups mounted opposition to clean air revisions, the administration delayed and eventually switched strategy. Officials initially had promised to send Congress a legislative package by June 30, but Henry A. Waxman, D-Calif., chairman of the House Energy Subcommittee on Health and Environment, denounced an early draft that leaked to Capitol Hill. By August the administration backed away from committing itself to specific proposals.

Instead, Reagan Aug. 5 submitted a set of 11 broadly worded principles for Congress to consider in revising the clean air laws. The shift in strategy was seen by many on Capitol Hill as a shrewd decision by the president not to stake his prestige on a bid for major revisions in the anti-pollu-

tion law in the face of polls showing massive public support for the act.

The administration's principles would continue the nation's progress toward cleaner air, but "at a more reasoned pace," said EPA Administrator Anne M. Gorsuch. The principles — which called for relaxing pollution standards and delaying some cleanup deadlines — were adopted Aug. 4 by Reagan and the Cabinet. They were met with enthusiasm by industry groups, but with suspicion by environmental organizations.

## Background

The Clean Air Act of 1970 directed the federal government to protect the American public's health by cleaning up polluted air. Taken together, the 1970 act and the 1977 amendments formed the nation's most complex and far-reaching environmental protection law.

Enforced by EPA, the Clean Air Act regulated virtually all air-polluting activity by U.S. industry, transportation, real estate development and the production and use of energy. The 1970 law had compelled industry and electric utilities to spend billions of dollars on emission control equipment and automobile manufacturers to equip cars with costly anti-pollution devices. The law imposed controversial duties on state and local governments. Its restrictions on building new plants that would degrade air quality may have altered the pace and distribution of economic growth among different cities and regions across the country.

Environmental groups considered the Clean Air Act the foundation of the federal government's commitment to environmental protection. By vast majorities the American people generally backed government efforts to clean up polluted air and make sure that pristine airsheds remained unspoiled. But as EPA imposed the law's requirements, corporation and labor group leaders heatedly

# Major Air Pollutants and their Health Effects

| Pollutant | Major Sources | Characteristics and Effects |
|---|---|---|
| Carbon Monoxide (CO) | Vehicle exhausts | Colorless, odorless poisonous gas. Replaces oxygen in red blood cells, causing dizziness, unconsciousness or death. |
| Hydrocarbons (HC) | Incomplete combustion of gasoline; evaporation of petroleum fuels, solvents and paints | Although some are poisonous, most are not. React with $NO_2$ to form ozone, or smog. |
| Lead (Pb) | Anti-knock agents in gasoline | Accumulates in the bone and soft tissues. Affects blood-forming organs, kidneys and nervous system. Suspected of causing learning disabilities in young children. |
| Nitrogen Dioxide (NO$_2$) | Industrial processes, vehicle exhausts | Causes structural and chemical changes in the lungs. Lowers resistance to respiratory infections. React in sunlight with hydrocarbons to produce smog. Contributes to acid rain. |
| Ozone (O$_3$) | Formed when HC and $NO_2$ react | Principal constituent of smog. Irritates mucous membranes, causing coughing, choking, impaired lung function. Aggravates chronic asthma and bronchitis. |
| Total Suspended Particulates (TSP) | Industrial plants, heating boilers, auto engines, dust | Larger visible types (soot, smoke or dust) can clog the lung sacs. Smaller invisible particles can pass into the bloodstream. Often carry carcinogens and toxic metals; impair visibility. |
| Sulfur Dioxide (SO$_2$) | Burning coal and oil, industrial processes | Corrosive, poisonous gas. Associated with coughs, colds and bronchitis. Contributes to acid rain. |

Source: Environmental Protection Agency

objected that the government was forcing entire industries to install expensive pollution control equipment at the cost of jobs and profits. State and city government officials also protested the agency's sometimes halting efforts to mandate compliance.

In setting federal air standards, Congress and EPA made technical judgments that in effect dictated how American industry operated factories, how it designed its products and where it could build new plants or install modern facilities. The clean air law and EPA regulations also attempted delicate economic and political trade-offs, protecting Eastern and Midwestern "Frost Belt" industrial centers and coal fields against competition from Southern and Western "Sun Belt" states with cleaner air and clean-burning coal deposits.

Since the early 1970s the law's requirements in fact had reduced some types of air pollution and kept others from growing worse. But progress was uneven, and many industries resisted complying with EPA standards by challenging them in court or persuading Congress to extend the law's deadlines.

**1970 Law.** Congress began taking note of air pollution problems just after the Korean War. By 1970, a landmark year for environmental action, public concern about declining air quality prompted President Richard Nixon to request a stronger federal clean air program. In his 1970 environmental message, Nixon proposed that the federal government set national standards to limit specific air pollutants, regulate smokestack emissions from stationary sources, such as factories and utility power plants, and test emission control devices on motor vehicles. Congress complied later that year, passing the Clean Air Act of 1970 by a unanimous vote in the Senate and only a single dissenting vote in the House.

The 1970 law directed EPA, the independent pollution control agency Nixon had created earlier that year, to set national standards for major air pollutants, without regard to economic costs. Even while calling for nationwide air quality goals, the law left to the states the responsibility to draft plans for meeting those standards within 247 air quality control regions across the country. State governments and EPA shared responsibility for enforcing the standards.

As a first step, the law directed EPA to determine the maximum permissible concentrations for at least seven common air pollutants that the agency found harmful to human health or the environment. It required EPA to set two types of "national ambient air quality standards," without considering compliance costs: primary standards to protect human health, with a margin of safety for the elderly, infants and other vulnerable persons, and secondary standards to keep pollutants from impairing visibility or damaging crops, buildings and water supplies. Congress set a 1977 deadline for the entire nation to meet the primary health standards.

The law also ordered EPA to set maximum emission standards, on an industry-by-industry basis, for newly built plants and factories (new source performance standards). It required state governments to draw up state implementation plans, subject to EPA approval, for meeting federal air quality standards. The law required states to order factories in "non-attainment regions" that failed to meet the standards to retrofit their plants with pollution control equipment, without regard to cost. To expand plants or build new plants, companies had to install equipment that limited pollutants to the lowest level emitted by any similar facility in the country.

In a separate title the law set a detailed timetable for reducing hydrocarbon, carbon monoxide and nitrogen oxide emissions by trucks and automobiles. The law gave the EPA administrator authority to waive the deadlines for meeting those standards for about one year.

**1977 Amendments.** In the early 1970s Congress backed away somewhat from its ambitious air quality goals by revising the 1970 law. Congress and EPA waived auto emission compliance deadlines in 1973, 1974 and again in 1975. In 1977, with the deadline for meeting primary standards approaching but many regions still out of compliance, Congress approved major Clean Air Act amendments.

**Addressing air pollution from industrial sources is a major goal of the Clean Air Act. Pictured is a plant in Birmingham, Ala., in 1972.**

Under pressure from President Carter and the automobile industry, Congress extended auto emission standards for new cars for two additional years, then set tighter limits for 1980, 1981 and 1982 models. Congress also delayed the deadline for meeting national air standards until 1982 and gave cities with especially severe oxidant and carbon monoxide pollution an additional five years, through 1987, to meet EPA goals.

In addition to extending the deadline, Congress allowed states to issue permits for new stationary sources in non-attainment regions after mid-1979 only if pollution from existing plants or factories had been reduced enough to offset the new facility's emissions. To put a new plant into operation

in an area that failed to meet national standards, a company thereafter had to purchase emission offsets from previously operating factories, either by buying and closing down an old plant or by buying equipment to reduce its emissions.

Congress in 1977 also approved a system to prevent development from spoiling the pristine air above national parks, wilderness areas and other regions where lack of industry had left the air much purer than national standards. A 1973 Supreme Court decision, on a case brought by environmental groups, had interpreted the 1970 Clean Air Act as requiring EPA to prevent significant deterioration in air quality in areas without major pollution. EPA in 1974 drew up regulations to implement that requirement. Congress largely wrote those regulations into the 1977 amendments, over objections by some Western senators who contended that stricter air quality standards would discourage economic growth in the region.

As approved by Congress, the prevention of significant deterioration (PSD) standards established three categories for regions where air quality was better than national EPA standards. The 1977 law classified most large national parks and wilderness areas in the strictest Class I category, allowing only small increments over brief periods in sulfur dioxide and particulate emissions that might obscure their scenic vistas. The law assigned all other clean air regions to a less restrictive Class II category, and it allowed states to petition EPA to designate some as Class III regions, where even more pollution could be tolerated to accommodate economic growth. In no case could pollution in Class III areas exceed national ambient standards, however, and the law required companies building plants in PSD regions to install the best available control technology, regardless of how expensive that equipment was.

## Clean Air Act Controversies

The 1977 Clean Air Act amendments were 180 pages long, three times the length of the original law. The revised act set forth an immensely complicated scheme for cleaning up polluted air in urban and industrial centers and preserving air quality throughout the rest of the country. But in the early 1980s the nation remained sharply divided over whether EPA was enforcing the law fairly and whether the resulting air quality improvement justified the economic cost to U.S. industries and regions.

Ten years after passage of the 1970 law, the process of implementing federal clean air standards was still proceeding slowly. EPA moved cautiously in enforcing the law, yet it was forced to base acceptable pollutant standards on scientific data and technical conclusions that environmentalists and business groups often challenged. Major industries — notably automobile manufacturers, steelmakers, metal smelters and electric utilities — complained that EPA requirements forced them to spend billions of dollars on non-productive emission control equipment that raised consumer prices and made their products less competitive.

State government agencies objected that EPA officials delayed approving state air quality programs while meddling in local enforcement issues. Environmental groups, on the other hand, maintained that EPA's delays in setting standards and congressional deadline extensions had needlessly allowed companies to continue polluting the air.

**National Air Standards.** The national ambient air quality standards set by EPA formed the heart of the Clean Air Act. The rest of the law was designed to force states to meet those EPA goals within deadlines set by Congress. By 1981, however, industrial groups were calling for changes in the way EPA arrived at those standards, which they viewed as unnecessarily strict and costly.

In the existing Clean Air Act, Congress gave EPA authority to set the standards at levels providing "an adequate margin of safety," not just for the general population, but for infants, the elderly and other persons with health problems that made them especially sensitive to air pollution. The law also directed EPA to determine the standards without taking costs into account, although it allowed states to consider costs when imposing emission limits on specific plants.

Critics of EPA standards within business and industry argued that the government should set clean air goals to protect the general population against major risks, instead of trying to prevent any danger to vulnerable groups. Many business groups had argued that the benefits of environmental control should outweigh or balance the costs of pollution control equipment.

Environmentalists feared that changing EPA standards would alter the law's basic thrust. They argued that the administration's proposals for cost-benefit analysis of the standards were smokescreens for gutting the 1970 act. Opponents of the cost-benefit approach charged that it would be nearly impossible to put accurate price tags on intangible benefits from cleaner air.

**Mobile Sources.** The act set limits for automobile emissions of hydrocarbons (HC), carbon monoxide (CO) and oxides of nitrogen (NOx) and required a 90 percent reduction from uncontrolled levels for HC and CO by 1982. NOx was to be reduced by 75 percent. The EPA could waive certain standards if public health did not require the statutory standards or if the technology to meet them did not exist.

The major auto manufacturers wanted the 1981 CO standard of 3.4 grams per mile to be relaxed to 7.0 grams per mile and the 1.0 gram per mile NOx standard changed to 2.0 grams per mile. The proposal was tough to sell to Congress because it would mean rolling back standards that already could be met. One reason industry wanted a weaker NOx standard was to allow production of more diesels. But environmentalists were concerned about the proliferation of diesels because their emissions were suspected of causing cancer.

**Industrial Growth.** Along with automobiles, factories, electric power plants and other industrial plants were the major contributors to air pollution over U.S. cities. Industrial smokestacks produced nearly all sulfur dioxide emissions, more than 80 percent of particulates and more than half of

nitrogen oxides that were spewed into the air. As a result, EPA efforts to curb pollution were directed at emissions from both existing and newly built plants.

In regulating those emissions, EPA indirectly influenced where new plants were built, how much they cost to operate and how long older factories were kept running. Some business and labor leaders protested that the government, in setting air quality standards, in effect was setting limits to economic growth in both older industrial centers and in fast-growing Sun Belt states.

To meet EPA ambient air standards, the Clean Air Act required state governments to order existing factories in polluted regions to retrofit furnaces, power plants and other equipment with devices to reduce emissions. The law also gave EPA and the states power to review all plans to build new plants or improve existing facilities to make sure that their owners installed the best possible pollution control technology.

Throughout the 1970s business officials complained that the expensive equipment they installed to reduce emissions from existing plants was often balky, was costly to run and consumed a great deal of energy. Industry also said that EPA and state procedures for granting permits for new or expanded facilities were time-consuming and duplicative.

Before building a new plant in a clean air area, a company had to obtain a permit from the state air pollution board requiring the best possible pollution control equipment for every emission source at that plant. In certain dirtier areas the requirements were even tougher. Owners of new factories not only had to promise to install the best control equipment but also to clean up emissions at existing plants.

**Non-Attainment Areas.** In polluted urban areas, Congress and EPA set up a complicated regulatory system to allow companies to build new plants or modernize existing facilities without making air quality worse. In the 1977 amendments Congress devised an "offset" system to encourage economic growth in industrial centers even while already contaminated air was cleaned up. To build a new plant that would emit a pollutant for which the area already exceeded national standards, a company could in effect buy a right to pollute the air by cutting back similar emissions from an existing facility previously in operation.

The offset system sought to reduce total emissions by requiring that the resulting reductions more than offset the sulfur dioxide a new plant produced. A company could obtain offsets by buying new pollution control equipment for an existing plant, or it could buy an old factory and close it down if its emissions would be too expensive to correct. A firm wanting to build or modernize a plant also could buy "pollution reduction credits" from another company that earned them by installing cleanup equipment.

Congress hoped that the offset system would give companies market incentives to develop new ways to control air pollution. But industry complained that offsets in practice were often unavailable in areas where companies wanted to expand. Opponents of the system also charged that existing industries that controlled offset rights could keep competitors from moving into an area and control the region's economic growth.

Industry wanted to eliminate the offset system and extend the 1982 deadline for achieving national standards in non-attainment areas that were showing improvement over the long term. Some industry groups also proposed that Congress terminate EPA authority to ban plant construction in non-attainment areas that lacked state plans showing they could meet the 1982 deadline. Business leaders complained that EPA often applied the bans to new factories when

automobile pollution was the major cause of poor air quality.

**PSD System.** The Clean Air Act imposed its most widely felt restrictions through the 1977 amendments to prevent air pollution from growing worse in areas that already met federal standards. Those provisions, known as the prevention of significant deterioration program, were designed to keep the air in regions that met standards for specific pollutants from deteriorating beyond pre-set ceilings, or "increments," that would keep it cleaner than national standards. Since nearly every U.S. city and county already met federal standards for at least one pollutant, the PSD system applied virtually across the nation. But its economic impact was potentially heaviest in fast-growing regions in the West and South that were attractive to industries seeking to build new plants and expand into new markets.

Environmental groups maintained that the PSD system would keep growth from degrading the pure air above less-developed regions to the extent that industrialization had polluted older cities. But some critics charged that Congress designed the PSD system to limit economic growth in the Southern and Western Sun Belt states, thus protecting the economic base of the industrial Frost Belt states in the Northeast and Midwest.

The act established three classes of PSD areas ranging from Class I, having the cleanest air, to Class III, where the air was allowed to become the dirtiest. Besides installing the best pollution control equipment and showing its pollution would not violate the increments, companies wanting to build near PSD areas had to show that their emissions would not impair visibility in nearby Class I national parks or wilderness areas. Because most of the West's oil, coal and oil shale reserves were located right

Heavy automobile traffic is still a major source of air pollution, despite required use of emission controls in cars and trucks.

next to such Class I areas, a conflict was anticipated between the clean air law and the nation's goals of energy independence.

The National Commission on Air Quality in 1981 found that the PSD program would not hamper energy development in the Southwest through 1995. But the commission, following its final report, concluded that only the Class I PSD program had been successful in maintaining air quality. Class II and Class III programs, according to the commission, were causing delays in permitting new industries, and red tape involved in the process held up industrial progress to some extent. Business representatives joined the commission in maintaining that the location of industries in the West would be adversely affected if the standard was retained.

**Coal-Burning Utilities.** Coal-fired power plants that U.S. utility companies operated to generate electricity in the early 1980s discharged more than half of the dangerous sulfur dioxide emissions into the nation's air. EPA's efforts to reduce those discharges, both from existing and newly built power plants, produced continuing controversy over whether clean air regulations impeded development of the nation's abundant coal reserves as dependable energy supplies.

The Clean Air Act controlled sulfur dioxide, along with nitrogen oxide and particulate emissions, from coal-fired power plant smokestacks. Sulfur dioxide gas caused respiratory difficulties, mixing with other air pollutants to cause coughs, bronchitis, asthma and emphysema. Sulfur dioxide emissions from coal-burning boilers in Ohio Valley and other Midwest plants were also prime suspects as the source of acid rain precipitation as they drifted over New York, New England and eastern Canada. *(Acid rain, p. 115; map, p. 93)*

Utility plant operators identified several ways to reduce sulfur dioxide emissions: by burning coal with low natural sulfur content, by chemically cleaning coal to reduce its sulfur components before burning or by installing flue gas "scrubbers" to remove sulfur dioxide as a liquid or solid precipitant from the gases given off by coal combustion before it was released to the air through plant smokestacks.

EPA, with backing from Congress and environmental groups, prescribed installation of flue-gas scrubbers throughout the electric power industry as the preferred way to curb sulfur dioxide pollution. During the 1970s the agency pressed state air pollution officials to force utilities to retrofit previously built power plants with these costly scrubbers. As mandated by Congress in the 1977 amendments, EPA in 1979 set uniform new source performance standards that required that all coal-fired plants built after 1978 be equipped with scrubbers.

In the 1977 amendments Congress protected markets for high-sulfur Eastern and Midwestern coal by in effect requiring utilities to install scrubbers on new plants even if the facility could meet sulfur-dioxide standards without them by burning low-sulfur Western coal. In a compromise between coal-producing regions, the "percentage reduction" standards required utilities to remove between 70 and 90 percent of sulfur dioxide from flue gases, depending on coal sulfur contents. But utility executives, Western mining firms and economists objected that EPA's scrubber policy arbitrarily saddled power plants with costly and cranky emission control methods and restricted development of the nation's ample and easily mined Western coal reserves.

EPA argued that scrubbers had worked well in Japan and for U.S. utilities that bought and maintained high-quality equipment. Environmental groups insisted that sulfur dioxide was so dangerous that the government should force utilities to remove as much of it as possible from the air. Clean air proponents also said officials could more easily enforce emission reductions by technological controls such as

scrubbers rather than through content of fuel.

With a scrubber for a 500-megawatt power plant costing $50 million, according to the Edison Electric Institute, utilities resisted installing them on existing plants through lawsuits, deliberate delay, lobbying state agencies and other strategies. In the Ohio Valley, where 21 aging plants produced the most concentrated source of sulfur pollution in the country, utilities fought hard for exemptions. State pollution control plans in many Midwestern states allowed utilities to bring coal-fired plants into compliance with local ambient air standards by building tall stacks that discharged pollutants high in the air, where prevailing winds blew sulfur dioxide over the eastern United States and Canada. To avoid building costly scrubber-equipped plants some utilities kept older power plants in operation longer than previously planned, prolonging pollution from their smokestacks.

# Environmentalists' Agenda

National environmental groups, in addition to opposing major weakening in existing clean air rules, in the early 1980s pushed for the federal government to crack down harder on some forms of air pollution that EPA had yet to regulate. In particular, conservationists demanded faster action to control airborne toxics and fine particulates in the air. And they urged Congress to force even stricter limits on sulfur dioxide emissions from coal-fired plants in response to growing concern about the destructive effects of acid rain.

## Particulate Control

Environmentalists wanted Congress to put EPA on a "fast track" in controlling cancer-causing pollutants. From 1970, when it was first directed to start regulating hazardous pollutants, to early 1981, EPA

had issued regulations for only four pollutants, although dozens had been found to
cause diseases such as leukemia and lung
cancer.

Environmentalists urged Congress to
direct EPA to start controlling emissions of
fine particulates — those less than 1/1000
of an inch in diameter — that were easily
inhaled deep into the lungs. These particles
hamper breathing, cause respiratory disease
and aggravate heart and lung disease. EPA
had promised since 1973 to control these
pollutants, but so far only had set up a 100-
station monitoring network to study the
problem.

## Acid Rain

During the early 1980s scientific evidence continued to accumulate indicating
that power plant and automobile emissions
from the industrial Midwest produced acid
rain — a weak solution of sulfuric or nitric
acid — that damaged forests and lakes
hundreds of miles downwind in the northeastern United States and eastern Canada.
Environmental groups, Northeastern congressional delegations and the Canadian
government demanded federal action to
combat that pollution. But electric utilities
and government officials from the Midwest
and from Appalachian coal-producing
states objected to proposals that would sad-
dle those regions with heavy economic costs.

Acid rain formed chiefly from sulfur
dioxide spewed into the air by coal-burning
electric power plants or from nitrogen oxide
from automobile exhausts. Once aloft, those
pollutants traveled hundreds of miles downwind, crossing state, regional and international boundaries. Falling to the ground as
rain or snow, the weak acid solutions were
blamed for damaging trees and killing off
fish in streams and lakes that lay beneath
the path followed by prevailing winds.

Acid rain damage was most prominent
in New England, upstate New York and

eastern Canada. Most observers attributed
acid rain in that region to a complex of coal-
fired power plants along the Ohio River
Valley in Ohio, Indiana, Illinois and Ken-
tucky that burned high-sulfur coal from
surrounding Appalachian coal fields. Some
studies suggested that acid rain produced
by coal-fired power plants and copper smelters in the Southwest and Mexico also
threatened forests and lakes in the Rocky
Mountain region.

Total U.S. sulfur dioxide emissions
from man-made sources amounted to about
24.1 million metric tons a year, according to
an Interagency Task Force on Acid Precipitation formed by 12 federal agencies. To
combat acid rain, U.S. environmental
groups and the Canadian government urged
the federal government to cut those emissions in half, by about 12 million metric
tons. With existing technologies, sulfur dioxide emissions could be curtailed by installing scrubbers to remove sulfur dioxide
from smokestack gas or by switching to
burning coal with lower sulfur content.

Demands to curb acid rain pollution
complicated economic and political debates
over federal clean air regulations. Reagan
had been elected in 1980 after pledging to
curtail government regulation of U.S. business and industry, and members of Congress were questioning whether EPA's efforts to force business to make expensive
pollution control investments were costing
the nation more than was justified in lost
jobs and industrial production. But even as
Congress began re-evaluating the economic
costs of enforcing the Clean Air Act's requirements, environmental groups and state
and local officials from the Northeast were
urging tough action against acid rain that
could cost electric utilities and their ratepayers billions of dollars.

Choosing a strategy for controlling acid
rain involved difficult political problems.
Some approaches placed the burden of

cleanup costs on the utilities emitting the most pollution — and ultimately on their customers. Others spread the cost by charging utility users nationwide, raising protests in Western areas, where utilities said they were not causing problems.

Utility industry groups said control costs would be huge, and they warned that electric bills in some places could rise by 50 percent. But environmentalists said government studies put costs far lower, involving rate increases of 2.5 percent to 10 percent.

One of the cheaper ways to reduce emissions of sulfur dioxide was to burn low-sulfur Western coal. But West Virginia, Ohio, Indiana and Illinois, states that produced high-sulfur coal, feared this could cost miners' jobs and hurt their economies. Consequently, many in Congress favored bills that required use of an expensive control technique — scrubbers that remove sulfur dioxide from smokestack gas.

# Reagan Clean Air Policies

Although Congress failed to act, EPA moved administratively to ease federal clean air regulations during Reagan's first two years in office. At the urging of the administration's Task Force on Regulatory Relief, chaired by Vice President George Bush, EPA in 1981 began reconsidering regulations adopted during the Carter administration to tighten controls on motor vehicle exhausts. Under EPA Administrator Anne M. Gorsuch, a conservative former Colorado legislator appointed by Reagan, the agency also slowed the process of developing hazardous air pollutant standards and prescribing specific standards for different categories of pollutants that newly built factories could emit.

### Motor Vehicles

In April 1981 EPA listed 18 administrative actions that officials intended to take "to reduce the regulatory burden on the motor vehicle industry." The agency maintained that those actions would save automobile makers $800 million and cut prices by $4 billion through 1986 without increasing air pollution. Under President Carter EPA had turned down industry appeals to consider most of the changes that the new administration proposed.

In August 1981 the vice president's task force asked EPA to consider relaxing a regulation that was scheduled to force gasoline refiners to cut back on the amount of lead they added to boost octane ratings. The administration contended that new evidence on lead's health effects and falling demand for leaded gasoline made the tighter standard too stringent. The task force also urged EPA to extend an exemption that Congress had granted for small refineries, giving them until 1982 to reduce lead additives.

Congress stepped in to question EPA's objectivity on the lead issue. Rep. Toby Moffett, D-Conn., chairman of the House Government Operations Subcommittee on Environment, called oversight hearings to disclose that Gorsuch had met with representatives from Thriftway Co., a small New Mexico refinery, and allegedly gave assurances that EPA would not enforce scheduled lead restrictions. After medical experts opposed relaxed lead standards during agency hearings, EPA in 1982 withdrew the proposed rules and imposed tighter lead standards. In early 1983 the agency started enforcement actions against Thriftway for violating lead-in-gasoline rules in 1981 and 1982.

### Bubble Concept

EPA in 1981 revised its regulations, at the Bush task force's urging, to let industries modernize old plants in polluted areas without first obtaining government approval to install new equipment. In its new rule, formally adopted in October 1981, EPA gave states authority to regulate industrial facilities in non-attainment areas under the so-called "bubble concept."

Under its initial interpretation of the 1970 Clean Air Act, EPA had directed states to regulate emissions from each boiler, furnace or other installation that was a source of emissions. In the 1977 Clean Air Act amendments Congress required states to conduct strict reviews of plans to build new emission sources in an area with unhealthy air before construction could proceed. Before building a new source a company had to demonstrate that the facility would reduce emissions to the lowest possible rate and that those levels would be offset by reduced emissions from other sources.

Under the bubble concept EPA allowed states to treat an entire plant, or every unit within a plant, as a single emission source, as if it were enclosed in a bubble that released emissions at a single point. Under that approach a company planning to modernize or replace a unit within a plant was no longer required to undergo review prior to construction so long as reduced emissions from another part of the plant offset the increased emissions from the new unit.

Administration officials and industry leaders contended that the bubble concept was consistent with the intent of Congress, which did not define emission "sources" in the 1970 law. By freeing industry plans to revamp facilities from detailed and costly EPA and state reviews, they added, the concept encouraged companies to replace old polluting equipment with cleaner-burning units.

EPA had considered adopting the bubble concept under specified circumstances during the Carter administration but eventually dropped the proposal. The Reagan administration revived it as part of its drive to reduce federal regulations on business and industry. By 1984, 31 states had opted for the bubble concept in enforcing clean air standards within their boundaries.

Environmentalists feared the policy would slow progress in cleaning up the air. In 1982 the U.S. Court of the Appeals for the District of Columbia, acting on a suit brought by the Natural Resources Defense Council, blocked EPA's revised clean air rules, finding the bubble concept inconsistent with the Clean Air Act's purpose. But the U.S. Supreme Court, in a 1984 ruling on the administration's appeal, upheld the bubble concept and reinstated the EPA rule.

## 1983 Cabinet Clash

Reagan's second EPA administrator, William D. Ruckelshaus, in 1983 began efforts to build a consensus within the administration behind a legislative initiative on acid rain. Reagan himself had listed acid rain as a top priority for quick action in a speech at the May 18, 1983, ceremony when Ruckelshaus was sworn in to replace Anne M. Burford (Anne M. Gorsuch, before her February 1983 marriage), who had resigned under congressional fire for EPA's handling of toxic waste programs. *(Burford resignation, p. 157)*

Ruckelshaus in September outlined a range of options to Reagan's Cabinet Council on Natural Resources and Environment, recommending a plan for experimental reduction of 3 million to 4.4 million tons in sulfur dioxide emissions in a handful of Ohio Valley states. Ruckelshaus' proposal was more limited than most acid rain bills before Congress. Stockman, Energy Secretary Donald P. Hodel and other administration opponents contended that it would be too costly to electric power companies and their ratepayers.

Turning down Ruckelshaus' plan, Reagan instead urged more research, arguing that not enough was known about acid rain to justify an expensive control program. Democratic contenders for their party's 1984 presidential nomination condemned the administration's stand, making it an issue during early primary campaigns in New England, a region where concern about acid rain was growing.

### Threatened EPA Sanctions

As amended in 1977, the Clean Air Act set a Dec. 31, 1982, deadline for meeting EPA's "national ambient air quality standards" — goals for the quality of air in general circulation, rather than for the gas coming out of smokestacks. In certain areas with severe auto-related pollution, an extension to 1987 was allowed.

On Feb. 3, 1983, EPA put approximately 200 communities around the nation — including a number of big cities — on notice that they faced the threat of sanctions as a result of various air act violations. Gorsuch had put the sanctions machinery into motion in January, claiming existing law gave her no choice. She said communities that missed the deadline would face bans on new construction and a cutoff of federal grants for highways and clean air programs.

Environmentalists charged that the administration was using the threat of sanctions as a way of pressuring Congress to act quickly on a clean air reauthorization bill.

# Congress Maintains Status Quo

With key congressional allies in the Democratic House and Republican Senate, enviromentalists fought a successful holding action against relaxing air quality goals. House and Senate environment committees grappled for months during 1981-82 with complicated clean air issues, but neither sent a bill to the floor.

In 1982, less than a month before the congressional elections, the president listed Clean Air Act revisions as one of five economic policy priorities, contending that a less stringent law, "while protecting the environment, will make it possible for industry to rebuild its productive base and create more jobs." EPA officials meanwhile prepared to ban new industrial construction and cut federal clean air assistance to hundreds of counties that were unable to meet national air quality standards by a deadline that Congress had set for the end of 1982.

But by then both the House and Senate had given up efforts to draft legislation to extend deadlines and adjust existing clean air standards. In August, Sen. Robert T. Stafford, a moderate Republican from environment-conscious Vermont and chairman of the Environment and Public Works Committee, fashioned a modest bill to "fine-tune" the law without gutting national air standards.

In the Democratic House, however, the Energy and Commerce Committee deadlocked in often bitter maneuvering between two key leaders over how much to ease clean air regulations. Committee Chairman Dingell, representing an auto manufacturing district, pushed hard for industry-backed legislation to ease federal auto emission standards, to relax industrial cleanup goals, to allow more pollution in pristine regions' air and to extend nationwide EPA deadlines. But Waxman, a Democrat from smog-ridden Southern California, chaired the panel's Subcommittee on Health and Environment. He fought a steady delaying action against Dingell's goals, in alliance with environmental lobbyists. The panel split badly between Dingell and Waxman factions and eventually broke off markup sessions.

Some House Democrats, convinced clean air would be a good campaign issue in 1982, were upset at Dingell's push for action in 1981. Environmentalists also favored waiting, believing the closer it got to Election Day, the less willing Congress would be to weaken the law — an opinion shared by some industry spokesmen.

Neither the House nor the Senate committee could reconcile demands by industry, environmental and regional interests that wanted to rewrite the landmark law. Clean Air Act authorizations expired at the end of fiscal 1981, but EPA regulations remained on the books. Congress continued funding EPA enforcement through annual appropriations bills for other government agencies.

Environmentalists concluded that the next Congress would be more receptive to retaining tough clean air regulations, while industry and its allies opposed a simple extension of existing law that might reduce pressure on Congress to consider major revisions.

## EPA Sanctions Moratorium

The deadline for states to comply with national air quality standards passed as scheduled on Dec. 31, 1982. EPA in 1983 began procedures for imposing sanctions, including the cut-off of federal highway funds, on communities that violated those limits. The threatened sanctions put pressure on Congress to extend or relax EPA standards for meeting national air quality goals. Congress instead imposed a one-year moratorium that banned sanctions on as many as 110 areas, through an amendment to a fiscal 1984 appropriations bill.

Many supporters and critics of EPA clean air standards joined to grant a reprieve to communities that had missed the deadline for complying with the agency's goal for the general quality of their air. But some proponents of revising the 1970 law objected that extending the deadline would also let members of Congress off the hook by reducing incentives for action. With the moratorium on sanctions in place, "you can forget about having clean air legislation" even reported out of committee "during this

Congress," Rep. David O'B. Martin, R-N.Y., predicted during House deliberations.

## 1984 Senate Committee Measure

As in 1981-82, committees in both the House and Senate worked for two years without results on proposals to overhaul the 1970 act. The act's existing clean air standards were controversial by themselves, and pressure to expand the law to control acid rain only compounded regional and philosphical differences over how to pay for improving the nation's air quality.

The Reagan administration itself was sharply split on acid rain issues and offered Congress little guidance. On one side was the newly appointed EPA Administrator Ruckelshaus, who recommended that the White House propose modest reductions in power plant emissions. Opponents, led by Hodel and Stockman, persuaded the president to call for further acid rain studies. With the administration still divided, neither the House nor the Senate took clean air bills to the floor.

As a result the original Clean Air Act and its 1977 amendments remained on the books, even though funding authorizations under the law had expired in 1981. Congress continued to provide money in annual appropriations for EPA to enforce clean air standards. And industry, labor unions, state and local governments and economists continued to complain as the law forced them to make costly investments to cut industrial pollution and curtail emissions from automobile tailpipes.

Environmental groups and their allies in Congress, bolstered by Democratic gains in the 1982 elections, hoped to take the offensive during the 98th Congress to extend the Clean Air Act with existing EPA authority largely intact, while expanding the law to address acid rain pollution.

Sen. Stafford grew impatient with administration waffling on an issue that was a prime concern among environment-minded New England voters. Early in 1983 he introduced a bill that would raise the reductions required in utility sulfur dioxide emissions from 8 million tons to 10 million tons a year. That goal would force utilities to cut emissions well below the levels that met EPA's health-based standards under the existing law. Following a "polluter pays" formula, the bill would have forced Midwestern and Ohio Valley states to bear the major costs of controlling acid rain.

The proposal allowed utilities to achieve those further reductions without installing expensive smokestack scrubbers by burning low-sulfur coal. To protect markets for Appalachian and Midwest high-sulfur coal fields, Congress in the existing Clean Air Act required all utilities to remove sulfur dioxide gas from smokestack gas, no matter how clean it was to start with. Members from Appalachian and Midwestern states stoutly defended that "percentage reduction requirement," which neutralized cost advantages for Western low-sulfur coal producers by forcing all coal-burning power plants to install expensive stack gas scrubbers.

Stafford's committee delayed a year before ordering its bill reported in March 1984. The panel agreed to abandon percentage reduction for meeting acid rain goals, but it headed off an amendment by Max Baucus, D-Mont., to repeal the scrubber requirement in existing law for complying with EPA health standards.

**Auto Pollution Controls.** The Senate committee measure retained existing automobile pollution standards that most new cars already met. But the committee approved an amendment, offered by Dave Durenberger, R-Minn., with Stafford's support, that for the first time would have made it illegal for individual car owners to disconnect auto pollution control devices or burn leaded gasoline in engines equipped with catalytic converters requiring unleaded fuel. Existing law made it illegal for manufacturers or dealers to remove pollution devices, but EPA reported that misfueling and tampering with equipment still contributed seriously to air pollution from cars.

**Bill Stalled.** The Environment Committee formally reported its bill on May 3, but the measure went no farther. Despite the comfortable 16-2 committee margin, the bill faced widespread opposition in the Senate. Jennings Randolph, D-W.Va., the committee's ranking minority member, had cast one of the two votes against reporting it. Randolph, who represented a coal-producing state in the Ohio Valley, based his opposition on the acid rain provision. Senators from Midwestern states had called for delaying acid rain controls or spreading costs throughout the nation, and their numbers were stronger in the full Senate than in the Environment committee.

## House Subcommittee Efforts

As the Senate panel prepared its report on the legislation in 1984, Waxman gave up efforts to draft clean air legislation after his House Energy and Commerce subcommittee May 2 scrapped his acid rain proposal.

Waxman had authored a clean air bill to force the nation's 50 dirtiest utility plants to install expensive scrubbers but to spread the cost beyond their ratepayers by imposing a nationwide tax on electric bills. But Waxman was unable to overcome objections by Democrats from Midwestern states where the 50 plants were concentrated and by Western members who opposed forcing their region to pay for correcting pollution that it neither created nor suffered from.

Waxman called off further markups, terming the acid rain vote "a likely death knell" for clean air legislation in the 98th Congress, as indeed it proved to be.

# 7

# Water Development

Water is not only the nation's most common natural resource but also the most essential. Without adequate supplies of water for agriculture, industry and residential use, large areas of the United States would have remained undeveloped.

Since 1824 the U.S. government has played a major role in building dams and other structures to develop the country's water resources. The federal government spends billions of taxpayers' dollars on irrigation, flood control, power generation and navigation along the nation's rivers and streams. The projects have opened many areas, notably in the West and South, for settlement and economic growth. But by the late 1970s economic and environmental concerns prompted a broad national debate over whether federal water projects produced more costs than benefits. While no one was predicting that the United States would run out of water, there was a growing awareness of the need to conserve.

Water has always been precious in the West, a land where barren deserts and treeless plains surround snow-topped mountain ranges. Fed by melting snow, the region's few river systems provide most of the renewable supplies of surface water. But runoff varies from year to year, and the region's prosperity depends on damming rivers to store water.

Blessed with more dependable precipitation, the East, South, Midwest and Pacific Coast have fewer water problems. But occasional droughts and decaying municipal water systems cause expensive problems in these regions. Eastern and Midwestern congressional delegations, dismayed by the wealth and power shift to the South and West, have been questioning federal programs that supply cheap water for the growing Sun Belt.

Throughout President Reagan's first term, debate in Congress reflected these regional differences. One important issue was cost sharing — what proportion of the expensive federal projects should be borne by beneficiaries and when and how should they pay. Within the federal government, the power to make decisions about water policy was also debated.

## Water Policy Planning

Congress in 1981 shelved a proposal to create an independent federal board to set national water policies. House and Senate committees that authorized federal water projects drafted legislation to set up the board to coordinate water planning by federal and state government agencies. But four Western senators thwarted the panels' attempt to write the measure into 1981 budget reconciliation legislation.

The committees proposed the board in part to prevent Secretary of the Interior James G. Watt from taking control of federal water policy-making programs. In fiscal 1982 budget revisions President Reagan proposed abolishing the existing federal Water Resources Council and consolidating federal water planning duties under Watt's direction.

Congress in the late 1970s had fiercely resisted President Carter's efforts to tighten executive branch control over costly water development projects. Still eager to preserve congressional freedom to fund new irrigation, flood control, inland waterway and other water projects, members feared that Reagan's reorganization plans would put Watt in position to dominate water resource program decisions.

As interior secretary, Watt directly supervised Bureau of Reclamation irrigation and electric power generation projects. As chairman of Reagan's Cabinet Council on Natural Resources and Environment, Watt also could influence water development programs run by the Army Corps of Engineers, a Defense Department agency, and by the Agriculture Department's Soil Conservation Service. Reagan's budget proposed assigning water planning functions to the Cabinet Council, which established a "working group on water resources" to advise the president on water policy and to draw up guidelines for determining which water projects the federal government should build.

Many senators and representatives strongly protested that the Cabinet Council would freeze Congress out of water policy deliberations until after key decisions had been made. As an alternative, House and Senate committees approved separate bills to set up an independent board, outside Interior Department control, that would report policy recommendations directly to

Congress as well as to the president. In creating the new board, Congress also would make a long-overdue start toward developing a "strong, comprehensive water policy for this nation," Sen. James Abdnor, R-S.D., chairman of the Senate Subcommittee on Water Resources, declared.

## Background

The federal government began developing the nation's water resources for economic purposes in 1824. Over the following 150 years Congress gave three Cabinet departments, one semi-autonomous regional authority and an executive branch agency major responsibilities for managing the flow of rivers, streams and harbors, and for improving water quality.

Interior's Bureau of Reclamation, the Army Corps of Engineers, the Soil Conservation Service (SCS) and the Tennessee Valley Authority (TVA) conducted separate programs to build, maintain and operate dams and other structures that stored water for irrigation, controlled floods, generated electric power, controlled soil erosion and created lakes for recreation. Since 1972, moreover, another government agency influenced water policy. The Environmental Protection Agency (EPA) regulated industrial effluents and municipal sewage discharges to control water pollution throughout the nation.

In establishing water development programs, Congress used its broad constitutional power to regulate navigation on navigable streams. Despite its massive spending on water projects, the federal government generally conceded to state governments the power to regulate water use within their borders and allocate scarce supplies among competing users. But with authority thus fragmented among 50 state governments and several federal agencies, the nation never developed comprehensive plans for managing water resources.

**Pork Barrel Politics.** Over the years Congress expanded federal water development efforts into classic "pork barrel" programs. In drafting water project authorization bills, the House and Senate took care to ensure support by distributing government-financed construction among members' states and districts. State and local community leaders were eager to share in the federal largesse. They formed regional alliances to support federal dam-building projects, which promoted economic growth by developing rivers and streams. Seven Western states along the Colorado River system, for example, reached an interstate compact in 1921 allocating its waters for use within their borders. Then, led by powerful congressional leaders such as Rep. Wayne N. Aspinall, D-Colo. (1949-73), and Sen. Carl Hayden, D-Ariz. (House, 1912-27; Senate, 1927-69), the Colorado River states persuaded Congress to finance a system of massive dams along the river.

But environmentalists and economists charged that in cutting such political deals, Congress often approved construction of water developments that had little economic justification. After Congress authorized federal construction grants to help local governments upgrade sewage treatment plants, members began practicing similar distributive politics to assure that their constituents benefited from the program. As a consequence Congress reacted suspiciously when presidents or executive branch officials proposed that the government coordinate its water development programs with national resource policy objectives.

**Research, Planning Programs.** In the mid-1960s Congress attempted to develop federal machinery to coordinate water policy and to promote research on water conservation and technology.

Since 1908 dozens of commissions, studies and reports had called for a unified national water policy. In 1961 the Senate Select Committee on Water Resources recommended that the federal government expand water planning programs, periodically assess regional water supplies and draw up comprehensive management plans for all the nation's river basins. Congress incorporated most of the select committee's suggestions into two laws — the Water Resources Research Act of 1964 and the Water Resources Planning Act of 1965.

The laws were touted as the long-sought answer to the coordination problem. Sponsors said they would put an end to the fragmented, project-oriented approach to water planning. But the acts failed to achieve that goal. Environmentalists continued to criticize water programs as riddled with economically unsound projects built at the behest of politically powerful constituents or members of Congress.

The 1964 law set up an Office of Water Research and Technology, which provided grants to universities to develop better water conservation methods.

The 1965 act established the Water Resources Council (WRC), which was to be the focal point for national water planning. It was to encourage conservation and coordinate water quantity and quality programs. The law also established six river basin commissions to manage rivers on a regional basis.

But the council and the river basin commissions proved ineffective largely because neither had authority to enforce planning efforts. The WRC was unable to coordinate quantity and quality programs, mostly because it could not control two powerful water agencies — the Army Corps of Engineers and the EPA. In addition, the council was chaired by the secretary of the interior, whose agency concentrated on Western water issues. That led states and other federal agencies to distrust the council's objectivity.

Water from Lake Sakakawea surrounds the Snake Creek pumping plant, part of the Bureau of Reclamation's Garrison Diversion Project. Water is lifted from here to Audubon Lake and from there flows to irrigate land and to supplement municipal water supplies.

**Carter Water Policy Review.** In the late 1970s mounting environmental concerns combined with persistent federal budget deficits to slow federal construction of new water projects. Carter attempted a thorough overhaul of federal water policy between 1977 and 1981. But Carter's administration, heavily staffed with former environmental activists, got off on the wrong foot with Congress when the Interior Department announced in February 1977 a "hit list" of 19 partly built projects that the president wanted to cancel.

Carter's plan infuriated members from states where the planned projects would be located. Although Congress eventually terminated funding for nine of the projects and modified plans for four others, the "hit list" contributed to a lasting impression that Carter's administration would ignore legitimate proposals to develop water resources.

In 1978 Carter unveiled plans for national water policies that would tighten executive branch control over federal spending on dams and other projects. The administration proposal stressed water conservation measures as an alternative to costly construction projects to augment regional supplies. Carter proposed tough standards to make sure that future federally financed projects protected the environment, promoted water conservation and produced economic benefits that exceeded costs.

The administration sought to subject those projects to uniform procedures to assess their costs and benefits. In its major legislative request the administration proposed a cost-sharing plan to require states to pay 10 percent of the costs of projects that produced water, power and other resources for sale. For flood control projects and other facilities that produced no salable resources, the administration proposed requiring states to pay 5 percent of construction costs. *(Cost sharing, p. 129)*

To implement those goals Carter announced that the Water Resources Council Congress had established in 1965 would review all projects proposed by federal water development agencies before they were submitted to Congress.

Carter's proposal for comprehensive water policies stirred opposition in Congress. Five days after he disclosed his plan, the House passed legislation to abolish the council and transfer its duties to the Interior Department. Congress eventually reauthorized the council but slashed its budget. In 1980, however, the House passed an omnibus water projects authorization bill that ignored Carter's reform proposals.

## Watt Water Policies

Taking over as interior secretary in 1981, Watt promised Western water interests that the Reagan administration would resume funding for new water construction. But the new administration, struggling to close the federal budget deficit, was reluctant to devote funds to dam-building projects until Congress and the states agreed on a cost-sharing formula. The administration's internal debate on cost-shar-

ing proposals lasted throughout Reagan's first term, stalling congressional deliberations on water project authorizations.

The administration in the meantime proposed consolidating under Watt's control the water planning and research programs the government had launched in the 1960s. Reagan's budget proposed saving $111.5 million in fiscal 1981 and 1982 by eliminating the Water Resources Council, the Office of Water Research and Technology and the six regional river basin commissions.

Congress, however, was reluctant to give Interior sole power over national water policy and resisted Reagan's plan to abolish those programs.

## Water Board Legislation

House and Senate committees responded to Watt's consolidation plan by proposing a new national water policy board to replace the council. The panels also sought to continue funding for the river basin commissions and for state water planning programs.

In the Senate the Environment and Public Works Committee May 15 reported legislation creating a five-member board. The House Public Works and Transportation Committee proposed a seven-member board.

Reviewing the measure in July, the House Interior and Insular Affairs Committee added a proposal to create a 21-member blue-ribbon commission — to include 12 members of Congress — to provide advice on what kind of water policy the country should have.

Both the House and Senate measures continued state planning grants and river basin commission funding. The Senate measure also continued federal water research grants to universities, although it accepted Reagan's plan to abolish the Office of Water Research and Technology. Neither measure reached the floor.

## Water Policy Funding

Congress in 1981 insisted on funding the existing Water Resources Council and the Office of Water Research and Technology. In a fiscal 1982 energy-water appropriations bill, Congress appropriated $3.8 million to keep the existing water council operating. That appropriation, however, was far below the $19.8 million the council received in fiscal 1981.

In appropriating fiscal 1982 funds for the Interior Department and related agencies, Congress also ignored Reagan's proposal to abolish the water research program by providing $10.6 million for the Office of Water Research and Technology. In its fiscal 1983 Interior appropriations bill, however, Congress accepted the water research office's demise and provided no further funding.

The House Appropriations Committee in 1982 recommended that Congress appropriate $500,000 in fiscal 1983 to continue the Water Resources Council. Neither the House nor the Senate acted on fiscal 1983 energy-water program appropriations, however, and Congress in 1983 accepted the council's elimination.

## University Research

Congress in 1984 overrode President Reagan's veto and continued federal funding for state university water research institutes. By overriding the veto, Congress March 22 enacted legislation authorizing $36 million a year in fiscal 1985-89 for Interior Department support for water research at land grant colleges in 50 states and some U.S. territories.

Congress first authorized federal water research support in 1964. Operating with a mix of federal and state funding, many university institutes focused their research on state or regional water problems. Massachusetts researchers had studied acid rain, Pennsylvania studied mine drainage, and New Mexico specialized in desalinization technologies for making briny groundwater in arid regions usable for irrigation.

Arguing that states should finance those programs, Reagan had proposed ending federal financial support in his budget proposals for fiscal 1982 through 1985. But Congress kept the program alive through year-to-year appropriations, then reauthorized the program over the president's veto.

In a concession to the administration, the House and Senate revised the final authorization measure in 1983 to require states to contribute a rising share of financial support for water research institutes. Interior Department officials then dropped their objections to the bill, but Reagan nonetheless followed an Office of Management and Budget (OMB) recommendation by vetoing the bill on Feb. 21, 1984.

The Senate May 25, 1983, passed an original version of the bill authorizing $21.1 million a year for water research. The House Oct. 31 passed its own version boosting annual authorizations to $60 million. House and Senate managers then worked out a compromise version authorizing $36 million a year.

The compromise authorized $10 million a year for matching grants to state university institutes and $20 million for matching grants for specific research projects selected by the interior secretary. The compromise raised the state matching requirement for the water institutes in stages, from one state dollar for each federal dollar in fiscal 1985-86 to two state dollars for every federal dollar by fiscal 1989.

The Senate approved the compromise version on Nov. 18, 1983, and the House agreed to the revisions unanimously on Feb. 7, 1984. Reagan vetoed the legislation on Feb. 21, contending that state research institutes had reached a point where "they

**Buckskin Mountains Tunnel under construction in the late 1970s. Tunnel is part of the Central Arizona Project, a 400-mile-long system of dams, aqueducts and other facilities to pump water from the Colorado River to serve Phoenix and Tucson.**

can stand and succeed on their own."

Hill strategists supporting the bill took their time before mounting an override attempt, giving state university officials an opportunity to contact their House and Senate delegations and slowly building support on an issue that they admitted excited little political passion. The Republican-controlled Senate acted first, on March 21, and its 86-12 vote gave the House impetus to override by a 309-81 vote the following day.

## Reclamation Law Revision

Congress in 1982 revised the Reclamation Act of 1902 to provide federally subsidized water to irrigate private farms up to 960 acres in size. Legislation cleared Sept. 29 raised a 160-acre limit set by the 1902 law on the amount of farmland irrigated by Interior Department reclamation projects that a single farmer could own. The measure also repealed the 1902 law's requirement that farmers who received federal project water live on or near their fields.

By revising the law, Congress recognized that the Bureau of Reclamation, the Interior Department's dam-building agency, had never enforced the 160-acre limit. In the process Congress headed off a long-running campaign by environmentalists and California land reform advocates to force Interior to deny low-cost water to wealthy individuals and corporations who irrigated thousands of acres, including some of the nation's richest farmlands, from federal reclamation projects.

Secretary Watt had warned that he had no choice but to start enforcing the 160-acre limit unless Congress changed the 1902 law. Backed by a 1976 federal court ruling, critics of federal reclamation programs pressed for strict enforcement of the acreage restriction to break up large agricultural operations and redistribute their land to small farmers. Environmental groups also charged that existing reclamation programs, by pricing water far below its market value, subsidized giant corporate farms and encouraged wasteful irrigation practices.

In lifting the limit to 960 acres, Congress agreed with Western farming interests who contended that a 160-acre farm was too small for modern agricultural operations. The revised law made individuals and small corporations eligible for federal project water to irrigate another 960 acres leased from other owners. But it required them to pay the government for the full cost of building projects and delivering water to the leased land.

## Background

Congress passed the Reclamation Act of 1902 to promote economic development in the arid Western states. With President Theodore Roosevelt's enthusiastic backing, Congress in the 1902 law gave the Interior Department authority to build dams to store water and canals to distribute it to irrigate deserts and plains where rainfall was too sparse for farming. Congress expanded the law's objectives in subsequent decades to permit the Bureau of Reclamation to build massive multipurpose dams — including Hoover and Glen Canyon Dams on the Colorado River, Grand Coulee Dam on the Columbia River, the Central Valley Project in California and other projects — that

generated electric power, supplied water for cities and industry and created lakes for recreation, in addition to irrigating farmlands.

When Congress passed the 1902 law, federal officials envisioned that the West should be settled by families living on small farming operations. Throughout the 19th century the government had been selling or giving away the lands it acquired in Western territories in 640-acre sections, each one mile square. In the famous Homestead Act of 1862, Congress granted free title to 160 acres, a quarter section, of public lands to any citizen who settled the land and cultivated it for five years.

To focus benefits from federal reclamation projects on family-size farms, Congress in 1902 limited the amount of land an individual could water to 160 acres, the conventional homestead unit. The 1902 law allowed a farmer and spouse to receive federal project water for up to 320 acres, a half section of land. The law permitted a farmer to receive federal project water to irrigate more than 160 acres only if the owner signed a "recordable contract" with Interior, promising to sell excess acreage within a specified period, usually 10 years, at the "dryland" price the acreage was worth before it could be irrigated.

Congress financed initial reclamation projects from receipts from public land sales, but the 1902 law required farmers to reimburse the government for the cost of irrigation water, without interest, over a 10-year period. Congress subsequently extended the repayment period for different projects to up to 60 years. In 1939 Congress limited farmers' obligation to repay the government for water project construction costs to their ability to pay, further expanding the below-cost irrigation water subsidy.

In the 80 years after Congress passed the 1902 Reclamation Act, the bureau built hundreds of projects in the 17 Western states where it operated. Bureau reclamation projects supplied water to irrigate about 10 million acres that produced more than 10 percent of the nation's total crop value. Federal projects supplied water to the West's richest agricultural regions, including the productive Central Valley in California, the leading agricultural state.

The 160-acre limit remained on the books, although it had been evaded on many water projects. Some of the nation's largest federally irrigated farms, particularly in California, covered thousands of acres, although much of the acreage was operated under lease. The question of whether lease arrangements violated the spirit of the 1902 law was at the heart of the dispute. The old acreage limit had been poorly enforced because of federal laxity, confusion created by later statutes and contradictory interpretations by courts and federal officials.

In 1976 a California group, Land Is for People, won a federal court ruling that the group interpreted as an affirmation of the 160-acre limit. President Carter's interior secretary, Cecil D. Andrus, set about enforcing the limit with a vigor that alarmed much of the farm community and the large corporations with interests in massive farms, particularly in California.

Congress had grappled periodically with the issue since then. The Senate passed a reclamation rewrite in 1979, and the House committee reported a bill in 1980.

### Legislative Action

Congress in 1982 raised the acreage limitation to 960 acres after bitter debate in both the House and Senate. To win its approval, Western members pushing to revise the 1902 limit had to overcome environmentalists' opposition and delaying tactics by Sen. Howard M. Metzenbaum, D-Ohio, a critic of reclamation subsidies.

It took elaborate maneuvering before the House and Senate settled on compromise legislation. House Interior Committee Chairman Morris K. Udall, D-Ariz., refused to go to conference on the reclamation bill until Congress settled an unrelated water rights dispute between the Papago Indian tribe and Tucson water users in his district. Once agreement was reached on the Papago dispute, Congress incorporated a compromise reclamation law revision along with the Indian water settlement into a bill that authorized the Bureau of Reclamation to enlarge the Buffalo Bill Dam and Reservoir in Wyoming. *(Papago dispute, p. 136)*

Conference negotiations on the acreage limit were stormy. Metzenbaum repeatedly told conferees that farmers should pay more for water than either the House or the Senate bill required. Conferees settled on a 960-acre ownership limit for an individual or small corporation, with a separate 640-acre limit applied to corporations with more than 25 stockholders. The compromise permitted farm operators to receive irrigation water for an unlimited amount of leased land but required the government to charge them a full-cost rate based on unpaid construction costs and a minimum interest rate of 7.5 percent.

## Cost Sharing

Congress in 1983-84 again fell short in its drive to launch new federal water development projects. Constrained by economic and environmental concerns, Congress had failed to pass an omnibus water projects authorization bill since 1976. It came close in 1984, but an $18 billion House-passed measure died in the closing days of the session.

Ever since President Carter in 1977 tried to cancel previously approved projects, Congress had been struggling to justify funding to start new irrigation, flood control, navigation and other water project construction. Environmentalists challenged federal dam building programs that they contended wasted scarce water while ruining fish and wildlife habitat. Economists meanwhile questioned whether economic benefits from costly projects justified the expense to the federal taxpayers.

For four years the Reagan administration had tried to come up with a "cost-sharing" formula acceptable to Congress that would weed out the most wasteful projects by requiring local governments or water users to pick up more of the construction costs. Protests by powerful Republican senators from the water-short West in 1983 headed off President Reagan's approval of a uniform government cost-sharing policy.

The House in 1984 approved tougher cost-sharing requirements when it passed an $18 billion omnibus bill authorizing the Army Corps of Engineers and the Interior Department's Bureau of Reclamation to start building more than 300 dams, locks, levees, harbor improvements and other water development and conservation projects. In the Senate, however, differences among three committees on cost sharing and other issues thwarted a time agreement allowing floor action on an $11 billion water projects authorization.

After waiting nearly four years for an authorization bill to settle on a cost-sharing plan, the House late in the 1984 session tried to tack funding for new projects onto a fiscal 1985 continuing appropriations measure. Despite last-minute negotiations, the Senate abandoned the effort after David A. Stockman, director of the White House Office of Management and Budget, opposed legislation funding any water projects until Congress approved basic cost-sharing reforms.

## Background

The Army Corps of Engineers, the Bureau of Reclamation and the U.S. Soil Conservation Service, an Agriculture Department agency, built or maintained water projects in nearly every congressional district. The corps and SCS operated throughout the nation, but the bureau served only 17 Western states. The SCS primarily helped farmers and ranchers build small dams and other facilities to curb soil erosion, but the corps and bureau built and operated huge projects that often served multiple purposes, including irrigation, flood control, recreation and electric power generation.

These projects provided tangible economic benefits: municipal and industrial water supply, hydroelectric power, ports and waterways for shipping, irrigation water for farmers, recreational lakes, flood protection — and, in some cases, fish and wildlife habitat.

No less tangible were the political benefits available to members of Congress who could deliver such projects to their districts.

Since the early 1970s, however, funding for new projects had slowed to a fraction of what it was in the 1950s and 1960s, and Congress had not approved an omnibus water projects authorization bill since 1976. President Ford signed that law authorizing $742 million worth of planning, design and construction in 36 states only weeks before the 1976 election.

Even without new projects, however, the backlog of unfinished water projects, plus those authorized but not yet funded, approached $50 billion in value. Appropriations for the corps, reclamation bureau and SCS actually rose in nominal dollars during the 1970s, but most funds were going to finish projects already under construction and to maintain and operate existing facilities.

By the early 1980s members of Congress, state and local officials, farmers, barge operators, shipping companies and numerous other interests, especially in the South and West, were eager for approval of new project "starts." The East and the Midwest were demanding federal assistance to replace or repair crumbling municipal water systems in older cities and other water facilities.

### Cost-Sharing Debate

Reagan was expected to push for new starts after defeating Carter in 1980 with solid support in Western states. But the Reagan administration was slow to develop a clear policy for selecting and financing new projects. Administration officials were determined to force state and local beneficiaries to assume a far greater share of the costs, but the White House also worried about the political fallout in Reagan's Western stronghold.

The administration in May 1982 proposed fiscal 1983 funding to start nine new projects where state and local sponsors had agreed voluntarily to pay a greater share of costs than had historically been the case. But members of Congress saw the projects as a stalking horse for a controversial cost-sharing policy and the House and Senate Appropriations committees refused to approve the funds.

In June 1982 Reagan's Cabinet Council on Natural Resources and the Environment began considering a comprehensive proposal to drastically increase state and local funding requirements on all federal water projects. The policy at issue called for a 100 percent non-federal share in financing of hydropower and both municipal and industrial water supply, a 50 percent non-federal share for recreation and a 35 percent non-federal share for flood control and irrigation. Under existing laws cost-sharing rates differed from project to project and agency to agency.

The new policy would have required beneficiaries to pay a major share of project

Hoover Dam seen from the Nevada side. Contracts setting prices for the dam's power will expire May 31, 1987, but so far Congress has resisted raising prices to users accustomed to cheap power.

costs — and pay up front, while projects were being built. Up-front local payment would have cut out the hefty hidden subsidy that resulted from the artificially low interest rates the federal government used to calculate local paybacks.

Joined by OMB, Corps of Engineers officials pushed throughout 1983 for administration approval of a uniform cost-sharing formula that would apply both to the corps projects throughout the nation and to Bureau of Reclamation projects in the West. But Interior officials balked at a uniform policy, maintaining that the government should negotiate cost-sharing agreements separately for each project, taking into account the beneficiaries' ability to pay. Led by Sen. Paul Laxalt, R-Nev., a close Reagan friend, senators from Western states wrote the president in 1983 to warn against "an up-front financing scheme even more

Draconian" than one proposed by the Carter administration. Reagan in January 1984 finally rejected any fixed cost-sharing formula in a letter that Reagan's second secretary of the interior, William P. Clark, personally delivered to Laxalt.

# Water Project Funding

During President Reagan's first term Congress continued to appropriate funds for several controversial federal water projects that environmental groups wanted to halt.

One of these projects was construction of the Tennessee-Tombigbee (Tenn-Tom) Waterway, a partly built 232-mile barge canal to connect the Tennessee River to the Gulf of Mexico at Mobile, Ala. Congress also funded ongoing work on the Garrison Diversion project, which was designed to send water from a Missouri River reservoir to irrigate farmland in North Dakota. A federal court had temporarily blocked construction on the $1 billion project. In 1983 Congress also maintained funding for the Stonewall Jackson Dam in West Virginia, although the representative from the district where the dam was being built recommended that it be stopped. Each year Congress voted to spend more money than the Reagan administration wanted.

In drawing up fiscal 1984 and fiscal 1985 appropriations bills, Congress provided no funding for "new starts" to launch construction of planned water projects. The House and Senate Appropriations committees instead waited for the Reagan administration and congressional authorizing committees to settle a continuing dispute over cost-sharing arrangements to require regions that would benefit from new projects to pay part of up-front construction costs.

Congress nonetheless appropriated $3.6 billion in fiscal 1984 and $3.8 billion in fiscal 1985 for the Army Corps of Engineers and the Bureau of Reclamation to continue construction and to maintain previously authorized hydropower, flood control, irrigation and inland waterway projects. Those measures provided no additional appropriations for Tenn-Tom. However, $180 million in unspent funds carried over from fiscal 1983 provided sufficient financing essentially complete construction of the project's navigation features.

Congress in 1984 again moved relatively speedily in approving a regular fiscal 1985 water bill. Cleared by June 28, that bill appropriated $2.8 billion for the Corps of Engineers and nearly $1.1 billion for the Bureau of Reclamation.

The corps built, operated and maintained water projects throughout the nation, but mainly in the East. The bureau operated only in 17 Western states. The Senate, with more representation for sparsely populated Western states than in the House, generally shifted appropriations from the corps to the bureau.

### Tenn-Tom Project

Critics in both the House and Senate came close during 1981 and 1982 to denying further appropriations to complete the $3 billion Tennessee-Tombigbee Waterway. But powerful congressional delegations from Alabama and Mississippi, the states where the canal was being built, fought off proposals to terminate funding.

First authorized in the 1940s, Tenn-Tom would be the largest water project in U.S. history. Sen. John C. Stennis, D-Miss., and other supporters had pushed the project to develop an inland waterway as a shortcut that barges could take from the Tennessee River along the Tombigbee River through Mississippi and Alabama to the Gulf port at Mobile. Proponents maintained that the canal, being built by the Corps of Engineers, would promote U.S. coal exports by providing a route for barge traffic from Appalachian coal fields to the sea.

Environmental groups had been fighting the Tenn-Tom project for years, contending that the economic benefits fell far short of the project's cost and the damage it would cause to the environment. The Association of American Railroads also lobbied against continued funding. If completed, the Tenn-Tom canal would compete for coal traffic with an existing rail system.

By 1982 the corps had spent about $1.3 billion building the Tenn-Tom project. In supporting completion of the waterway, the House Appropriations Committee estimated its total cost at $1.8 billion. Opponents said the cost could reach $3 billion because the lower part of the waterway would have to be straightened to accommodate expected barge traffic, but Congress had yet to authorize that work.

The Reagan administration requested $201 million for the project in its fiscal 1982 budget, but it made no major lobbying effort to defend its funding. The House Appropriations Committee cut $11 million from the Tenn-Tom proposals. But Rep. Tom Bevill, D-Ala., chairman of the Appropriations Subcommittee on Energy and Water Development, led the fight for the project on the floor.

During floor debate the full House defeated, 198-208, an amendment to delete the $189 million Tenn-Tom appropriation that was offered by Joel Pritchard, R-Wash., and Bob Edgar, D-Pa. Freshman House members voted 42-30 for the amendment, suggesting that support for costly water projects would continue to decline. Tenn-Tom supporters contended that Congress should complete a project in which the government already had made a large investment, but opponents maintained that it was time to rectify Congress' past mistake in authorizing the project in the first place.

After the House passed the bill with the Tenn-Tom funds, the Senate rejected, 46-48, a floor amendment to delete the project's appropriation that was offered by Charles H. Percy, R-Ill. In contrast to new House members, freshman senators elected in 1980 voted 7-11 against Percy's amendment.

Calling the waterway an "economic dinosaur," Percy said the coal companies were not seeking it and that the eventual traffic would not be enough to pay for operating it. Daniel Patrick Moynihan, D-N.Y., called it a perfect example of pork barrel abuse. If Congress did not start "acting responsibly" by killing it, the country would never support any more public works projects, he warned.

While J. Bennett Johnston, D-La., led the floor defense for Tenn-Tom funds, Stennis lobbied undecided colleagues. On the floor Johnston contended that the basic issue was "an age-old fight" between railroads and barge transportation. The railroads "have a monopoly, and they want to keep it," Johnston said.

Congress then continued to appropriate funds for the Tenn-Tom project through the fiscal 1983 continuing resolution. As cleared, however, the resolution carried a Senate amendment that prohibited use of funds either to study or to build improvements in the Tombigbee south of Demopolis, Ala., the portion that critics maintained would have to be straightened to allow barges to navigate.

### Garrison Diversion Project

Congress had authorized the Garrison Diversion project as part of the Pick-Sloan Plan for developing the Missouri River system in 10 states under the Flood Control Act of 1944. The Garrison project was a $1.1 billion system of aqueducts and irrigation canals designed to carry water from a Missouri River reservoir across North Dakota to irrigate about one million acres of farm land in the state. Its purpose was to compensate North Dakota for 500,000 acres of farm land flooded by Missouri River mainstream dams that the Corps of Engineers built to control floods in downstream states.

Although many Pick-Sloan projects had been completed, construction on the Garrison Diversion was only about 15 percent finished in the early 1980s. Congress regularly appropriated money for the project in the 1960s and 1970s, but a 1979 lawsuit and environmental group lobbying slowed work. Environmental groups objected that the project would destroy wetland habitat for waterfowl, and the National Taxpayers Union contended that the costs far exceeded benefits to North Dakota farmers.

For years the Canadian government had joined environmental groups in opposing the Garrison Diversion. The Canadians maintained that water draining north across the border from irrigated farm lands to the Souris River would alter the Hudson Bay region ecosystem.

In 1981 Congress appropriated $4 million for Garrison as part of the fiscal 1982 energy/water appropriations bill. Rep. Silvio O. Conte, R-Mass., a critic of what he considered pork barrel water projects, had led the fight to get the funds deleted from the bill. Opponents came closer to killing the Garrison project in 1982. Before passing the fiscal 1983 continuing resolution, the House approved Conte's attempt to delete Garrison funding by a 252-152 margin. The Senate restored the funds, however, and the conferees kept them in the final measure. The conference agreement added provisions barring use of the money to build facilities that would affect water draining north into Canada.

In both 1983 and 1984 the Senate forced the House to accept appropriations to continue construction of the Garrison Diversion. To keep the project going, however, the North Dakota delegation in 1984 had to negotiate a compromise with environmentalists who set up a special commission to study redesigning the project to reduce threats to wetlands, waterfowl and fish both in the state and in Canada.

The House Appropriations Committee again omitted Garrison funds from its fiscal 1985 recommendations, passed by the House on May 22, 1984, but proponents counted on the Senate to keep the project alive. As expected, the Senate panel approved the administration's full $53.6 million request for Garrison construction.

### Stonewall Jackson Dam

Despite an unusual split within the West Virginia delegation, Congress in 1983 maintained funding for the Stonewall Jackson Dam in that state. Breaking with congressional pork barrel traditions, Rep. Bob Wise, D-W.Va., persuaded the House to delete $26 million that the House Appropriations Committee had recommended for a project being built in his district.

First authorized in 1965, the project's initial cost estimate of $34 million had risen to $205 million, and Wise argued there were cheaper methods of flood control that should be considered before the dam was finished. Although every other West Virginia member backed the project, the House by a 213-161 vote on June 7 accepted Wise's proposal to delete the funds.

Led by Senate Minority Leader Robert C. Byrd, D-W.Va., however, the rest of the state's delegation convinced House-Senate conferees to restore the funds in the final water projects appropriations. Despite his assault on the dam, Wise won re-election in 1984 with 69 percent of the vote in a safely Democratic district.

# Central Arizona Project

Congress in 1981 authorized an additional $350 million to $500 million to build

A section of the Teton Dam broke in June 1975, causing 11 deaths and $400 million in damages.

Central Arizona Project (CAP) distribution systems to deliver water to Phoenix and Tucson residents.

To take account of rising costs, Congress Dec. 9 cleared legislation under which authorizations for Bureau of Reclamation spending on the systems were indexed to offset inflation since the project was approved in 1968. In approving the indexing bill, however, Congress attached an amendment to force state and local governments in the region to pay 20 percent of the distribution system's cost.

The House wrote the cost-sharing provision into the bill with the support of Republican fiscal conservatives and Democratic environmentalist members who had long complained that expensive federal water projects financed by federal taxpayers in effect subsidized wasteful water uses by residents in the arid Southwest without requiring them to pay part of construction costs. Congress authorized the $2.8 billion

CAP system in 1968 to enable Arizona to develop its share of Colorado River water. The Bureau of Reclamation designed the CAP as a 400-mile-long system of dams, aqueducts and other facilities to pump water from the Colorado on the state's western border to serve Phoenix and Tucson. Those fast-growing cities depended on groundwater supplies that were being depleted by rapid population growth. The CAP system also included facilities to deliver water to Arizona Indian tribes that had won a share of Colorado River water under a 1963 Supreme Court decision.

The 1968 law authorized $100 million for building non-Indian distribution systems. The bureau had yet to begin construction on those facilities, however, because CAP water was not expected to be available for irrigation until fiscal 1985. In the meantime inflation since 1968 had driven estimated construction costs up to $300 million-$500 million. Congress in 1968 had indexed costs for other parts of CAP, but not for distribution and drainage canals.

Congress passed legislation approving indexing for non-Indian delivery systems, including an amendment requiring state and local governments to pay 20 percent of construction costs up front. Under previous laws the beneficiaries of federal reclamation projects repaid the government, at artificially low interest rates, after water deliveries started.

## Papago Indian Water Rights

Lawmakers in 1982 approved legislation to settle an Arizona water rights dispute between Tucson water users and the Papago Indian tribe. House Interior and Insular Affairs Committee Chairman Udall maneuvered through Congress a revised settlement to resolve Papago claims to groundwater reserves from which the Tucson area drew its water supplies. By settling the seven-year-old legal challenge out of court, the measure cleared the way for further construction of the $1.7 billion Central Arizona Project (CAP).

President Reagan June 1 had vetoed an earlier bill, contending that it provided a federal bailout for Tucson residents, local governments and commercial interests that were fighting the Papago claims. Udall, whose district included Tucson and surrounding areas, took the lead in negotiating a compromise settlement that Congress accepted as part of a major reclamation law reform legislation.

Under the settlement the Papago tribe relinquished all further claims to water in the basins underlying the Tucson area and agreed to cooperate in regional water management plans. In return Congress authorized nearly $40 million in federal appropriations to build irrigation facilities and provide the tribe with adequate annual water supplies.

## Western Dam Repairs

Congress in 1984 agreed to charge local beneficiaries for 15 percent of the cost of repairing aging and faulty federal dams in the West. Settling a four-year controversy over cost-sharing arrangements, Congress Aug. 10 cleared legislation that authorized $650 million in new spending on repairs by the Bureau of Reclamation. The House completed action on the bill by accepting a Senate compromise that required recipients of water and other benefits from the dams to repay the government for 15 percent of the costs, some at market rates of interest.

Critics of federal water project subsidies hailed the decision as an important precedent for sharing the costs of building new dams and other structures. The Reagan administration and Congress had been deliberating since 1981 over proposals to force state and local beneficiaries to pay much larger shares of water projects that the Bureau of Reclamation and U.S. Army Corps of Engineers built to promote navigation, control floods, generate electric power or supply water to farmers and cities in their regions.

By requiring cost sharing for dam repairs, "I believe we establish the principle that virtually no federal water investment shall be immune from cost sharing," Sen. Metzenbaum declared.

Reversing a 1982 stand, the House in passing the legislation had accepted its Interior and Insular Affairs Committee's proposal that the federal government assume the full costs of repairing dams built by the Bureau of Reclamation. Chairman Udall led Western delegations in insisting that the Treasury should be responsible for repairing safety defects in dams that had been mostly built and designed by the government.

But Metzenbaum, a critic of federal subsidies for water development projects in the West, forced Senate Energy and Natural Resources Committee Chairman James A. McClure, R-Idaho, to agree to a compromise cost-sharing plan to assure Senate approval of the House dam repair funding.

In clearing the bill, Congress provided the bureau with funding authority to repair about 40 dams, some built as long ago as 1911, that had been found unsafe. Well over half of the funds could be required to repair or replace six Salt River dams upstream from Phoenix, Ariz.

## Background

Concern about the safety of federally built dams in the West had grown since 1976. The Bureau of Reclamation's Teton Dam in Idaho broke that year, and the resulting floods killed 11 people and caused about $400 million in damages. By 1984 the federal government had paid out $350 million in damage claims from the Teton Dam disaster.

Congress in 1978 authorized $100 million for safety repairs on federal dams. But the bureau in the following years identified additional dams needing repairs that would be more costly. The bureau had been building dams in the 17 Western states since Congress passed the Reclamation Act of 1903. Bureau officials judged 40 of the dams unsafe because of faulty or obsolete engineering designs, new forecasts that upgraded flooding or earthquake risks, or structures that had simply rusted or crumbled with age.

The House in 1982 passed a bill authorizing $550 million for dam repairs after adopting an amendment imposing a cost-sharing requirement. But the Senate Energy Committee rejected the cost-sharing amendment, and the proposal died at the end of the 97th Congress.

The Reagan administration meanwhile continued to debate whether to apply uniform cost-sharing policies to Bureau of Rec-lamation projects. In 1982 the administration had urged Congress to require beneficiaries to share the costs of dam repairs. But influential Republican senators from Western states resisted cost-sharing formulas that would apply to bureau projects in the West as well as Army Corps of Engineers projects in other regions. President Reagan reversed direction from the administration's 1982 stand by declaring that the federal government should bear the entire costs of repairing faulty dams.

## House Cost-Sharing Switch

As it had in 1982, Udall's Interior Committee May 16, 1984, reported legislation authorizing dam repair funds without any cost-sharing requirements. Environmentalists and taxpayer groups again joined in backing a floor amendment to require water users to contribute to repairs. This time, however, the House followed the administration's reversal by rejecting the proposal.

Existing law required beneficiaries to pay for routine maintenance costs on federal projects, but the Interior bill required the government to pay for any additional repairs to correct safety problems. On the House floor two members from the Northeast — Edgar, an environmentalist, and Gerald B. H. Solomon, R-N.Y., a fiscal conservative — teamed up to offer a proposal to force beneficiaries to repay some repair costs over a 50-year period. But by a vote of 194-192 the House March 20 instead chose a substitute offered by Abraham Kazen Jr., D-Texas, chairman of the Interior Subcommittee on Water and Power Resources, that required cost sharing only if repairing a dam produced new economic benefits.

Contending that very few repair projects would provide additional economic benefits, Solomon argued that Kazen's amendment would recoup little, if any, of the government's $650-million repair bill.

### Senate Cost-Sharing Provision

At Metzenbaum's insistence, however, the Senate tacked on compromise cost-sharing requirements before passing the House bill. With Metzenbaum's objections to the House bill jeopardizing Senate passage, McClure and other Western senators negotiated an agreement with the Ohio senator for sharing part of repair costs.

The compromise allocated 15 percent of the costs of repairing a dam to various users of the water and power it supplied. Existing laws generally allowed beneficiaries to pay back dam construction costs at artificially low interest rates, conferring a substantial subsidy. But the Senate compromise required most users to repay repair costs at market rates — with an exception for irrigation farmers, who could pay their share back without interest, depending on their ability to bear the cost.

Without further committee action, the Senate Aug. 9 passed the bill by voice vote after adopting Metzenbaum's amendment to implement the compromise. The House Aug. 10 agreed to the Senate revisions, clearing the legislation for President Reagan to sign into law on Aug. 28.

# Hoover Dam Power Pricing

Lawmakers in 1984 shrugged off conservationists' objections and approved a 30-year extension in low-cost rates for electric power from Hoover Dam on the Colorado River.

In a crucial test for federal power and water policy, Congress July 31 cleared legislation that kept expiring contracts for Hoover Dam power in effect until 2017. Those contracts sold electricity to Arizona, Nevada and Southern California at bargain rates that had been computed when the federal government finished building the dam in 1937.

Before passing this bill on May 3, the House defeated a proposal backed by conservationists that would have canceled the Hoover Dam contracts and auctioned power to the highest bidders, at current market rates. Conservationists contended that higher rates would encourage energy conservation and reduce federal deficits by producing $3.5 billion during the first 10 years in additional power revenues. But senators and representatives from Western states that benefited from low-cost federal electricity maintained that it would be unfair to boost rates that had been based on what it cost the government to build the dam that generated the power.

### Background

In the Boulder Canyon Project Act of 1928, Congress authorized the Bureau of Reclamation to build Hoover Dam where the Colorado flowed through Boulder Canyon, on the Arizona-Nevada border near Las Vegas, Nev. The government's first massive multiple-purpose water project, the dam controlled floods, stored water for farmers and cities in the Southwest, and generated hydroelectric power for Los Angeles and other fast-growing Southern California communities. It set a precedent for other huge dams that the bureau, the Army Corps of Engineers and the Tennessee Valley Authority built in the following decades to spur economic growth along the Columbia, Missouri, Tennessee, upper Colorado and other major U.S. rivers.

The Boulder Canyon Project Act, like other laws authorizing subsequent dam-building projects, required farmers, municipalities, industries and electric utilities that received water or power from a dam to repay the government for construction costs attributed to those functions. Those laws all set generous terms for repayment, usually over a 50-year period, setting interest rates by methods that usually conferred substantial subsidies at taxpayer expense. The 1937 contracts accordingly set prices for power from Hoover Dam at a low level — four-tenths of 1 percent per kilowatt hour — based on construction costs and prevailing interest rates during the 1930s. By the 1980s, when the Congressional Research Service calculated the average national price for electricity at 6.5 cents per kilowatt hour, Hoover Dam electric power was one of the greatest energy bargains in the world.

Hoover Dam was one of the first major federal power projects to near the end of its 50-year payback period. Contracts allocating and setting prices for the dam's power were due to expire on May 31, 1987, and a congressional decision on whether to extend or overhaul the existing price formula set a precedent that could influence future economic conditions in regions, especially the West, that depended heavily on federally built dams for water and cheap electric power.

The Reagan administration in 1981 had begun studying ways to raise power rates on federal dam projects. But the Senate, through amendments to appropriations legislation, blocked a review that delegations from big public power states in the Southeast and West feared would produce a recommendation to close federal budget deficits by raising federal power prices.

### House Debate

As originally passed by the Senate in 1983, the legislation ratified the agreement on reallocating Hoover Dam power but preserved existing prices. The House passed its own version on May 3, 1984, by a 279-95 vote, after turning down a floor amendment to make Hoover Dam power available to the highest bidder.

Barbara Boxer, D-Calif., from the San Francisco area, led the challenge to existing power pricing. Hoover Dam contracts supplied power to Los Angeles but not to San Francisco or San Diego, California's other major cities. Boxer offered an amendment to auction power to any utility willing to bid for it at current market rates, contending that the Senate bill would set "Depression-era prices for a 21st-century resource." Boxer also said Congress should break up "the exclusive Hoover club" by giving utilities a chance to bid on the power for Utah, Colorado, New Mexico and the rest of California.

Udall opposed Boxer's amendment. Not only would the amendment raise prices for 11 million ratepayers who now consumed Hoover Dam power, Udall maintained, but it also would disrupt pricing arrangements for other federal projects around the country. The House defeated Boxer's amendment by a 176-214 vote.

### Senate Cloture

When the House version of the bill was sent back to Senate, Metzenbaum and other critics prepared to fight final action on the measure. They argued that low Hoover power rates discouraged energy conservation, induced industry to relocate to the Southwest from other regions, and could cost the Treasury $6 billion in the following 10 years.

Metzenbaum drafted amendments to shorten the contract extension period to give Congress time to study and debate the issue, but the amendments were either tabled or ruled out of order. Metzenbaum had barely begun his fight before Senate leaders, after four hours of debate, moved to invoke cloture to end the debate. The July 30 vote went down to the wire as the leadership rounded up 60 votes, the minimum required to invoke cloture. The final tally was 60-28.

Metzenbaum gave up the following day after taking a bitter parting shot at his opponents' tactics. The Senate then voted

# 8

# Water Protection

The United States has made some progress toward cleaning up polluted rivers and lakes: the Potomac River is no longer a disgrace to the nation's capital, fish have reappeared in Lake Erie and Lake Ontario and all across the country once-contaminated streams and ponds are again clear and alive. But some still ask: "What have you done for me lately?" Most of the progress toward fishable and swimmable waters had been made before 1977, the year Congress amended the Water Pollution Control Act of 1972, renaming it the Clean Water Act.

Those who believe the legislation to be working well point to the fact that water pollution has become no worse despite the growth indicated by a 40 percent increase in the gross national product since 1970. Fifty-seven million acres of new cropland are under cultivation, and 20 million to 30 million acres of land have been converted to urban uses. But other observers are becoming alarmed at the higher incidence of a less obvious kind of water pollution. Groundwater pollution — caused by toxic substances seeping into underground aquifers — is the water issue of the 1980s.

## Clean Water

Congress during President Reagan's first term put off revising the federal water pollution control program. The Clean Water Act of 1977 gave the EPA broad powers to regulate polluted discharges into the nation's lakes and rivers. Industry and environmentalists generally recognized that the law could stand some improvement, but neither the Reagan administration nor the 98th Congress gave clean water legislation high priority.

Congressional deliberations on water pollution issues were relatively low key, in contrast to frequently angry clashes on proposals to combat acid rain and strengthen the Clean Air Act of 1970.

The House in 1984 passed a compromise bill that offered concessions to environmental groups, industry and officials who ran municipal sewage treatment programs. But the administration objected to its potential cost, and the Senate never took up its own less expensive version.

Some U.S. lakes and rivers had been dramatically cleaned up since the Water Pollution Control Act of 1972 went into effect, although there was little evidence that overall national water quality was improving. Congress revised and renamed the law in the Clean Water Act of 1977. But industry protested the law's "technology-based standards," while municipal governments and local developers wanted increased federal assistance for sewage system construction. Although some environmentalists acknowledged that parts of the law were working poorly, they resisted major changes in the existing Clean Water Act that might endorse the Reagan administration's drive to reduce the Environmental Protection Agency's (EPA) authority to regulate pollution by industry.

Congress in 1981 had yielded to the president's demand for major cutbacks in EPA grants under the 1972 law for municipal sewage treatment facilities. But to environmentalists' relief, the White House never followed up by challenging the basic strategy that the Clean Water Act set for cleaning up polluted waters. EPA in 1982 sent Congress a "wish list" for extending deadlines and easing requirements that industry, particularly chemical manufacturers, found burdensome. But Anne M. Burford (formerly Gorsuch), then EPA administrator, signaled Congress that clean water legislation ranked low on the administration's environmental agenda by declaring the existing law "fundamentally sound as it stands without need for major or extensive revision at this time."

With little administration pressure for action, Congress moved slowly in debating clean water issues. Authorizations for spending to carry out part of the Clean Water Act expired in 1982, but Congress continued to fund enforcement through annual appropriations bills.

## Background

In the Water Pollution Control Act of 1972, Congress directed the federal government to take responsibility for cleaning up the nation's polluted streams, lakes and underground supplies of water.

Disillusioned with state water pollution control efforts, Congress in the 1972 law spelled out a specific federal strategy for reducing discharges into water bodies throughout the entire nation. It set two

ambitious goals for the 1980s: to make all U.S. waters safe for swimming and fishing by 1983, and to end all polluted discharges into navigable waters by 1985.

The law assigned the federal government, through EPA, the task of regulating water pollution by cities, towns and factories to meet those objectives. It set up a multibillion-dollar federal program, managed by EPA, to provide matching grants to finance municipal sewage treatment plants. It required EPA permits for every public and private facility that discharged wastes into U.S. waters. The law also ordered the government to set technology-based standards for water quality, forcing industry to equip factories with costly equipment to cut polluted discharges, without taking account of how clear or dirty the water was where the facilities released treated effluents.

Other provisions of the law extended U.S. Army Corps of Engineers power over dredging-and-filling operations to cover most of the nation's streams and wetlands and enlarged potential federal control over groundwater contamination and "nonpoint" precipitation run-off from cities, farms and rangelands. In combination, the 1972 law and its 1977 amendments dictated a strong federal presence in water pollution control programs that ran counter to President Reagan's belief that the national government should turn most such responsibilities back to state and local governments.

**Technology-Based Standards.** The 1972 law required every industry that released water to install the best practicable control technology (BPT) by 1977. It followed up by requiring them to cut polluted discharges even more by installing the best available control technology (BAT) by 1983. In 1977 amendments to the law Congress granted industry an additional year, until 1984, to install BAT equipment for removing toxic pollutants and set a new treatment standard, called best conven-

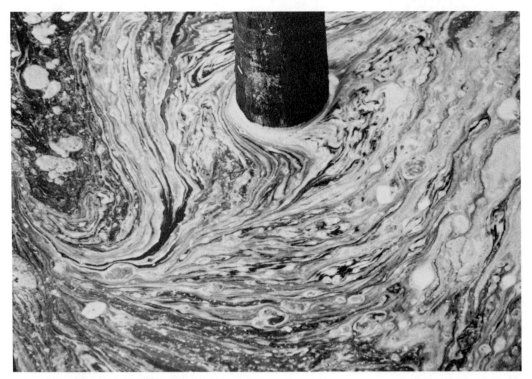

**Water from a pulp mill in Bellingham Bay, Puget Sound, Washington in 1973. Clean water legislation is designed to prevent this type of pollution.**

tional technology (BCT), for reducing common pollutants like suspended dirt, nitrogen and phosphorous, with a 1984 deadline. The 1977 amendments also gave industry until 1987 to install BAT equipment for a third category, called unconventional pollutants.

Before 1972 Congress had left it to states to regulate water pollution. In the Water Quality Act of 1965, Congress required states to set standards for the average level of pollutants allowed in rivers, streams and lakes. The state standards classified streams according to the quality of their water and set different categories for how much pollution was allowable. Environmentalists contended that states simply reclassified dirty streams downward instead of taking measures to clean them up.

In response, Congress decided in the 1972 law to substitute technology-based standards to force industries throughout the nation to clean up discharges into any water, regardless of its quality to start with. An estimated 80 to 90 percent of U.S. industry met the law's 1977 deadline for installing "best practicable" pollution control equipment. But business owners objected that meeting the 1984 deadlines for installing devices for treating effluents would cost industry perhaps $60 billion with only incremental improvements in water quality.

Critics maintained that technology-based standards ignored the varying natural capacity of different streams and lakes to assimilate organic wastes. By requiring uniform technology for discharges into all water, they argued, the law forced industry to treat some wastes that streams could handle themselves. In its 1973 report the National

Water Commission objected to technology-based standards, contending that the policy ignored the capacity of water to cleanse itself, raised pollution control costs and forced industry to dispose of wastes in other ways, increasing air and land pollution problems. The National Commission on Water Quality in 1976 also called for replacing technology standards with standards for water receiving wastes. Although technologies existed for eliminating all discharges into U.S. streams, the 1976 commission concluded that putting them to use would be prohibitively expensive, demand intensive energy use, and generate large quantities of residual materials that had to be disposed of in other ways.

The Reagan administration favored a return to receiving-water standards to take account of the different characteristics of water bodies, their use, and the preferences of local residents. Environmentalists, while conceding some difficulty with technology standards, objected that varying standards might be impossible to monitor and enforce.

**Discharge Permits.** The 1970 law required every public and private facility that discharged wastes directly into waters to obtain a permit declaring the discharge lawful. By 1984 EPA regional offices and 33 state governments with EPA-approved programs had issued more than 64,000 National Pollution Discharge Elimination Systems (NPDES) permits.

EPA in theory could take legal action against permit holders who violated the pollution levels authorized by their permits. Environmentalists criticized EPA for negotiating settlements and avoiding litigation. Federal and state budget cuts hindered efforts to monitor compliance with permit requirements.

The Reagan administration made several proposals to relax the permit system. It requested that Congress extend the term of industrial permits to 10 years from the existing five-year term. EPA also developed plans for a "bubble system" that allowed increased pollution from one outfall at an industrial plant so long as compensating controls at another emission source kept total polluted discharges from rising.

**Non-Point Runoff.** In implementing the 1972 law EPA focused on controlling industrial and municipal discharges that could be traced to the end of a single pipe. But Section 208 of the law also called for steps to control pollution that flowed into streams and lakes from water running off farms, rangelands, logging areas, mines, construction sites, city streets and highways.

Since such non-point pollution could not be regulated through a discharge permit system, Congress envisioned that state governments should control polluted run-offs through land-use planning, building codes and zoning laws. Section 208 directed state governments to develop area-wide waste treatment plans emphasizing controls on non-point sources. But EPA concentrated staff and budget resources on regulating point sources of water pollution, and funding for state and local planning was limited.

State and local officials remained reluctant to impose politically unpopular zoning building and restrictions, and EPA lacked authority and resources to force them to require land management practices that would reduce non-point pollution. While Congress in the early 1980s considered proposals to strengthen EPA's non-point program, a vigorous program to control polluted run-off would run counter to historic political resistance to federal government intervention in local land use decisions.

## 1983 Senate Committee Bills

In 1983 the Senate Environment and Public Works Committee drafted two measures extending the Clean Water Act and adjusting some provisions. Although the measures made few changes in existing law, neither reached the Senate floor in 1983 or 1984.

The Senate panel Sept. 21 reported a clean water reauthorization bill, drafted by John H. Chafee, chairman of the Subcommittee on Environmental Pollution, that amounted to a minor tuneup instead of a major overhaul of the 1972 law. The committee followed up Oct. 26 by reporting a second bill that dealt with one controversial area by attempting to prod quicker action to control pollution produced by water running off farm lands, streets and other non-point sources. Both measures were reported by unanimous votes.

The first bill reauthorized Clean Water Act enforcement for four years, at slightly higher spending levels and extended various deadlines for complying with EPA standards. It granted a Reagan administration proposal to extend the term of EPA pollution discharge permits for industry from five years to 10 years.

During markups Dave Durenberger, R-Minn., withdrew a proposal to strengthen federal controls on non-point water pollution carried into lakes and streams by water running off farms, mines, construction sites and city streets. Although the Clean Water Act directed states to draw up land use plans to control polluted runoff, EPA had given the program low priority.

In reporting the second bill, however, the Senate committee recommended legislation authorizing $300 million over fiscal 1985-87 in grants for state planning to control non-point pollution.

## House Legislation

The legislation the House passed in 1984 would have more than doubled authorized spending levels for EPA water pollution programs to more than $24 billion for fiscal 1985-88. For fiscal 1985 the House measure set a total spending ceiling of $6.2 billion, up from $2.6 billion under existing law. Responding to Reagan's demand for budget restraints, Congress in 1981 had cut annual authorizations for sewage treatment construction grants from $5 billion to $2.4 billion. In its bill, however, the House approved incremental increases in sewage grants that, in combination with a new $1.6 billion state-run revolving loan program, would restore total support for sewage construction to $5 billion a year by fiscal 1986-88.

While welcoming expanded funding, environmental groups opposed the legislation as reported by the House Public Works and Transportation Committee on June 6. Ed Hopkins, a lobbyist for the Clean Water Action Project, an environmental group, said the committee in effect was trying to reverse a number of reforms that Congress made in the construction grants program in 1981.

Among other things, the panel made new "collector" sewer lines under residential streets eligible for grants, conferring what environmentalists regarded as a subsidy for new housing developments that could further overload municipal sewage treatment capacity.

The House bill passed by a 405-11 vote on June 26. Before passing the bill, however, the House adopted a substitute to the committee measure offered by Robert A. Roe, D-N.J., chairman of the Public Works Subcommittee on Water Resources, with support from committee leaders. Roe's amendment embodied a compromise, concluded June 20, that defused most of the environmental groups' objections to the committee legislation. Although some opponents remained dissatisfied, the final House bill offered concessions to most groups with interests at stake in the water pollution program.

# Safe Drinking Water

Congress in 1984 fell short in a late-session drive to impose tougher federal standards for drinking water purity. In the last weeks of the session, the House Sept. 18 approved legislation to spur EPA into more aggressive enforcement of the Safe Drinking Water Act of 1974. The House-passed bill, a compromise among industry and environmental groups, also set up a $50 million-a-year program to force state governments to prevent contamination of groundwater formations that supplied half of the nation's drinking water supplies.

But the White House Office of Management and Budget (OMB) opposed the bill, objecting both to the cost of expanding EPA regulation and to the precedent of federal control over state groundwater management programs. The Senate Environment and Public Works Committee drafted a less ambitious bill as the session drew to a close, but House and Senate negotiators were unable to agree on compromise legislation that all sides could accept before the 98th Congress adjourned.

## Background

The Safe Drinking Water Act empowered EPA to set national purity standards for drinking water systems, to be enforced by the states or directly by the agency if states did not do so. The national standards were to be based on recommendations by the National Academy of Sciences about what levels of pollution were acceptable if human health were the only consideration. EPA was to adjust these ideal levels to take feasibility and cost into account.

Implementation of this ambitious scheme lagged for several reasons. The academy, in 1977, declined to say how much of any given contaminant could be considered safe. The modestly funded water program was not always a top EPA priority,

and agency efforts during the Carter administration to move ahead aggressively on several fronts were battered in court actions.

Rep. Dennis E. Eckart, D-Ohio, a co-sponsor of the 1984 legislation, said he had learned that "you can lead the EPA to water but you can't make them regulate it." The bill, he added, "will make them do it."

## House Legislation

Key members of the House Energy and Commerce Subcommittee on Health and the Environment drafted the House bill in private sessions with environmentalists and water industry officials. Subcommittee Chairman Henry A. Waxman, D-Calif., said EPA officials consulted on technical questions during negotiations had been "quite sympathetic to our position" on tighter drinking water standards.

Reported by the full Energy and Commerce Committee by voice vote Sept. 18, 1984, the bill imposed specific deadlines for EPA to set drinking water quality standards. The measure gave EPA expanded power to order compliance with the standards and required the agency to monitor water quality more frequently. Another major section barred injection of toxic wastes above or into underground aquifers holding drinking water supplies. The bill directed states to adopt EPA-approved plans for preventing contamination in underground drinking water supplies. It authorized $35 million in matching grants for state and local programs to protect aquifers that served as the sole source of drinking water for entire towns or regions.

The House Sept. 18 passed its bill, by a 366-27 vote, as members shrugged off administration opposition to the bill.

## Senate Compromise Negotiations

Senate Environment and Public Works Committee members drafted their own version in an effort to skirt OMB objections to the House bill. Reported on Sept. 28, the Senate bill also set deadlines for EPA standards, strengthened enforcement powers, expanded monitoring and barred injection of hazardous wastes near drinking water supplies.

But the Senate committee dropped House provisions requiring states to launch groundwater protection programs and settled for a $15 million-a-year demonstration program for keeping sole-source aquifers pure. It also reworded language in several provisions that House sponsors had drafted to limit EPA's discretion or make it easier for the agency to take action against pollution. Environmental groups disliked the Senate proposal and Waxman declared, "I'd rather have no bill at all."

Through informal negotiations House and Senate sponsors worked out most differences by Oct. 4. But Waxman refused to agree to a Senate amendment, backed by Alan K. Simpson, R-Wyo., that allowed a court decision on drinking water regulations to be appealed to the U.S. appeals court in the region where the dispute arose. Existing law required that such appeals be heard by the federal appeals court in Washington, D.C. Waxman and Sen. Max Baucus, D-Mont., also rejected a demand by Sen. Steven D. Symms, R-Idaho, to retain existing law by dropping stronger health-related language for setting water purity standards that appeared in both the House bill and the compromise proposal.

Lobbyists for environmentalists expressed regret at losing the legislation but claimed that both the judicial review amendment and existing health standards would cause lengthy delays in setting national drinking water standards. Such delays, they said, would defeat the basic purpose of the legislation, which was to force quick standard setting by EPA. *(Groundwater contamination, p. 149)*

# Sewer Grants

Lawmakers in 1981 sharply curtailed federal grants for building municipal sewage treatment systems. Prodded by the president, Congress on Dec. 16 cleared legislation that cut in half authorizations for the $5 billion-a-year program. To curb fast-rising federal costs, Congress also overhauled the system by which the government distributed financial assistance to force local governments to correct water pollution from municipal sewage wastes.

Environmentalists credited the federal grants with encouraging cities and towns throughout the nation to install or upgrade systems to collect and treat human wastes before dumping them into streams, lakes or oceans. Since authorizing the grants in 1972, however, Congress continually had expanded authorized spending to finance proposed projects in members' states and districts.

In its 1981 measure Congress authorized $2.4 billion a year for fiscal years 1982-85 for EPA grants for sewage treatment construction. But it revised the formula for distributing those grants in ways that reduced the federal government's obligation to finance projects that local officials wanted to build. Starting with fiscal 1985, the legislation cut federal contributions to 55 percent of construction costs. It also denied, starting in fiscal 1985, new EPA grants for expanding sewage treatment capacity to prepare booming regions for future population growth.

## Background

Congress launched the ambitious sewage plant construction program in 1972. The Federal Water Pollution Control Act, enacted over President Nixon's veto, authorized the federal government to make construction grants for up to 75 percent of the cost of upgrading municipal sewage treat-

Scientist at Amarillo, Texas, water treatment plant collects samples to test water purity.

ria that consumed organic wastes, by 1977. The law also required municipal governments to install the "best practicable" technology by mid-1983.

Congress amended the 1972 law when it passed the Clean Water Act of 1977. With the 1977 deadline for secondary treatment arriving, Congress gave municipalities that had yet to receive federal assistance an additional six years, until 1983, to clean up sewage discharges. Recognizing the need for more flexibility in effluent treatment methods, the 1977 law allowed cities to adopt "innovative and alternative technologies," such as recycling treated water or using it for irrigation, to comply with federal standards. The 1977 law authorized $5 billion a year through fiscal 1982 for EPA grants.

Congress amended the law again in 1980 to revise a requirement that industries discharging wastes into city-owned plants pay part of construction costs for those facilities. The 1980 measure also allowed states and cities to pick up more than their traditional 25 percent share of construction costs if their governors chose to do so.

## Construction Grant Criticisms

In the 1970s the sewage treatment plant construction grants grew rapidly into a multibillion-dollar program. Between 1972 and 1981 Congress authorized $38.98 billion and appropriated $33.3 billion for construction grants. EPA awarded 13,000 grants by 1981, and 3,200 plants were in operation.

Yet nearly every interest involved in the program — state governments that disbursed federal construction grants, engineers who built sewage treatment plants, congressional investigators, the congressional General Accounting Office (GAO) and EPA officials who administered the grants — criticized how it operated. Escalating costs were a major problem. Initial estimates were that the program would

ment plants throughout the nation to remove most pollutants from municipal wastes before discharging them into bodies of water.

The 1972 law replaced federal water pollution laws dating back to 1899. It set two goals: to make all waters fishable and swimmable by 1983 and to eliminate all polluted discharges into navigable waters by 1985. It required both industry and municipal governments to install modern treatment facilities to meet the goals. For industry, Congress set deadlines for installing improved pollution control equipment by 1977 and for cutting discharges further by using more sophisticated technology by 1984.

To improve public sewage treatment, the law directed local governments to begin secondary treatment of sewage wastes, removing 85 percent of pollutants with bacte-

require a total investment of $63 billion in 1972 dollars. But because of inflation, bureaucratic delays and population growth, EPA estimated that by the year 2000 it could cost $120 billion to reach the cleanup goals, with the federal share approaching $90 billion.

Critics contended that state governments, in allocating funds for sewage facility construction, had given low priority to municipalities that contributed the most to water pollution. Readily available federal construction grants encouraged city governments to build costly and sophisticated plants. But Congress provided no federal subsidy to operate and maintain the equipment. Without adequate funds and technically qualified operators, some local governments operated new plants well below their design capacity.

### Reagan Demand for Overhaul

Two months after taking office in January 1981, Reagan announced that he did not want to spend another penny on federal sewage construction grants until Congress overhauled the program. Reagan demanded and got a $1.7 billion rescission in fiscal 1981 grant appropriations but announced he would approve $2.4 billion for fiscal 1982 grants if Congress made the program more cost-effective.

In proposals sent to Congress in April 1981, Reagan sought to reduce the federal government's future potential obligation from a projected $90 billion to $23 billion. The administration wanted to eliminate federal funding for new collection systems, for "reserve" treatment capacity to serve future population growth, for replacing or repairing existing sewers or leaking pipes and for storing overflows from combined storm and sanitary sewer systems.

The administration requested a one-year authorization, through fiscal 1982, to make the timing of construction grants consistent with the rest of the Clean Water Act, which came up for review in 1982. State water program administrators sought a six-year reauthorization to make funding for the grant program more predictable. Environmentalists also favored extending the construction program for more than one year, giving Congress a chance to review national water standards, clean water deadlines, and other controversial provisions of the existing law without the threat of changes in the construction grant formula hanging over its deliberations.

### Congressional Action

Reagan's plan in effect called for shifting federal sewage construction grants from rural and high-growth regions in the South and West to older cities in the Northeast. It set off a bitter regional struggle in Congress between Sun Belt and Frost Belt state delegations.

Congress set the stage for overhauling the construction grant program in the budget-cutting reconciliation package it cleared in July 1981. By the end of the year Congress and the administration reached agreement on a four-year reauthorization bill that cut funding for construction grants in half and narrowed the scope of federally funded sewage treatment projects.

In the budget reconciliation measure, signed by the president Aug. 13, Congress limited fiscal 1981 construction grant authorizations to $2.5 billion. Yielding to Reagan's demand to revise the program, the House and Senate Public Works committees also agreed to language providing no fiscal 1982 funds unless legislation trimming federal grant commitments were enacted.

## Groundwater Contamination

For every gallon of fresh water flowing in the nation's rivers and confined by lakes, roughly 24 more are hidden underground — enough to fill the Great Lakes at least four times. Groundwater forms a vast natural resource that has grown in importance even as it has become increasingly endangered. U.S. consumption of groundwater rose from 34 billion gallons a day in 1950 to 88 billion gallons a day in 1980. Approximately half the nation now depends on groundwater — often untreated — for drinking water. Yet contaminated groundwater has been reported in every state. Household, farm and industrial wastes are being detected in the nation's underground water supplies with increasing frequency.

Groundwater protection is limited in part because there is no explicit national policy to protect its quality. There are, however, numerous federal and state laws that affect groundwater quality by regulating activities and substances that pollute it. At least 16 federal statutes authorize programs that in some way touch on groundwater protection. All 50 states have groundwater programs of some type; some have tougher regulations than those required under federal laws. Taken together, these programs have made significant strides in detecting, correcting and preventing groundwater contamination, particularly pollution caused by hazardous wastes.

Achievements under these programs have been significant but have not solved the problem. Cleanup responsibility is part of EPA's "superfund" program, which so far has cleaned up relatively few of the abandoned hazardous-waste sites scattered across the country. Instead of encouraging waste recycling and incineration, restrictions on land dumping have increased the use of deep-well injection to get rid of hazardous waste. But there is no guarantee that wastes pumped deep into the earth will not eventually pollute nearby groundwater supplies. And scientific uncertainty about the health consequences of waterborne chemicals has made federal standard-setting difficult, leaving disposal of many known contaminants uncontrolled. *(Superfund program, p. 163)*

Nonetheless, Congress in recent years has attempted to strengthen hazardous-waste laws to prevent further groundwater pollution. The House twice has approved measures that would require states to develop groundwater protection plans.

There is some doubt in the environmental community, however, that separate legislation is necessary. "I'm not convinced that what is needed is a single, comprehensive bill versus amendments to existing laws," said Velma M. Smith, director of the Environmental Policy Institute's groundwater protection project. Strengthening current laws may meet less political resistance than developing a new groundwater package, she added.

### Background

Groundwater collects in permeable strata of rock, sand or gravel called aquifers that usually lie within half a mile of the surface. The upper level, called the water table, can rise or fall depending on seasonal precipitation cycles and withdrawals by wells. The water in an aquifer flows with the slope of the underground formations at rates that range from a fraction of an inch to several feet per day, an important consideration in tracking groundwater pollution. Typical daily flow covers only a few inches. Contaminants most often reach groundwater by percolating down through the soil and spreading out in a plume, like smoke emerging from an upside-down smokestack. The course of the plume is determined by the general groundwater flow.

For most of this century, concern among health officials focused on drinking water contaminants, such as viruses and bacteria, that entered public supplies drawn from rivers and lakes. Chlorination was

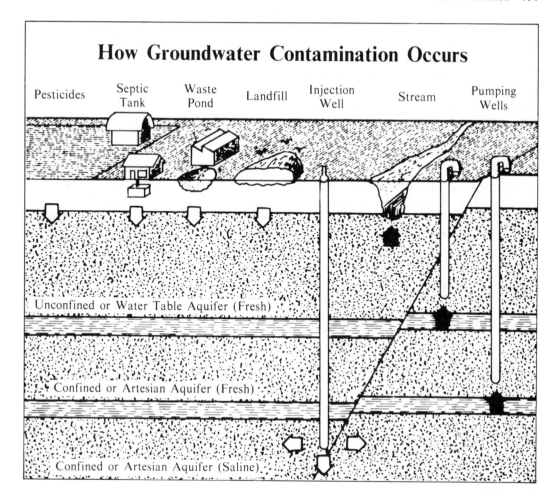

# How Groundwater Contamination Occurs

Pesticides | Septic Tank | Waste Pond | Landfill | Injection Well | Stream | Pumping Wells

Unconfined or Water Table Aquifer (Fresh)

Confined or Artesian Aquifer (Fresh)

Confined or Artesian Aquifer (Saline)

introduced as early as 1908 to rid drinking water of waterborne diseases such as cholera and typhoid. Chlorine works well as a disinfectant, but it has no effect on inorganic contaminants such as heavy metals — chromium, lead, mercury, tin and zinc — or on man-made organic chemicals, many of which are toxic at levels registering in parts per billion. These are the contaminants that are turning up not only in surface water but also in water pumped from underground.

Groundwater contaminants often reach much higher concentrations than surface water pollutants because there is little mixing and dispersal of toxic substances underground. Once contaminated, groundwater may remain so for hundreds of years. Cleaning a polluted aquifer is extremely difficult, if not impossible, with existing technology. Not surprisingly, the best solution to the problem is prevention.

## Magnitude of Pollution Problem

Estimates of the extent of groundwater contamination are based on educated guesswork. True levels may never be known because of the cost and technical requirements involved in developing quantitative assessments. Most experts believe that the level of contamination is relatively low. The

Office of Technology Assessment (OTA) reported in 1984 that only 1 or 2 percent of the nation's groundwater is believed to be polluted. An EPA survey found that only about 3 percent of public water systems drawn from groundwater are contaminated at levels that exceed standards the agency is considering setting for many contaminants — 5 to 50 parts per billion. But even these levels of contamination are significant because they appear in heavily populated areas where groundwater use is increasing.

Many of the pollutants are known or suspected to cause adverse health effects, including skin and eye damage, damage to the central nervous system, kidney and liver disease, and cancer. Accurate information linking specific contaminants to specific health problems frequently is not available. People often do not know they are drinking bad water because many contaminants are colorless, odorless and tasteless. Even when it is known that people drank polluted water, medical science seldom can establish a definitive link between the bad water and disease.

One exception occurred in Woburn, Mass., where two city water wells were contaminated with chloroform and TCE (trichloroethylene). In February 1984 doctors reported that there was a statistically significant relationship between the contamination and an increased incidence of childhood leukemia, birth defects and childhood disorders.

## Sources of Contamination

Improper or unsafe disposal of hazardous waste is a major source of groundwater contamination. More than 19,000 abandoned hazardous-waste dumps have been reported to EPA; it is not known how many are polluting groundwater. Landfills not licensed to accept hazardous wastes may nonetheless contain substances that contaminate groundwater. EPA has identified

75,000 industrial landfills, about which little is known. In addition, there are 18,500 municipal landfills, but few states require regular monitoring of groundwater quality at these facilities. No one knows how many are leaking contaminants. The number may be high because landfills frequently have been located on terrain regarded to have little commercial value, such as marshland, abandoned sand and gravel pits, old strip mines or limestone sinkholes, all of which act as conduits for contaminants.

Similar problems affect 181,000 ponds and lagoons used to treat, store or dispose of wastes generated by oil and gas production, mining, numerous industrial processes, agricultural activities and urban populations. Most are not lined with a protective shield to prevent wastes from percolating into the soil. EPA has reported that about 40 percent of the industrial and municipal impoundments are located in areas with thin or permeable soils, over aquifers that are or could be used for drinking water.

Leaking storage tanks, primarily those below ground, pose another threat to groundwater. Tanks are used to store everything from gasoline and toxic chemicals to waste products. Some experts say that between 75,000 and 100,000 of the estimated 1.4 million gasoline storage tanks buried at service stations nationwide are leaking.

These "point sources" of pollution are the most thoroughly documented and regulated. "Non-point" sources generally escape regulation but also pose serious hazards. Major non-point pollution sources include highway de-icing salts, pesticide and fertilizer runoff from fields, tailing piles used in mining operations to dispose of rock and dirt, and accidental spills and leaks.

The nation's 20 million household septic tanks and seepage from livestock manure and agricultural fertilizers are major sources of nitrate contamination. The U.S. Geological Survey's 1984 National Water

Summary reported that about 8,000 of nearly 124,000 wells surveyed contained nitrate concentrations that exceed federal standards for drinking water. Nitrate by itself is relatively harmless, but it can be converted to nitrite in the human body, causing a life-threatening disease in some infants and cancer risks among adults. The implications of the Geological Survey report may be more significant than the nitrate levels themselves. "The question is, if you have nitrates, what else do you have?" asked David W. Moody, chief of the agency's Water Summary and Long Range Planning Office.

### Curbing Contaminants

A comprehensive federal groundwater protection policy does not exist. In 1980, the last year of the Carter administration, EPA proposed a national protection plan that would have classified groundwater according to use and encouraged states to develop their own protection plans. Many states, especially those in the arid West, objected to what they considered federal interference in state water issues. The Reagan administration — already committed to reducing federal regulation — withdrew the proposal in 1981 for revision.

In August 1984 EPA issued its new "Ground Water Protection Strategy." The agency affirmed its belief that contamination is a severe problem growing worse, but it proposed no comprehensive federal legislation. Instead it said that EPA should provide support to state and local governments to help them develop their own programs. Environmental groups said the agency had ducked the issue. "This is EPA's non-strategy," said Jackie Warren, who heads the Toxic Waste Project at the Natural Resources Defense Council in New York.

The following month the House approved a reauthorization of the 1974 Safe Drinking Water Act that required EPA to monitor regularly underground drinking water sources and required the states to adopt plans, approved by EPA, to protect those groundwater sources from contamination. Disagreement with the Senate over those and other provisions killed that bill. The Senate in May 1985 and the House a month later passed another reauthorization bill containing similar language. Many of the provisions in the two bills were designed to push EPA to issue regulations in a more timely fashion. The differences between the two bills (the Senate version did not require states to draw up plans for protecting groundwater) must be resolved before a final bill can be sent to the president. The Reagan administration opposes both measures in their present form.

The Safe Drinking Water Act is the only federal law designed to ensure safe water at the tap. In that law, Congress gave EPA the authority to set quality standards and testing requirements for ground and surface water used by water systems serving more than 25 people and to regulate the disposal of liquid wastes into deep wells. The agency has been criticized for moving too slowly in both areas.

Since 1974 EPA has set 22 drinking water standards covering coliform bacteria, turbidity (cloudiness), man-made and naturally occurring radioactive materials, six pesticides and trihalomethanes — organic chemicals that contain chloroform, a carcinogen frequently found in drinking water. Environmental groups contend that EPA has been too cautious in issuing regulations to remove many other contaminants from drinking water.

Arnold Kuzmack, acting deputy director of EPA's Office of Drinking Water, explained the agency's caution: "The regulatory process requires more and more detailed backup that will stand up to court challenges. That means it takes a lot longer to make certain any piece of regulation is absolutely right." He added that the agency intends to issue standards for a number of additional organic chemicals in 1985. Both the House and Senate reauthorization bills would require EPA to set standards for more than 60 contaminants within three years.

### Cleaning Up Abandoned Dumps

Five years after Congress first passed superfund legislation, it is clear that waste dump contamination of soil and water is far more pervasive, more expensive to handle and more difficult to remedy than initially believed. EPA estimates indicate that there are from 1,400 to 2,200 waste sites that eventually will require cleanup. OTA puts the figure as high as 10,000. Depending on the actual number of sites, the cleanup could cost between $10 billion and $100 billion and take up to 50 years to complete, according to OTA. Funding for the first five years was set at $1.6 billion.

Of the 800 sites on EPA's priority cleanup list at the end of 1984, only six have been fully restored. The agency has begun to clean up 62 more sites and won commitments from private parties to clean up 72 others. In some cases, the problems have only been transferred elsewhere. "Some restoration efforts have consisted merely of transferring wastes from the contaminated areas to landfills, which themselves could be leaking," the Congressional Budget Office (CBO) said.

OTA has urged EPA to change its cleanup strategy. Rather than trying to clean permanently a limited number of the worst sites, leaving most abandoned dumps untouched, OTA advised a limited cleanup of all sites on the priority list. "Initial responses that accomplish the most significant and cost-effective reduction of risks and prevent sites from getting worse might cost about $1 million per site for most

sites," OTA said. To minimize groundwater contamination, the strategy emphasized covering sites and storing wastes, and excavating wastes only where technically and economically feasible. Phase two of the strategy would focus on permanent cleanup once specific goals were set and technologies available to remedy the problem.

### Deep-Well Disposal

The RCRA amendments imposed relatively few restrictions on deep-well injection operations. Environmental groups consider this a loophole in the law that could result in greater groundwater contamination. Deep-well injection already handles 58 percent of the nation's hazardous wastes, an estimated 10 billion gallons a year. With land disposal limited by the 1984 RCRA amendments, deep-well injection has become more attractive as a cheap alternative to recycling or destroying hazardous wastes. "I've personally witnessed a flood of deep-well injection permit requests [nationwide] since passage of the RCRA amendments," said Suzi Ruhl, a lawyer with the Legal Environmental Assistance Foundation in Tallahassee, Fla. EPA has estimated that it costs roughly $8 a ton to inject wastes into deep wells, $28 a ton to impound them in ponds and $50 a ton to dump them into landfills. Resource recovery and treatment technologies can run into hundreds of dollars a ton, although many of these techniques are in a competitive range with deep-well and surface disposal.

Injection of hazardous wastes into deep wells began in the 1950s as environmental laws began to protect surface waters from pollution. The wells carry wastes to porous sedimentary formations, typically sandstone, that lie between one-quarter mile and a mile below the surface. The wells are separated from drinking water aquifers by an impermeable layer of rock that theoretically seals the waste in an underground tomb. In practice, however, liquid waste occasionally has found its way to the surface, raising the specter of major groundwater pollution problems. Leaks also have been found in well casings, allowing pollutants to escape into the soil.

A 1984 EPA survey found 525 active hazardous-waste deep wells at 90 separate sites nationwide. Approximately two-thirds of the wells are in Texas and Louisiana. The next largest grouping, about 20 percent, are in the Great Lakes region. The chemical industry is the biggest user of deep-well injection, followed by the petroleum refining and petrochemical industries. EPA reports that about 41 percent of the injected wastes are corrosive and 36 percent are organic compounds. It is feared that corrosive waste may eat its way through the impermeable overlying rock and escape into groundwater.

It is the inability to ensure that wastes injected underground will remain where they are placed that most troubles those opposed to the method. "Great gaps in our knowledge of the subsurface and our inability to predict accurately the movement of wastes underground make it difficult, if not impossible, to ensure that, once pumped down the well, hazardous wastes will permanently remain within the zone of confinement," wrote Jane L. Bloom, an attorney for the Natural Resources Defense Council. In Vickery, Ohio, it was discovered in 1983 that 20 million gallons of waste had leaked from a commercial deep-well injection facility.

The House version of the Safe Drinking Act reauthorization would bar disposal of hazardous waste by underground injection above or into any geological formation within one quarter mile of a drinking water source. Environmentalists contend that at the least deep-well operators should be subject to the same standards as operators of land disposal facilities. Currently, deep-well operators are not required to demonstrate financial responsibility for cleanup activity or payment of damages to those harmed by leaks. Nor are they required to monitor groundwater near injection sites for contamination. Although monitoring of the well casing is required under the Safe Drinking Water Act, slow leaks often escape detection.

At congressional direction, EPA studied deep-well injection operations, issuing an interim report in May 1985. "The critical item of information is that we have found only three cases of drinking water contamination [from deep-well injection]," EPA's Arnold Kuzmack explained later. "And all three would have been prevented under current regulations. We have no cases of contamination that the current regulatory framework wouldn't handle. We find it difficult to conclude that there is a terrible problem. We certainly don't have the problem with deep wells that we have with landfills."

"The only way they haven't found problems is they haven't looked," said Ruhl, who has traveled extensively in her work on deep-well problems. Richard C. Fortuna, executive director of the Hazardous Waste Treatment Council, said EPA surveyed only 20 of the 90 deep-well injection sites nationwide when the agency should have surveyed them all.

## Alternative Solutions

Discouraging land disposal of hazardous wastes, the 1984 RCRA amendments were intended to promote the use of safer methods, such as chemical treatment to reduce hazards, incineration to destroy wastes, and chemical stabilization to neutralize hazardous wastes so they are no longer harmful. Yet, current incentives for waste reduction and treatment may be inadequate, CBO warned in its hazardous-waste report. "[W]aste reduction incentives could easily disappear in an atmosphere of regulatory uncertainty," the report said. If industry delays investments in waste reduction measures until the last minute, or commercial treatment facilities cannot be built fast enough to keep up with demand, the landfill ban might have to be eased, CBO analysts said. If industry makes no effort to reduce its volume of hazardous waste, national production may rise from the 266 million metric tons recorded in 1983 to about 280 million metric tons in 1990, according to the budget office.

Disturbed by this prospect, some have urged Congress to approve a waste disposal tax to prod industry to generate less waste and to force development of treatment technologies. The tax on wastes disposed of in landfills would be higher than the tax on safer disposal methods. Twenty states already have imposed various types of waste-end taxes on hazardous-waste generators. But EPA, after surveying eight states, said it is unclear if these taxes have had their intended effect.

The Reagan administration has proposed a waste-end tax to help finance superfund. It would tax waste disposal on land at $10.78 a metric ton; waste disposed of by other methods would be taxed at $2.87 a metric ton. To maintain a stable revenue base for superfund cleanup operations, waste-end tax rates would go up each year as waste production went down.

CBO, however, questioned whether the proposal would bring about the anticipated shift toward safer waste management practices, saying an $8-a-ton tax difference was "too small to erode the cost advantage currently held by landfills over more advanced technologies." The budget office said at least a $20-a-ton difference was needed to accomplish the goal of recycling and incineration.

It suggested a schedule of $25 a metric ton for untreated wastes placed in landfills, $5 a metric ton for treated wastes, $4 a metric ton for wastes injected into wells, and no tax for wastes that are incinerated, recycled or reused.

Environmental groups contend that the administration's proposal would only encourage the continued use of deep wells. "Taxing deep-well injection at one-third or one-fifth of what you tax land disposal isn't the way to encourage recycling or destruction of wastes," said Warren of the Natural Resources Defense Council. "As long as deep-well injection is cheap, we won't see much change."

# 9

# Hazardous Waste

In the 1970s environmental legislation was aimed at cleaning pollutants such as raw sewage and industrial wastes from waterways and smog and dirt from the air. By the end of the decade, with improvement in these areas, the emphasis shifted to different problems, some of them less visible but more insidious. Toxic substances in thousands of dumps scattered around the country posed enormous threats to public health and safety. Moreover, many of these sites were hidden from view in underground dumps where toxic substances leaked from their containers to pollute nearby soil and groundwater.

Love Canal, the site of a long-forgotten chemical dump on the outskirts of Niagara Falls, N.Y., became the national symbol in 1978 of the hidden health threats posed by toxic substances. More than 200 families were evacuated from their homes because dozens of chemicals had seeped into their basements. Four years later dangerously high levels of dioxin were found in Times Beach, Mo. The state and federal governments eventually bought the homes of about 700 families, permanently evacuating them and essentially closing down the town.

These incidents strengthened public support for action to clean up hazardous waste. But the then-new Reagan administration did have the same environmental goals.

The president, committed to getting the government "off the backs" of industry, attempted to deregulate by cutting back on funds for environmental programs. Several years later one result was a major scandal at the Environmental Protection Agency (EPA).

## EPA Scandal

Congressional investigations into the Reagan administration's handling of toxic waste cleanups forced EPA Administrator Anne M. Burford (formerly Anne M. Gorsuch) to resign her post in 1983. Burford quit on March 9 after months of controversy and a bitter constitutional clash with Congress. For more than a year six congressional panels had been investigating charges of mismanagement and improper conduct by EPA officials in running a $1.6 billion "superfund" program for cleaning up abandoned hazardous waste dumps.

The highly publicized scandals threw EPA into its worst turmoil since Congress created the agency in 1970. In addition to Burford, 20 top EPA aides either resigned or were fired as Congress probed allegations of political manipulation, "sweetheart" deals, conflicts of interest, perjury and destruction of documents by agency officials.

The resulting disclosures added to congressional misgivings about administration policies that stressed voluntary industry compliance with environmental laws in place of vigorous EPA legal action against abuses. The superfund fracas also focused congressional attention on the administration's deep cutbacks in EPA's operating budget. Public alarm over the scandals and environmental group pressure for tougher EPA enforcement contributed to congressional approval of sharply increased agency budgets for fiscal 1984 and 1985.

On the day Burford resigned, the White House agreed to meet House subcommittee demands for access to EPA superfund documents. In return, the House later dropped a 1982 contempt citation against Burford for refusing — on Reagan's orders — to turn the papers over to a House oversight committee.

Former EPA Assistant Administrator Rita M. Lavelle, director of the superfund program, was the only agency official who faced criminal charges as a result of the controversy. Lavelle, who was fired by Reagan on Feb. 7, 1983, was sentenced to six months in prison and a $10,000 fine in 1984 after being convicted on charges that she lied under oath during congressional testimony.

Trying to repair political damage from the revelations, the president March 21, 1983, picked William D. Ruckelshaus, who had been EPA's first director in 1970-73, as Burford's replacement. Before resigning at the end of 1984, Ruckelshaus restored public and congressional confidence in an agency that held responsibility for implementing key federal air, water and toxic pollution control programs.

## EPA's Mission

In the Resource Conservation and Recovery Act of 1976 Congress directed EPA to regulate how business handled and disposed of dangerous liquid and solid waste materials. In 1977 officials discovered that chemicals leaking from an abandoned dump were poisoning residents in the Love Canal subdivision, near Niagara Falls, N.Y. As more abandoned chemical wastelands were found in states throughout the nation, Congress drew up the superfund law to give EPA authority to clean them up to protect public health and the environment.

Congress cleared the superfund law on Dec. 3, 1980, a month after the presidential election. It fell to the Reagan administration to begin implementing the program that President Carter had proposed. In the 1980 law, known as the Comprehensive Environmental Response, Liability and Compensation Act, Congress created the $1.6 billion superfund to pay for immediate cleanup costs, avoiding time-consuming lawsuits to establish which persons or companies should be held responsible. The law contained liability provisions for government action to recover the cleanup costs and collect damages from dumpers who were responsible for hazardous waste contamination. It financed about 86 percent of the fund through a tax on the chemical and oil industries, with the remainder provided through congressional appropriations.

The law required EPA to draw up a list of priority cleanup sites by July 1981, then update that list at least every year. But the agency took nearly two years, until the end of 1982, to compile a list of 418 dump sites that officials considered most dangerous to public health. Those sites received top priority, making them eligible to be cleaned up with superfund money as soon as EPA completed a two-month comment period.

## Congressional Investigations

In the meantime, however, congressional critics charged that EPA had been dragging its feet on cleaning up dangerous wastes while officials compiled the list. In addition, they questioned settlements that EPA had negotiated with chemical companies to recover costs of cleaning up wastes for which those firms were responsible. Two House subcommittees — the Public Works and Transportation Subcommittee on Investigations and Oversight and the Energy and Commerce Subcommittee on Oversight and Investigations — began investigating the superfund program.

The committees sought EPA superfund program documents as part of their investigations. On Nov. 22, 1982, Burford was served with a subpoena that sought virtually every EPA document on 160 priority waste sites. Burford said the subpoena covered 787,000 pages, and she refused to turn over 74 documents. She said she acted on written orders from President Reagan, dated Nov. 30, in which he instructed her to withhold certain documents because their dissemination outside the executive branch "would impair my solemn responsibility to enforce the law." The White House contended that some of the subpoenaed documents concerned potential litigation and could jeopardize enforcement of the superfund law.

As other committees joined in with their own investigations, the scope of inquiry widened to include additional charges:

—Possible conflict of interest, as in the case of superfund director Lavelle, who eventually legally removed herself from a California dumping case that involved her former employer, Aerojet-General Corp.

—Alleged political manipulation of superfund cleanup grants. Lavelle and Burford, for example, were accused of withholding a grant for the Stringfellow Acid Pits in California to avoid boosting the reelection campaign of Gov. Edmund G. Brown Jr., a Democrat.

—Possible destruction of evidence and obstruction of the congressional inquiry. One concern was raised by the installation of paper shredders at EPA's hazardous waste office after Burford refused to turn over subpoenaed documents.

**Anne M. Burford, President Reagan's first EPA administrator, was forced to resign her position March 9, 1983.**

—Alleged use of political "hit lists" to mark for termination EPA science advisers and civil service employees, as well as political appointees, who disagreed with the administration's policy of easing environmental regulation over industry.

### White House Stand

The White House initially took a hard-line stand on the congressional probes, resisting demands for internal EPA documents on grounds of executive privilege. After the controversy mushroomed in early 1983, however, the administration backed down and nudged Burford into resignation.

The dispute over congressional access to EPA documents meanwhile escalated a dispute over environmental policy into a confrontation over the constitutional powers of Congress and the president. Following Justice Department advice, Reagan claimed

Rita M. Lavelle, former director of the EPA superfund, was the only official prosecuted in the wake of EPA scandal. President Reagan fired Lavelle Feb. 2, 1983.

the documents were protected by executive privilege because they discussed sensitive enforcement strategy for pending legal cases on hazardous waste dumping. In response, the House voted 259-105 on Dec. 16, 1982, to hold Burford in contempt of Congress.

But the Justice Department refused to prosecute Burford. Instead, it filed suit on the day the House voted, seeking to block action on the contempt citation. The department claimed that the Constitution implied a privilege for the president to ensure that law enforcement files and the policy deliberation process remained confidential. On Feb. 3, 1983, however, the U.S. District Court in Washington, D.C., granted a motion filed by lawyers for the House of Representatives to dismiss the Justice lawsuit.

## Compromise on Documents

In the month after the Justice Department suit was dismissed, the administration and congressional subcommittees worked out compromise arrangements that gave members access to most EPA documents they had been seeking.

White House officials contacted Rep. Elliott H. Levitas, D-Ga., chairman of the House Public Works Subcommittee on Investigations, and they reached agreement on Feb. 18 to permit panel members and staff to see the disputed documents under conditions to make sure that they were kept confidential. At a news conference two days earlier, Reagan said he no longer would insist on executive privilege in the matter. The president also announced that the Justice Department would mount its own investigations into alleged wrongdoing in EPA's hazardous waste program.

In return, Levitas agreed to try to persuade the House to cancel the contempt citation against Burford. The documents dispute dragged on until March 9, until Burford resigned and the White House finally satisfied demands by four other House subcommittees for agency documents. The House Aug. 3 by voice vote approved a resolution dropping the Burford contempt citation. The resolution asserted the House position that executive branch officers must comply with congressional subpoenas and that federal prosecutors had a duty to proceed against anyone formally cited for contempt after defying such a subpoena.

## Outcome of EPA Investigations

Twenty major EPA officials ultimately resigned in the wake of Burford's departure, although barely half a dozen had actually been accused of wrongdoing and only Lavelle faced criminal charges. The Justice Department said its investigation had produced insufficient evidence to warrant criminal prosecution of Burford and five of her top aides.

Charges varied for each official. Most of the charges that Justice investigated involved conflicts of interest, destruction of subpoenaed documents and false testimony. Levitas used the term "whitewash" to describe the department's report.

The charges against Lavelle stemmed from agency decisions on the Stringfellow Acid Pits dump site in California. Lavelle's former employer, Aerojet-General Corp., was listed as a dumper at the site. On June 18, 1982, Lavelle recused (legally removed) herself from decisions on the Stringfellow case. She testified under oath at three congressional hearings that she learned of Aerojet's involvement only the day before.

But on Aug. 4, 1982, Lavelle was indicted on charges of perjury and obstructing a congressional investigation. The indictment charged that Lavelle had lied under oath about when she first knew about Aerojet's involvement, and trial witnesses testified that she had been told as early as May 28, 1982. The indictment also charged that Lavelle had lied when she denied that superfund cleanup grants had been used for political purposes. A federal jury in Washington, D.C., found Lavelle guilty on Dec. 1 of four of the five counts. Lavelle began serving six-month sentence on April 19, 1985.

Congressional panels slowed their EPA investigations after Ruckelshaus replaced Burford. The Oversight and Investigations Subcommittee issued a report on Aug. 30, 1984, revealing that Lavelle had repeated contacts with White House officials as she allegedly targeted superfund grants to help Republican and hurt Democratic candidates prior to 1982 congressional elections. The report also detailed charges that Lavelle removed or concealed documents from her office after Reagan fired her.

All four Republicans on the 13-member subcommittee disputed the report's conclusions and charged that the timing of its release during the 1984 presidential campaign was politically motivated. Dingell ac-

knowledged in transmitting the report to the full Energy and Commerce Committee that Ruckelshaus had improved EPA's performance. Dingell also noted that Reagan was opposing pending legislation to expand the superfund program while "only six of the 546 sites on the national priority list of the most hazardous sites in the nation have been cleaned up." *(Superfund, p. 163)*

## Hazardous Waste Controls

Responding to the EPA scandals, Congress in 1984 tightened federal controls over how business and industry handled hazardous chemical wastes. Completing action that the House had started in 1982, Congress Oct. 5 cleared a measure that strengthened EPA power to regulate "cradle-to-grave" storage and disposal of toxic, flammable, corrosive and explosive waste materials.

In passing this legislation, Congress was prodded by growing public concern about environmental contamination by hazardous waste products that leaked or were dumped into the nation's soil and water. The bill ordered EPA to enforce more aggressively the Resource Conservation and Recovery Act of 1976 (RCRA), the federal government's chief law regulating the handling of dangerous wastes that were generated by industrial and business activity.

In extending the 1976 law for four years, Congress tried to close loopholes that Rep. James J. Florio, D-N.J., the chief House sponsor of the 1984 measure, said had freed roughly half of the nation's hazardous wastes from EPA rules requiring safe disposal. In the most controversial crackdown, Congress directed EPA to begin regulating small business operations such as gasoline stations and dry cleaners that produced smaller quantities of dangerous materials. Other provisions regulated underground tanks for storing petroleum and other substances and imposed sharp restrictions on disposing of wastes in landfills, ponds, underground mines, caves and salt formations.

Through those and other provisions Congress took its most concrete legislative steps to correct what members viewed as EPA's mismanagement of the government's campaign to clean up hazardous wastes that threatened public health and safety throughout the country.

With the scandals in mind, Congress set tight deadlines for EPA to enforce rules for handling and disposing of hazardous materials that previously had escaped federal regulation. In drafting the legislation, House and Senate committees spelled out requirements in extensive detail, banning some practices by law unless EPA issued regulations finding them to be safe. The U.S. chemical industry and other critics of the legislation maintained that the authors were trying to write detailed regulations instead of law, going into areas where members of Congress lacked technical competence to make scientific judgments.

## Background

Congress passed the RCRA in 1976 to prevent future hazardous-dump problems. The act set minimum requirements for storage, treatment and disposal of corrosive, explosive, ignitible or toxic wastes. Facilities covered under the law included storage tanks; surface impoundments; waste piles; land treatment sites; landfills; incinerators; thermal, physical and biological treatment operations; and injection wells. It required those who generate or handle hazardous wastes to obtain an operating permit from EPA or from states with RCRA programs approved by the agency. Under the act, EPA has listed more than 400 specific wastes for regulation. A tracking system requires an EPA manifest to accompany each of these wastes at each stage of ship-

ment, storage, treatment, recycling and final disposal. The agency delegates most enforcement to the states.

EPA got off to a slow start in implementing RCRA. Final regulations for land disposal of hazardous wastes, for example, were not issued until Jan. 26, 1983. Through 1984, EPA and states with approved programs had issued only 968 final permits to the estimated 5,000 treatment, storage and disposal facilities that eventually must have permits to stay in operation. Moreover, even facilities that meet RCRA guidelines may not be safe over the long run. According to the Congressional Budget Office (CBO), 45 RCRA-regulated facilities have been closed and are now listed for cleanup under the Superfund. "[I]t is unclear whether the EPA can prevent more RCRA-regulated sites from becoming future superfund candidates," CBO said.

Congress attempted to strengthen RCRA with passage of the Hazardous and Solid Waste Amendments of 1984. The toughest new provision would ban land disposal of all bulk liquid hazardous wastes. It also set a series of deadlines for EPA to determine whether 400 hazardous wastes adversely affected health or the environment. If EPA did not act by the deadline for each specified contaminant, land disposal of that contaminant would be banned. Operators of hazardous-waste landfills were required to provide double liners, groundwater monitoring, leak detection and collection of contaminants that leach into the surrounding soil. The amendments also regulated underground storage tanks, primarily gasoline tanks, for the first time.

Under the original act, EPA did not require generators of less than one metric ton (2,200 pounds) a month of hazardous waste to dispose of their wastes in RCRA-approved facilities. Consequently, these wastes often were dumped into city landfills or sewers connected with city wastewater treatment plants. To protect both surface and underground public water supplies, the amended act lowered the regulatory threshold to 100 kilograms a month.

The cost of compliance with RCRA regulations runs into the billions annually and is expected to climb under the new amendments. CBO put annual industry expenditures, without considering available tax benefits, between $4.2 billion and $5.8 billion in 1983. The figure is expected to increase to between $8.4 billion and $11.2 billion in 1990.

### 1983 Action

Spurred by the EPA controversies, the House Energy and Commerce Committee and the Senate panel in 1983 drafted similar legislation to reauthorize and strengthen RCRA enforcement. The House passed its measure in November, but the Senate waited a full year before acting on its committee's proposals.

Both the House and Senate committees recommended that Congress expand EPA enforcement powers and strengthen the right of private citizens to sue violators of the 1976 law. Both bills placed tighter restrictions on landfill or pond disposal and set ambitious timetables for EPA to complete regulatory steps that had dragged on for years.

Despite objections by small business groups, the House and Senate measures also ordered EPA to start regulating firms and institutions that produced smaller quantities of hazardous wastes. Existing EPA regulations exempted generators of less than 1,000 kilograms, or 2,200 pounds, per month of hazardous waste. At least 20 states already regulated small-quantity generators more stringently than the federal government.

However, trade associations for dry cleaners, auto repair shops and other small businesses objected to proposals for bringing small-quantity generators under the reg-ulatory umbrella. To do so would mean unjustified costs and paperwork for their members, they said.

### 1984 Compromise Legislation

The bill reauthorizing RCRA for fiscal 1985-88 was signed into law Nov. 8, 1984. Most provisions of the House and Senate versions had aimed at closing loopholes in existing law, and their differences were minor. Conferees blended House and Senate provisions for regulating small quantity generators, giving EPA until March 31, 1986, to issue rules for businesses and institutions that produced between 100 and 1,000 kilograms (220 to 2,200 pounds) of hazardous wastes per month.

To limit disposal of hazardous wastes on land, the conference bill immediately banned depositing them in underground mines and salt formations until EPA took certain regulatory actions. It also set a statutory prohibition, effective six months after enactment, on placing bulk or non-containerized liquid wastes in any landfill. It banned land disposal of specified wastes entirely, although the measure allowed extension of the effective date if no alternative disposal means were immediately available.

Avoiding a last-minute snarl, Senate conferees agreed to drop Senate provisions revising the 1980 superfund law that House negotiators insisted be considered in separate legislation extending the superfund program. The House accepted Senate provisions to regulate underground storage tanks, a problem that the House had dealt with through a separate superfund bill it passed in August.

## Superfund Renewal

The Senate in 1984 blocked a House election-year drive to expand the federal superfund program to clean up abandoned hazardous waste dumps. Amid partisan bickering the House passed legislation to renew the superfund for five years and boost its funding to $10.2 billion. The program, financed by congressional appropriations and a tax on crude oil and raw chemicals, gave EPA power to clean up dangerous wastes that business and industry had left unattended at sites scattered across the country.

President Reagan opposed renewing the program until 1985, when taxes that Congress imposed to pay for the cleanup were due to expire. House Democrats, pushing for an expanded cleanup effort, excoriated the president and charged that the Republican-controlled Senate had "caved in" to administration pressure to bottle up the superfund legislation.

Under political heat from environmental groups, the Senate Environment and Public Works Committee in September drafted a separate $7.5 billion superfund reauthorization, but the full Senate never voted on the measure.

## Background

Before 1976, toxic, corrosive, flammable, and explosive materials could be legally dumped just about anywhere. Congress imposed federal regulation on hazardous wastes in the Resource Conservation and Recovery Act of 1976. By then, however, decades of abuse had left hazardous wastes scattered at thousands of neglected sites across the nation. In many dumps the hazardous materials had begun leaking into surrounding soil and underlying groundwater aquifers. At President Carter's urging, Congress created the superfund program in 1980. *(Groundwater contamination, p. 149)*

**1980 Law.** In the Comprehensive Environmental Responses, Compensation and Liability Act of 1980, Congress set up a $1.6 billion fund to cover the costs of cleaning up wastes that had been abandoned by those responsible for dumping.

The law gave EPA power to go after whoever had caused the problem — including companies that generated or hauled the wastes or that owned or operated dump sites. If dump owners had disappeared, EPA could hold companies whose wastes had ended up in the dumps completely responsible for cleaning them up. If those responsible refused to act, EPA could clean up wastes itself, then sue them for up to three times the actual cost of the cleanup.

To finance cleanups if EPA was unable to recover costs, Congress set up a Hazardous Substance Response Trust Fund — dubbed the "superfund" — with 12.5 percent of the funds from general Treasury revenues and the rest from a tax on petroleum and on raw chemical "feedstocks" used to manufacture chemical products. EPA estimated that 71 percent of the nation's hazardous wastes came from the chemical industry.

**Superfund Problems.** It fell to the Reagan administration to launch the cleanup program. But environmentalists and congressional backers of the program suspected that EPA officials whom Burford appointed were less than enthusiastic about forcing industry to pay for correcting hazardous waste problems.

Among the problems congressional investigators found was that EPA was slow in setting up procedures needed to get the program started and slow in spending the money in the fund. Another finding was that EPA preferred to negotiate rather than litigate against dumpers to collect costs, a preference that was delaying cleanup, recovering less than full costs and settling for inadequate cleanups at many sites. EPA was charged with making "sweetheart deals" with industry.

As EPA officials meanwhile found more and more abandoned waste sites, it became clear that the $1.6 billion that Congress provided for a four-year period

Dump sites such as this one with corroding metal containers are now considered the major environmental hazard.

fell far short of what was needed to correct threats to health and safety. By 1984 EPA estimated that the nation held at least 22,000 dangerous waste dumps, with as many as 2,200 requiring urgent cleanups at a cost of between $8.4 billion and $16 billion. In 1985 the congressional Office of Technology Assessment (OTA) estimated that the superfund program would require $100 billion over 50 years to complete its task.

In his January 1984 State of the Union message, Reagan said he would support extension of the superfund progam beyond 1985. EPA Administrator Ruckelshaus, Burford's successor, said in March that the administration would wait until 1985 to propose a reauthorization measure. The administration in 1985 proposed spending $5.3 billion on the superfund cleanup effort under a five-year extension.

## 1984 Action

With House Democrats eager to move ahead, Chairman Florio led a 1984 drive to renew and expand the superfund a year ahead of schedule. After the subcommittee in April rejected his initial proposal, Florio negotiated a compromise reauthorization measure that won backing from key Democratic committee chairmen and influential House Republicans, who often championed chemical industry positions on toxic waste issues.

**House Committee Action.** The compromise measure, approved by the full Energy and Commerce Committee June 20 by a 38-

3 vote, provided for a cleanup fund of approximately $9 billion for fiscal 1986-90. Florio initially had sought provisions to compensate toxic dump victims, but the compromise dropped them. It did authorize health studies and measures to mitigate victims' exposure to hazardous wastes, and it kept provisions to authorize private lawsuits in federal courts to seek compensation for injuries caused by toxic dumping. Victims could sue for damages under existing liability laws in most states, but standards of proof and other legal obstacles made it hard for them to win their cases.

Two other House committees considered the measure before it went to the floor. The Public Works and Transportation Committee July 31 accepted Florio's bill virtually unchanged. But the Ways and Means Committee, with jurisdiction over the bill's tax provisions, Aug. 2 approved by a 27-5 vote a package of amendments that shifted superfund tax burdens to oil companies from the chemical industry and other hazardous waste generators while boosting general Treasury revenue contributions. The Ways and Means amendments raised total funding for the five-year extension to $10.2 billion. The House approved the bill on Aug. 10.

**Partisan Sniping.** In the 323-33 vote, the superfund reauthorization drew overwhelming support from House Republicans as well as Democrats. Yet partisan sniping broke out during floor debate as Republicans objected to hasty legislative action while Democrats countered that the bill was needed to prod the administration into cleaning up more waste sites. "I don't know the genesis of this measure," Barber B. Conable, R-N.Y., complained Aug. 9, "but I suspect it was the San Francisco Democratic convention."

Vice presidential candidate Geraldine Ferraro, D-N.Y., had commented on "the sorry performance of the EPA," underscoring the political emphasis that Democrats placed on superfund reauthorization. She repeated her remarks before television cameras on the Capitol lawn, flanked by Florio and environmental group leaders.

**Senate Inaction.** After the August congressional recess for the Republican National Convention, the Senate Environment panel Sept. 13 approved a "bare-bones" $7.5 billion superfund reauthorization bill introduced by Chairman Robert T. Stafford, R-Vt., and Jennings Randolph, D-W.Va., the panel's ranking minority member. The Senate committee proposed basically to renew the existing superfund law with few changes. The Senate Finance Committee held mid-September hearings on extending superfund taxes, but it took no action on the legislation.

Although the tax that finances cleanup of hazardous waste dumps was due to expire Sept. 30, 1985, Congress had not passed legislation to reauthorize the superfund before the August 1985 recess.

# 10

# Federal Land Management

Through the 1970s environmentalists looked to the secretary of the interior as what Rep. Morris K. Udall, D-Ariz., called "the nation's conservationist. This is the guy who's guardian of the resources, this is the man who gets up in the morning and asks what he can do to preserve the endangered species and so on."

Secretary of the Interior James G. Watt had a quite different idea about the responsibilities of his office. As a former leader of the "Sagebrush Rebellion," Watt was committed to the "privatization" of the nation's vast natural resources, especially those on public lands in the West. "These public lands remain today among our greatest untapped assets," he said in testimony before the Senate Subcommittee on Energy and Mineral Resources in June 1983.

Congress was frequently at odds with Secretary Watt over policy for managing federally owned lands. In a series of budget battles, the 97th Congress rejected Watt's plan to halt federal land purchases for expansion of the national park system and divert funds to improving existing park facilities.

Under Watt's direction the National Park Service slowed the pace of land acquisition. In contrast to the late 1970s, moreover, the 97th Congress made only minor additions to the park system. Sharp differences between the Republican Senate and the Democratic House also slowed congressional action on the Carter administration's 1979 proposals for expanding the national wilderness system within U.S. national forests.

Following Watt's resignation in 1983, William P. Clark, President Reagan's close adviser, took over as interior secretary and quieted the angry protests that Watt's policies had stirred among House Democrats and environmental group leaders. Congress nonetheless continued to debate major policy choices between developing federally owned resources and preserving the environmental quality of national parks, forests and rangelands.

In what could prove one of its most lasting environmental decisions, Congress in 1984 settled some long-running disputes over preserving wilderness within the national forest system. Through 20 separate bills the House and Senate added more than 8.3 million acres to the federal wilderness system. In a compromise that environmentalists and timber companies negotiated as the 1984 presidential election approached, Congress at the same time released another 13.5 million acres of undeveloped national forest lands for logging, mining, oil and gas exploration and other commercial uses.

Clark defused another often bitter dis-

# Wilderness Legislation
## 1981-84

The 97th Congress gave federal wilderness protection to national forest lands in the following states.

| State | Acres Designated |
| --- | --- |
| Alabama | 6,780 |
| Indiana | 12,953 |
| Missouri | 6,888 |
| West Virginia | 47,800 |

The 98th Congress gave federal wilderness protection to national forest lands in the following states.

| State | Acres Designated |
| --- | --- |
| Arizona | 1,054,000* † |
| Arkansas | 91,100 |
| California | 3,210,560† ‡ |
| Florida | 49,150† |
| Georgia | 14,439 |
| Mississippi | 5,500 |
| Missouri | 16,500 |
| Montana | 259,000 |
| New Hampshire | 77,000 |
| New Mexico | 27,840* |
| North Carolina | 68,750† |
| Oregon | 859,300 |
| Pennsylvania | 9,705† |
| Tennessee | 24,942 |
| Texas | 34,346 |
| Utah | 750,000 |
| Vermont | 41,260† |
| Virginia | 55,984† |
| Washington | 1,038,878* † |
| Wisconsin | 24,339 |
| Wyoming | 884,049† |

* Includes acreage managed by Interior Department's Bureau of Land Management.
† Excludes additional protective designations, such as Wilderness Study Area or National Recreation Area, made in bill.
‡ Includes 1,418,230 acres of land already in national parks.

pute by resuming federal land purchases, which Watt had proposed halting, to expand national parks and wildlife refuges. The Senate again killed House legislation to impose tougher controls on development near national park boundaries, however. Congress also cleared measures that enlarged the federal wild river system.

While Clark scaled back Watt's ambitious mineral leasing plans, Senate Republicans from Western states in general remained pleased with the Reagan administration's emphasis on developing federal lands that were managed by the Interior Department's Bureau of Land Management (BLM) and the U.S. Forest Service, an Agriculture Department agency. *(Mineral leasing, p. 39)*

Clark on Jan. 1, 1985, announced that he was resigning the Interior post. Reagan named Energy Secretary Donald P. Hodel, who previously had served as an under secretary under Watt, to replace Clark.

## Forest Wilderness System

Congress progressed slowly during 1981-82 in expanding the federal wilderness system. By the end of its second session, the 97th Congress had cleared legislation to designate 132,011 acres in five Southern and Midwestern states as protected wilderness within U.S. national forests. But environmental groups continued to spar with the Reagan administration, timber companies and other commodity interests over how much of the 187-million-acre national forest system should be set aside for preservation.

As a result, separate legislation to protect much larger forest lands in California, Montana, Wyoming and Oregon died when the 97th Congress adjourned. And President Reagan on Jan. 14, 1983, vetoed a 1982 bill that designated wilderness in Florida, objecting to buying phosphate mining leases in Osceola National Forest.

The stalemate thus carried over to the 98th Congress as the House and Senate tried to decide the future of 62 million acres, roughly a third of the national forests, that the U.S. Forest Service had studied in the late 1970s for possible wilderness designation. Western economic interests, joined by the Reagan administration, were pressing Congress to clear the way for timber harvesting and other uses on 36 million acres that the Forest Service recommended be kept open for "multiple-use" management. Even as Congress debated those proposals, a 1982 federal court decision blocked development of those lands.

In 1984 Congress settled the status of more than 20 million acres of undeveloped land in U.S. national forests. Ending years of uncertainty, the Senate and House cleared bills setting aside more than 8.3 million acres of forest lands in 20 states as federally protected wilderness. Those laws vastly expanded the national system for preserving pristine lands that Congress created in the Wilderness Act of 1964.

In the same measures Congress freed huge tracts in the national forests for possible logging, mining, oil and gas exploration and other commercial ventures. Under a compromise accepted by environmental groups and timber companies, the bills released 13.5 million acres of roadless lands that had been studied — but not yet selected — as wilderness preserves for multiple-use management by the U.S. Forest Service over the following 15 years.

President Reagan signed all of the 1984 wilderness bills, although his administration generally objected to keeping federal lands off limits to development. After two decades of debate, however, the president's conservative Republican allies in the Senate were eager to wrap up a prolonged wilderness review that had tied up millions of acres in studies, planning, lawsuits and legislative maneuvering.

## Background

In the Wilderness Act of 1964, Congress established the national wilderness system to preserve, by law, federally owned lands that still were largely untouched by man.

The Interior Department and the Forest Service managed most federal lands under multiple-use policies that tried to balance commercial development, recreation, wildlife habitat and other values. The 1964 law put lands within the wilderness system off-limits to logging, mining, drilling, road building, motorized travel and other activities that would disrupt their natural silence and permanently mar their primeval qualities. Once added to the system, most wilderness lands could be used only for hiking, horseback riding, hunting, fishing, canoeing, nature study and other activities that left no lasting evidence that people had been there.

It took an act of Congress to designate public lands as part of the federal wilderness system. By preserving wild lands through law, wilderness advocates argued, Congress would prevent federal management agencies from later reopening them for development without congressional consent. While Congress had created most wilderness areas in the lower 48 states from the 187 million-acre national forest system, it also had designated large tracts within the national parks and federal wildlife refuges for preservation by statute. Through a 1976 law Congress also ordered BLM, an agency that controlled nearly 249 million acres in Alaska and Western states, to study 28 million acres of those public lands for possible wilderness status.

Most of the wilderness areas designated by the 1964 law tended to be high mountain peaks and remote forests in Western states that held sparse timber and few mineral resources. But conservationists, in

The Delaware Water Gap, a national recreation area authorized by Congress in 1965, runs along the river boundary of Pennsylvania and New Jersey and provides recreation for thousands of people.

of recreation and deny the U.S. mineral industry a chance to explore lands for potential oil and gas and other resources. Once Congress created a wilderness, they pointed out, it might be impossible to persuade the House and Senate to pass another law reopening lands for development.

Caught in the middle of the debate, the Forest Service twice during the 1970s surveyed unspoiled lands within the national forests in an effort to settle, once and for all, on final boundaries for the wilderness system. During the Ford administration the service conducted a study of 56 million acres of land where no roads had yet been built. The Roadless Area Review and Evaluation (RARE I), completed in 1976, recommended that Congress classify about 12 million acres as wilderness. But the Sierra Club challenged the RARE I study in court, and the Forest Service settled out of court by agreeing to complete a land use plan and environmental impact statement before allowing any use that would alter the wild characteristics of any roadless area.

After the Carter administration took office in 1977, M. Rupert Cutler, a former Wilderness Society official who was appointed assistant secretary of agriculture for natural resources and environment, directed the Forest Service to conduct a second roadless area study (RARE II). With the U.S. timber industry eager to harvest more federal forests, the Carter administration wanted to settle the status of 62 million acres and draft an environmental impact statement that could hold up under court challenges. Following the agency's recommendations, President Carter in 1979 proposed that Congress designate 15.6 million acres as wilderness while the Forest Service conducted further studies on another 10.6 million acres of roadless areas. Before sending the RARE II results to Congress, Cutler directed the agency to prepare for managing the 36 million acres it had found unsuit-

nominating other unspoiled lands for protection, urged the agencies and Congress to enlarge the wilderness system to preserve other types of ecosystems, at lower elevations in the West and in Southern and Eastern forests.

The Forest Service took a purist point of view, arguing that past timber harvests, cattle grazing, vehicle travel and other historic uses had eliminated many lands as candidates for preservation. Industry officals, joined by state and local officials in regions with large federal land holdings, often argued that the government had protected enough wild lands for hiking and other forms of recreation that only a relatively affluent minority of Americans could enjoy. They maintained that wilderness status would "lock up" valuable timber, exclude snowmobiles and other popular forms

able for wilderness for multiple uses, including timber harvests.

But wilderness groups, not satisfied with Carter's proposed additions, challenged the 1979 RARE II impact statement and filed lawsuits to block development on roadless lands that the Forest Service proposed to reopen for multiple-use management. Congress, meanwhile, moved slowly on wilderness designations, considering the RARE II proposals through state-by-state bills that usually were drafted in close consultation with each state's House and Senate delegations.

In 1979-80 the 96th Congress designated 4.2 million acres in seven states as wilderness. Action slowed in 1981-82 after President Reagan defeated Carter and Western conservatives such as James A. McClure, R-Idaho, took over key congressional posts when Republicans won control of the Senate. During the 98th Congress John B. Crowell Jr., former general counsel to Louisiana-Pacific Corp., a leading timber company, replaced Cutler and urged Congress to move more quickly to free RARE II areas for development.

Allied with Crowell, McClure and other Western conservatives proposed that Congress combine new wilderness designations with "hard release" language that would prohibit executive branch agencies from ever again considering wilderness protection for RARE II lands that Congress left out as it expanded wilderness system boundaries. Conservation groups, on the other hand, would accept only "soft release" provisions that would allow the Forest Service to review roadless regions once more in 1992-94, when management plans for national forests were due to be rewritten.

Even as Congress debated RARE II, the results were questioned by court decisions. In October 1982 the 9th U.S. Circuit Court of Appeals upheld a lower court decision, in a lawsuit brought by the California state government and environmental groups, to bar development in 46 roadless areas within that state that the Forest Service proposed for multiple-use management. The court found that the agency's environmental impact statement failed to assess adequately the environmental consequences of non-wilderness designation. The Reagan administration responded in February 1983 by announcing that the Forest Service would throw out its RARE II results and start over with yet another roadless area study.

## Wilderness Legislation

During its 1982 post-election session, Congress cleared five wilderness bills that stirred relatively less controversy. Those measures, all sent to the president between Dec. 13 and 20, enlarged the national forest wilderness system by designating wilderness areas in Hoosier National Forest in Indiana; Talladega National Forest in Alabama; Mark Twain National Forest in Missouri; Monongahela National Forest in West Virginia and Apalachicola, Ocala and Osceola National Forests in Florida. The president pocket-vetoed the Florida wilderness bill Jan. 14, 1983.

**California Wilderness Debate.** McClure's Senate committee sidetracked legislation that the House passed in 1981 to designate as wilderness 2.1 million acres of national forest in California, along with 1.4 million acres in national parks within that state.

The House passed the legislation, drafted by the Interior Committee, on July 17. Through maneuvering by Rep. Phillip Burton, D-Calif. (1964-83), who shepherded the California bill through committee, the House attached provisions on the floor that released 2.2 million acres in California from wilderness consideration until the Forest

Service began its next round of roadless area reviews in the 1990s. The release provision, a compromise that environmentalists and the timber industry had negotiated in 1980, prohibited further wilderness lawsuits on California national forests and removed a court injunction against developing 590,000 acres of disputed lands.

But with the election of a Republican-controlled Senate in 1980, the industry refused to support the California compromise. Instead, it backed national release legislation, offered by California Sen. S. I. Hayakawa, R, to set a 1985 deadline for Congress to act on RARE II recommendations, then bar future wilderness designations within national forests. Opponents of the California wilderness bill made no effort to defeat it during House committee and floor action, hoping to find the Senate more receptive to amendments. The Senate Energy panel held hearings on Hayakawa's bill in 1981 but took no action on the House-passed measure.

The Carter administration had proposed 1.3 million acres of national forest wilderness in California; the Reagan administration proposed protecting 1.2 million acres.

**Compromise.** The Democratic House, generally sympathetic to environmentalist causes, in 1983 passed California and Oregon wilderness bills substantially boosting the acreage the Reagan administration wanted to preserve. In the Senate, influential Western conservatives favored smaller wilderness designations and held out for language that would permanently release remaining roadless lands for commercial use, ruling them out for future wilderness expansions. Since environmentalists hoped they could persuade the Forest Service to recommend some of those lands for wilderness during the 1990s, the debate over releasing non-wilderness lands stalled final

action between 1979 and 1983 on major wilderness system additions.

By 1984, however, both sides stood ready to resolve the impasse that tied up millions of acres in uncertain status. Senate Energy and Natural Resources Committee Chairman McClure and Rep. John F. Seiberling, D-Ohio, chairman of the House Interior and Insular Affairs Subcommittee on Public Lands, May 2 agreed to set release terms that required wilderness reviews of forest lands every 15 years. The accord broke the logjam of wilderness bills, and Congress wrote the compromise language into most of the 20 state-by-state measures it cleared before adjourning its 1984 session.

In all, Congress in 1984 added an area larger than the state of Maryland to the national wilderness system. In 1983 Congress had cleared a single bill that created a 259,000-acre wilderness area in Montana. The 1984 legislation expanded the wilderness system in 21 states. The largest designations were in California, Arizona, Oregon, Washington, Utah and Wyoming — all Western states with huge expanses of federally owned national parks, forests and Interior Department rangelands. Major wilderness additions in the East were in New Hampshire, North Carolina and Virginia. *(Acreage designated, p. 168)*

The year's action brought to about 88.6 million acres the total amount of federally designated wilderness. Most of that, some 56.4 million acres, was in Alaska, with only 32.2 million acres in the lower 48 states. Alaska's wilderness was designated in a 1980 law after years of bitter arguments.

# National Park Expansion

Congress in 1981-82 overruled the Reagan administration's plan to stop buying land for the national park system. Secretary

Watt in 1981 proposed an indefinite moratorium on federal government land purchases to expand national parks and other public land holdings. At the same time Watt asked Congress for authority to spend the government's Land and Water Conservation Fund to repair and improve the country's 48 existing national parks, 78 national monuments, historic sites and other lands that already were part of the 73.6-million-acre national park system.

Watt reasoned that the National Park Service should first restore its existing parks before acquiring additional lands. But environmental groups charged that halting new park expansion would only force the government to pay more in the future for lands that should be protected by Park Service management. In the meantime, they went on, the government might forfeit the chance to keep those lands unspoiled by logging, mining or residential development.

Congress concurred, and both the Democratic House and Republican Senate substantially boosted the administration's fiscal 1981 and 1982 requests for land acquisition appropriations. Congress provided additional funds for Park Service maintenance, but it turned down Watt's proposal to divert the money from the conservation fund, which had been set up in 1965 to finance federal land acquisitions from offshore oil and gas revenues.

Congress went along, for one year only, with Watt's proposal to halt fiscal 1982 grants from the fund for state government park purchases. But it refused the administration's request to abolish federal grants for urban parks and preserving historic buildings.

### Background

Congress vastly expanded the national park system during the 1970s. The park system grew from 24.4 million acres in 1971 to more than 70 million acres as the government established new parks, monuments, historic sites and urban parks near or within major cities. Congress added most of those parks, notably in Alaska, by transferring public lands from other federal agencies to Park Service control. But lawmakers throughout the decade also created new parks and expanded existing areas, particularly in the East and around urban areas, by authorizing the Park Service to buy up privately owned lands with money from the conservation fund.

Congress first began protecting national parks when it established Yellowstone National Park in 1872. Over the following century it expanded the system by designating other federally owned lands and accepting private land donations to form extensive parks, monuments, historic sites, recreation areas, seashore and lakeshore areas under Park Service management. Before the 1960s, however, the Park Service had only limited authority and funds to purchase lands for the system.

In authorizing the Cape Cod National Seashore in 1961, Congress for the first time gave the Park Service authority to acquire a large area primarily by buying it. In 1962 President Kennedy set up a Bureau of Outdoor Recreation in the Interior Department to provide central planning for recreation area development. At the Kennedy and Johnson administration's request, Congress passed the Land and Water Conservation Fund Act of 1964 to earmark federal receipts from various sources, including federal recreation user fees, for land purchases by federal and state agencies.

The 1964 law provided 50 percent matching grants to the states for acquiring and developing recreation areas. It also provided funds for the Park Service, U.S. Fish and Wildlife Service, U.S. Forest Service and U.S. Bureau of Land Management to buy lands for parks, wildlife preservation areas and national forests.

As land costs rose in subsequent years, Congress expanded the fund and provided new sources of revenue. Because user fees provided less revenue than expected, Congress in 1968 authorized direct appropriations to bring the fund up to $200 million a year. As an alternative, the 1968 law also assigned federal revenues from Outer Continental Shelf (OCS) oil and gas leasing to the fund to raise authorized levels.

**Funding for Expansion.** Several times during the 1970s, Congress authorized substantial increases in conservation fund spending for federal land acquisition, state park purchase grants and historic preservation projects. Rapidly rising OCS receipts provided additional funds, and Congress through legislation passed in 1976 and 1977 increased annual authorizations for the fund to $900 million for fiscal 1978-1989.

With the fund expanded, Congress and the Nixon and Ford administrations began steadily enlarging the park system by expanding existing parks and creating new areas. In the 1970s the Park Service developed new types of recreation areas, including urban parks, national seashores, lakeshores and other units that often lay close to heavily populated metropolitan regions. Members of Congress were eager to expand the system, both to preserve unspoiled wild lands and to develop recreation areas for their constituents. In a 1978 omnibus parks bill, Congress authorized $1.2 billion for more than 100 parks and preservation projects in 44 states, the largest parks legislation in history. Pushed through by Rep. Burton, that measure approved so many projects in so many states that members referred to it as the "park barrel," a play on the congressional "pork barrel" practice of spreading federal public works projects among dozens of congressional districts.

Congress in 1980 added another 43.6 million acres to the national park system by creating new parks in Alaska, as part of legislation that settled the status of federal lands making up most of that state.

**Land Acquisition Debate.** Conservationists applauded the rapid expansion of the national park system in the 1970s. But the Park Service struggled during the decade to come up with the funds and manpower to manage its fast-gowing holdings. Some observers suggested that the designation of parks and recreation areas in crowded urbanized areas was eroding the park system's original purpose in preserving scenic wonders and unspoiled regions. Conservative critics and private landowners, especially those with homes and other property near or inside national parks, questioned whether the federal government ought to be adding to its already extensive public lands. Those groups were especially vocal in Western states, where the largest national parks were located.

Many national parks encompassed scattered private lands within the boundaries set by Congress. The Park Service followed a policy of buying up such privately owned "inholdings" within park boundaries to consolidate its lands and protect against development that would ruin natural values. Private owners often resisted selling to the government, and they protested what they regarded as pressure to sell. Such owners organized the National Inholders Association to lobby against Park Service land acquisition policies.

Watt, a Wyoming native, was also critical of federal land acquisitions. During the Nixon and Ford administrations, Watt had been director of the Interior Department's Bureau of Outdoor Recreation (renamed during the Carter administration the Heritage Conservation and Recreation Service), the agency that managed the Land and Water Conservation Fund and drafted plans for expanding national parks and other

The Indiana Dunes National Lakeshore is a unique natural area in the midst of one of the nation's largest urban centers. Thousands of people from Chicago and other cities in Illinois and Indiana visit the dunes every year.

recreation areas. Watt, after taking over as interior secretary, abolished the agency and transferred its functions to the Park Service. Ric Davidge, a former lobbyist for the National Inholders Association, was appointed aide to Ray Arnett, the assistant interior secretary for parks and wildlife, who supervised the Park Service.

Watt in 1981 proposed slowing the pace of federal land acquisitions for parks and other areas. In 1980 the congressional General Accounting Office (GAO) released a report that found that sewers, roads and buildings within existing national parks were deteriorating or inadequate to serve growing numbers of visitors. The report identified 172 facilities in 12 national parks that failed to meet the federal government's

own health and safety standards. Seizing on the GAO report, Watt proposed spending $105 million from the conservation fund for repairs and improvements in existing parks instead of for park expansion.

## Congressional Action

Watt's proposal to divert funds for park repairs required congressional action to amend the 1964 law that established the Land and Water Conservation Fund. Congress was unwilling to revise the law, although it appropriated additional funds for park repairs as part of the regular Park Service budget.

In drafting a 1981 budget reconciliation package, the House and Senate wrote in a statement declaring the "sense of Congress" that the government should continue acquiring land to expand national parks, forests and wildlife refuges, using money from the conservation fund.

The reconciliation law recommended that at least $105 million be spent each year for upgrading parks, but the money would come from the National Park Service's operation and maintenance accounts. The measure also recommended the continuation of federal grants to the states for historic preservation and acquisition of urban parks. The administration wanted them eliminated.

In addition to $105 million to restore and rehabilitate national park system units, the reconciliation measure recommended that annual appropriations targets for fiscal 1981-84 should be at least $275 million for the Land and Water Conservation Fund, $30 million for historic preservation grants and $10 million for urban park grants.

Congress followed up in December 1981 by clearing a fiscal 1982 Interior Department appropriations bill that appropriated $155.6 million for the Land and Water Conservation Fund. The measure appropriated an additional $105 million for Park Service maintenance to fund Watt's campaign for repairs and improvements. The administration had sought $45 million from the fund for land purchases along with the $105 million for existing park improvements.

The bill also provided $8 million for urban park grants and $26.5 million for historic preservation grants, programs the administration wanted to terminate. But House and Senate conferees dropped an amendment that would have provided $102.3 million for grants for state parkland purchases. These cuts were to be in effect for only one year.

Again in 1982 Congress insisted on substantially boosting the administration's requests for the national park system. Al-

though Watt did not press the plan to divert Land and Water Conservation Fund money for park repairs, the administration proposed spending only $69.4 million in fiscal 1983 for federal land purchases and sought to eliminate state grants entirely. In approving fiscal 1983 Interior Department appropriations, however, both the House and Senate voted more than $200 million for federal land purchases. For fiscal 1983 Congress provided $206.5 million from the fund for national park purchases and $75 million for state assistance.

## Wild and Scenic Rivers

Congress in 1984 protected five rivers by adding them to the federal Wild and Scenic Rivers System. Though various measures Congress expanded the system to take in parts of rivers in California, Arizona, Michigan and Oregon. It also temporarily protected New Hampshire, North Carolina and another Oregon river from proposed development while the government decided their status.

In the Wild and Scenic Rivers Act of 1968, Congress set up a federal-state system for preserving wild rivers for river-running, fishing and other recreation. Similar in some ways to the national park and wilderness systems, the program protected the natural, free-flowing quality of rivers by barring federal dam projects and restricting roads and other developments that would step up human activity along their courses.

Many wild rivers ran through national parks, forests and other federal lands, giving the government direct control over riverbank development. The 1968 law also gave the government authority to acquire private lands along their banks, in some cases by condemnation, and to buy "scenic easements" from landowners who agreed not to develop their holdings in ways that would spoil the river.

Objections from private landowners had made many proposals for designating wild and scenic rivers controversial. With energy costs rising, electric utilities and Western irrigation districts opposed protection for streams that were being considered for dams generating hydroelectric power.

Such disputes had forced Congress to move slowly in expanding the original eight-river system protected by the 1968 law. In addition to protection by act of Congress, the law gave the secretary of interior power to designate a wild or scenic river by approving a state request for its preservation. Just before the Carter administration left office, Interior Secretary Cecil D. Andrus on Jan. 19, 1981, added five northern California rivers totaling 1,235 miles to the system. Timber and water interests in California took a legal challenge to the designations to the U.S. Supreme Court.

Conservation groups faulted the Reagan administration for downgrading the river protection program through budget cuts and reorganizations. Interior Secretary Watt in 1981 abolished the department's Heritage Conservation and Recreation Service, which had managed the wild and scenic rivers program, and transferred its remnants to the National Park Service. The administration in 1982 unveiled a proposal to add eight new river segments to the system, but environmentalists contended that the administration's plan also would have made it more difficult to protect additional rivers and easier to develop them.

The Park Service had inventoried about 1,500 river segments totaling about 61,000 miles that the agency considered eligible for wild and scenic status. Through its 1984 additions, the first since Andrus' designations in 1981, Congress expanded the existing system to take in about 7,200 miles in 65 rivers or river segments.

In its most controversial 1984 step, Congress protected 83 miles of the Tuol-umne River in California as a wild and scenic river through a provision that the Senate Energy and Natural Resources Committee attached to legislation expanding the federal wilderness system in that state. Interior and the U.S. Forest Service in 1978 had proposed the Tuolumne for wild and scenic status, but in 1982 two California irrigation districts were granted a Federal Energy Regulatory Commission (FERC) permit to study building a massive hydroelectric project on the river's main stem. About two-thirds of the state's 45-member House delegation sponsored legislation to protect the Tuolumne, but the administration and Rep. Tony Coelho, D-Calif., who represented Modesto, opposed that action until dam studies were finished.

Coelho was chairman of the Democratic Congressional Campaign Committee, which funneled funds and other support for fellow Democratic members needing help in re-election campaigns. He also served on the House Interior and Insular Affairs Committee, which considered wild and scenic rivers designations. But wild river advocates bypassed the influential Coelho's opposition by adding the designation to the California wilderness bill in the Senate.

As part of separate Arizona wilderness legislation, Congress conferred wild and scenic status on 39.5 miles of that state's Verde River. In other legislation, Congress also designated 23 miles of the Au Sable River in Michigan, 112 miles of the Owyhee River in Oregon and 50 miles of the Illinois River in Oregon. Congress also gave protected study status to the North Umpqua River in Oregon, the Wildcat River in New Hampshire and the Horsepasture River in North Carolina.

## Forest Timber Contract Relief

Congress in 1984 granted logging companies in the Pacific Northwest relief from

The Rio Grande River flows through Big Bend National Park in Texas. Shown in the far background is the del Carmen Mountain Range, Mexico.

high-cost contracts to cut timber from national forests. The industry had bid up prices for federal timber during the late 1970s, expecting a housing boom that would keep lumber prices rising. But as inflation fell off, some small logging companies faced possible bankruptcy if those contracts forced them to buy timber at prices well above what they could sell it for after cutting down trees and sawing them into lumber.

After resisting pleas for relief for several years, Congress Oct. 1 relented by passing legislation that allowed the timber industry to "buy out" from contracts for up to 200 million board feet of federal timber. President Reagan somewhat reluctantly signed the measure, which Republicans in the Pacific Northwest maintained was es-

sential to restore the region's important logging industry to economic health.

The so-called timber "bailout" issue had dominated congressional debates in 1982-84 on national forest policy. The dispute highlighted a U.S. Forest Service backlog of an estimated 40 billion board feet of standing timber that the agency had sold to timber companies but still remained uncut. It gave members of Congress ammunition to oppose the Reagan administration's campaign to accelerate future harvests from national forests to supply timber industry demand.

### Background

The national forests held half of the nation's softwood sawtimber inventory, the bulk in Douglas fir, pine, spruce and other species growing in the Pacific Northwest region. The U.S. timber industry relied heavily on national forests in Washington, Oregon, northern California and Idaho to meet national demand for lumber and other forest products. The Forest Service managed most forests in the region, but the Bureau of Land Management also controlled rich productive timberlands in Oregon and Washington.

In the Southeast, the nation's other major timber region, logging companies grew most of their own trees on privately owned lands. Although major timber producers held extensive private forests in the Pacific Northwest, they bought most of the timber they harvested from the Forest Service and BLM. As the industry exhausted its own private forests, it began pressuring the agencies to accelerate harvests from mature "old-growth" stands of Douglas fir and other species to keep sawmills running until reforested trees planted on private lands were ready for harvest in the 21st century.

Alarmed by rapidly escalating new housing costs, the Carter administration in the late 1970s prodded the Forest Service to step up timber harvests, particularly from the towering "old-growth" national forests of Washington, Oregon and northern California. President Reagan in 1981 named Crowell as assistant secretary of agriculture for environment and natural resources, the official who oversaw the Forest Service. Crowell directed the agency to plan for accelerated harvests that would as much as double national forest timber sales. His former employer, the Louisiana-Pacific Corp., was a major purchaser of national forest timber.

But environmental groups and congressional critics — led by Rep. James Weaver, D-Ore., the chairman of the House Interior Subcommittee on Forest Management, challenged the need for increasing harvests

Logger working in Humboldt County, Calif. Economic and environmental conditions in the rural county were the subject of a PBS television documentary.

at a time when timber companies could not afford to cut a growing backlog of trees they already had signed contracts to buy.

Under existing law timber companies contracted with the federal government to buy and cut timber on publicly owned land. Contracts usually were awarded to the highest bidder, with proceeds going to the Treasury.

In the late 1970s inflation and heavy demand led companies to bid up contract prices for timber. But a subsequent collapse of the housing market coupled with sharp reductions in inflation left many firms stuck with contracts to buy timber at prices well above its current market value. A number of small companies faced possible bankruptcy unless relief was granted.

# Congress Moves to Halt...

Congress in 1981-82 ended federal government support for development in the barrier islands along the nation's Atlantic and Gulf of Mexico coastlines. As part of 1981 budget reconciliation legislation, Congress cut off federal flood insurance for new homes and other structures on undeveloped barrier islands. It followed up with separate 1982 legislation that curtailed federal spending to build roads, bridges and other structures on coastal islands that the Interior Department designated for preservation.

Those steps were among the few new environmental initiatives launched by the 97th Congress. The Reagan administration and environmental groups both backed the barrier island legislation, uniting to deny federal support for building homes and tourist facilities that threatened fragile dunes and wetlands, already vulnerable to flooding and erosion.

Barrier islands stretch along the Atlantic and Gulf coasts from Maine to Mexico. They act as buffers protecting the coastline, delicate wetlands and estuaries from the full force of hurricanes and ocean storms. These islands and other coastal landforms are unstable as a result of erosion, flooding and other natural forces. Consequently, they can be very poor places to build houses, roads and other structures. Not only were the houses likely to wash away, but human activity could damage dunes and wetlands.

The government often paid twice for barrier island development: once to subsidize the original construction and again to bail out property owners hit by disaster. By cutting off federal flood insurance and development assistance, Congress both protected the islands against damaging use and saved the government money.

## 1981 Flood Insurance Ban

Congress in 1968 had set up a federally backed flood insurance program as part of the Housing and Urban Development Act. In that law, Congress authorized the Department of Housing and Urban Development (HUD) to subsidize insurance premiums paid by homeowners and small businesses in flood-prone regions. Because the

---

Sagging lumber markets already had forced the industry to lay off workers and close down sawmills that formed the economic base of many small Pacific Northwest towns. To prevent further damage to the regional economy, Sen. Mark O. Hatfield, R-Ore., and other members backed legislation to allow timber purchasers to cancel up to 40 percent of their contract commitments to buy and harvest trees.

But the bailout proposal split the forest products industry. Southern timber operators opposed contract relief proposals that they contended would give their Pacific Northwest competitors an unfair advantage. Senate Agriculture Committee Chairman Jesse Helms, R-N.C., blocked Hatfield's legislation in 1982 and 1983. The administration also raised philosophical objections to "bailout" legislation and Crowell testi-

# . . . Barrier Islands Development

market was limited and potential losses from disastrous floods were great, private insurance companies had formed a pool to sell insurance against flood damages.

Environmentalists contended that the federal flood insurance program, however well-intentioned, encouraged developers to build homes, businesses and resorts in ecologically sensitive river flood plains and coastal islands that easily could be ruined by development.

During debate on the 1981 reconciliation bill, the House attached a proposal by its Banking, Finance and Urban Affairs Committee to halt federal flood insurance on undeveloped barrier islands after Oct. 1, 1983. The Senate reconciliation bill carried no similar provisions, but House-Senate conferees agreed to retain the House language.

## 1982 Legislation

In the 1982 legislation Congress established a Coastal Barrier Resources System under Interior Department supervision. After mapping out barrier landforms to be protected within that system, the law barred most spending for financial aid for building roads, airports, boat landings, bridges, causeways or other structures that would promote residential and business use of the islands. It also prohibited federal spending to stabilize barrier landforms or prevent erosion along inlets, shorelines or inshore lands within the system, except to protect life and property on adjacent areas.

The legislation moved smoothly through the House and Senate with backing from the administration and a diverse coalition of environmental, disaster relief and conservative groups. The measure sparked controversy only when the House and Senate mapped out precisely which lands would be included in the coastal barrier system. Developers and landowners in several states lobbied during House deliberations to keep their properties outside the system boundaries, and the map lines in the House and Senate versions differed somewhat. In a conference agreement House and Senate negotiators adjusted the boundaries to add land in Rhode Island, Delaware, North Carolina, Florida and Mississippi while deleting lands in Maine, New York, South Carolina and Alabama.

---

fied against Hatfield's bill in 1982.

The Senate Energy and Natural Resources Committee, which held jurisdiction over national forests in the West, nonetheless in 1982 approved a contract relief bill after Hatfield and J. Bennett Johnston, D-La., proposed revisions to defuse Southeastern timber interests' concerns about the competitive effects of Forest Service resale of timber at lower prices. But Howard M.

Metzenbaum, D-Ohio, objected to granting relief for major timber companies as well as small sawmill operations and questioned the bill's impact on housing prices. His filibuster threat blocked Senate floor action on the 1982 bill.

Relief legislation remained stalled in 1983, but the Forest Service took administrative steps to allow companies to extend the term of their contracts by five years without paying interest. That took some pressure off the industry, but many firms kept pressing Congress for longer-term contract relief.

## 1984 Congressional Approval

The Senate Energy Committee revived the bill in 1984, attaching contract relief provisions to an unrelated House-passed measure. The revised measure allowed logging companies to "buy out" contract obligations for up to 55 percent of the timber they had bought before 1982. It set forth a formula for calculating how much a company had to pay the government for contract relief, based on its potential loss and the amount of timber under contract. It set a ceiling of 200 million board feet on the total amount of timber under contract that the government could agree to take back.

To protect Southeastern logging companies, the measure set limits on national forest timber sales in Washington and Oregon through fiscal 1991.

The Senate passed the bill by a 94-2 vote on Sept. 26 after adopting four amendments that Metzenbaum offered to tighten contract buy-out terms. One Metzenbaum proposal set stiffer terms for larger companies to buy out from contracts than for smaller loggers that had bought less timber from national forests.

Office of Management and Budget Director David A. Stockman Oct. 1 urged the House to defeat a Senate proposal that he contended would "provide a small number of corporations with $400 million worth of special relief." But the House the same day cleared the legislation by voice vote, and Reagan signed it on Oct. 16.

# Index